Luke Milbourne

The Psalms of David in English Metre

Translated from the Original

Luke Milbourne

The Psalms of David in English Metre
Translated from the Original

ISBN/EAN: 9783337341022

Printed in Europe, USA, Canada, Australia, Japan

Cover: Foto ©Lupo / pixelio.de

More available books at **www.hansebooks.com**

THE PSALMS OF DAVID,
IN
English Metre;

Translated from the ORIGINAL,
And Suited to all the TUNES
now Sung in CHURCHES:
With the Additions of several NEW.

By *LUKE MILBOURNE*,
A Presbyter of the Church of *England*.

عند البرهان تعرف السواليد

Adag. Arab.

Thus by the Streams, the Spring is clearly shown;
And the Translation makes the Author known.
                                   Lord *Falkland*.
None can condemn the Wish or Labour spent,
Good Matter in good Words to represent.
                          Bishop *King*, to Mr. *Sandys*.

London, Printed for *W. Rogers* at the *Sun*, R. *Clavill* at the *Peacock*, and B. *Tooke* at the *Middle Temple Gate*, all in *Fleetstreet*. *J. Lawrence* at the *Angel* in the *Poultry*, and *J. Tayler* at the *Ship* in St. *Paul's* Church-yard, 1698.

TO
His Highness
THE
DUKE
OF
GLOCESTER.

May it please Your Highness,

THis little Book wants a *Protector*; And where could it find a Better, than in *Our other Hope?* Your Highness has here the *greatest King*, and the *best of Poets*, to

A 2 excite

The Epistle Dedicatory.

excite Your *Courage*, and enliven Your *Devotion*. You have the *Wit* and *Spirit* of a Court, without the *Follies* of the present Age; *Fineness* of *Thought*, without *Loosness* of *Fancy*; *Rapture*, without *Extravagance*; and *Piety*, without the Extreams of *Superstition* or *Idolatry*. These Hymns contain nothing but what may adorn the Innocence of *Youth* and the Vigour of a *Manly Age*. The Masters of Musick may try their Skill here, and sing *God's Praises* in as charming Notes as *common* and *despicable Amours*; and advance the Love of their Redeemer, above all the Atchievments of a *fancied Hero*.

From

The Epistle Dedicatory.

From *Your Highness's* Hand this Work may be acceptable to *His most Excellent Majesty*, and find Admission into the Closet of Your *Royal Mother*: If read by Your Self, it will be a *Divine Monitor* in Your Diversions, a *Companion* in Your Privacy, a *Support* under Uneasiness, and a *Security* to Your Religion: Those *Holy Truths*, convey'd through the Channels of *smooth* and *easie Verse*, will, with God's Blessing, make You *wiser than Your Enemies*, *more knowing than any Earthly Teachers*, and *more apprehensive than those of Elder Years*. May the God of Heaven bless Your Highness's *Pregnant Youth* with advancing

The Epistle Dedicatory.

Vertues, and unfading Years: May He crown You with *Love* and *Honour* here, and with *Love* and *Happiness* hereafter: Which is the most earnest Prayer of

Your Highness's

Most Humble, and

Most Obedient Servant,

Luke Milbourne.

To the Most Reverend Fathers in God the Archbishops, *the Right Reverend the* Bishops, *and the Reverend* Clergy *of Great Britain and* Ireland; *especially such as now do, or hereafter may represent that whole Body, in* Convocation:

The Preface of *Luke Milbourne, Presbyter,* and Author of this Translation of the *Psalms* of *David.*

Most Reverend, Right Reverend, and Reverend Fathers and Brethren!

THat Psalmody was, *amongst the Jews, a considerable Part of Divine* Worship, *that Book, of which this calls it self a* Translation, *is a sufficient Evidence; That it*

A 4 *was*

was used among Christians *of old, is unquestionable. And perhaps it is no Disparagement either to the Jewish or the Christian Church, that a great part of the old Heathen Worship consisted in Singing* Hymns and Praises *to their Gods. There is somewhat so truly Divine and Charming in* Well-set Notes, *and* Vocal and Instrumental Harmony ; *they are so apt to chear and revive* languid and drooping Spirits, *so likely to make strong Impressions on the* Memory, *and so extreamly affecting to the* devout Soul, *that as the Agreeableness of their Numbers made* Poets *of old the fittest* Treasurers of Divine Knowledge, *so the Softness and Sweetness of their Notes may make the* Masters of Sacred Musick *among our selves (were but their Lives as Heavenly as their Art)* the fittest Companions for happy Souls, and Blissful Angels : *With respect to whom, our excellent* Waller *says* ;

<blockquote>
All that we know of those above,
Is, that they sing, and that they love.
</blockquote>

What

The Preface.

What Thoughts our first Reformers *in this Nation had of this part of Divine Worship is not easie to conjecture. But whether they judged* Singing of Psalms *by the whole Congregation no neces-sary part of a* Publick Liturgy, *or sup-posed that the* Reading Psalms, *chaunt-ed in* Recitative, *or sung as at present in* Cathedrals, *(which seems favour'd by that Title they carry in our* Common-Prayer-Book, The *Psalter or* Psalms *of* David, Pointed as they are to be Said or Sung in Churches,) *was enough to answer that part of Worship, 'tis certain they took no Care for any* Metrical Trans-lation *of those sacred Hymns, for pub-lick Use. And though some pious and learned Men had taken pains to put them into* Verse, *the setled Liturgy took no notice of the Matter. Nor could I ever find any* Authentick Allowance *for sing-ing them in publick, whatsoever the* Com-pany of Stationers *pretend to, whose plausible Title had a Regard to their own Profit, more than the Church's* Edifica-tion.

The Preface.

tion. *However, the Practice of Singing prevail'd here every Day, in* Imitation *of the* Reformed *abroad, and certainly tended very much towards the advancing of the* Reformation *it self; but, after all, was only connived at, or tolerated: And after the* Restauration *of our Religion, and our Government, never Authorised, or so much as mentioned, as a Part of our* Publick Service: *And the present and constant Practice of our Cathedrals and Collegiate Churches, and our Colleges, not to mention the* Chapel Royal, *and other Places where Choirs are fixed, intimates, that such Psalms were never design'd to be setled by Authority; Prose-Anthems being there generally sung, taken out of the* Reading Psalms; *some short Parts of other Scriptural Hymns; some of private Composure; and, by chance, sometimes a Verse or two out of* Sternhold and Hopkins; *as, particularly, out of the 68th Psalm,* Let God arise, *&c. Set, I think, by Mr.* Laws. *Now the Cathedrals being*

The Preface.

ing Patterns to our Parochial Assemblies, *at least in the main parts of solemn Worship, they having* no Example *of such a Nature from them, could pretend to no* Right *of* Singing Psalms *in Verse by the entire Congregation.*

Hence, though the great Sir Philip Sidney *translated the whole Book of* Psalms *into* Rhyme; *and the pious Bishop* Hall, *and the renouned Lord* Bacon, *and it may be some others, turn'd several particular Psalms into Verse, more correct, doubtless, than the former, yet there never was any Motion towards* introducing them into Churches. *And since our* Convocations, *to whom that Work properly belongs, never took any such Cognizance of these, or of the* Ancient Version, *as to recommend them, with the* Liturgy, *to the* Parliament, *our* Common Psalmody *remains a* Matter *of* Liberty: *And it never yet was made an* Article of Enquiry *at any* Episcopal Visitation, *Whether any* Psalms *were sung, or what* Versions *of them were used in* Parochial Churches.

On this Account it was, that whereas no Man better understood his own Supremacy in Ecclesiastical Affairs than Charles the First, of blessed Memory, yet, though he designed the utmost Honour to the Memory of his Father, when the new Translation of King *James* the First *was made publick, he only allow'd and recommended it to common Use;* which, as Experience shew'd, was not enough to break in upon Inveterate Custom, *or to exclude* that *which had for so many Years gotten* Possession *of our* Bibles *and* Common-Prayer-Books *of all Volumes, and of our* Worshipping Assemblies.

The Standart *of our* English Language *having been so much alter'd of late; and* Poetry *especially having reach'd its utmost Height, by that noble Genius appearing in the Writings of Sir* John Denham, *Mr.* Waller, *and Mr.* Cowley, *and some later Authors, the Roughness and Uncorrectness of the* Ancient Version *has appear'd the more evident and notorious:*
The

The Preface.

...e *Observation of which made Mr.* San-
...ys, *Mr.* May, *Mr.* Burnaby, *Bishop*
...ing, *Mr.* Barton, *Sir* John Denham
...m*self, Mr.* Smith, *Mr.* Goodridge. *Dr.*
...trick, *Dr.* Woodford, *and Dr.* Ford,
...*d now very lately Mr.* Brady *and Mr.*
...ate, *make their several* Translations
...*ith different Success. Mr.* Burnaby*'s*
...ook, *and Mr.* May*'s Essay, I have seen:*
...*r.* Sandys*'s and the Reverend Dr.* Wood-
...rd*'s are above our ordinary* Musick,
...e *last especially, whose Author seems to*
...eath *with* David*'s* Spirit, *and to aspire*
...*Raptures almost equal with that* Divine
...Psalmist; *and whose Steps are as nobly fol-*
...*w'd by that Masculine* Poet, *as well as*
...ainter, *the incomparable Mrs.* Beal.
...*r.* Barton*'s Version is generally apposite*
...*ough to the Text, but exalted little above*
...e Old. *Sir* John Denham*'s I have not*
...en, *but find the admirable Dr.* Wood-
...rd *(a sufficient Judge) giving them a*
...ble *and, doubtless, a deserv'd* Chara-
...er. *That of the Right Reverend Bishop*
...Chichester *labours under the unhappy*
Choice

The Preface.

Choice of his Rhyme, *(as* O[t]
*observ'd) so far, as to render t[he]
wise* excellent Work *ungrate[ful]
Ear.* Mr. Smith *is very gay,[per-]
haps too affected, if the Rev[erend]
D[oct]or* Patrick *may be Judge, wh[ose]*
pious *indeed, and generally p[ious is]
an almost* Unpoetical Translat[ion of the]
most exalted Poetry. *For M[r. Brady]
and* Mr. Tate's, *since they are [pub-]
lishing a* New *and* Corrected [Edition of]
their Translation, *I shall pass [no Judg-]
ment on that Work, whose Er[rors and]*
Excellencies *I must be content [to be ig-]
norant of till it is published. [As for]
those which I have hitherto s[een, they]
are fitted to common* Tunes, *th[e]
most* Elaborate, *and the most [learned is]
that of* Dr. Ford; *that Reve[rend Per-]
son having a truly* Poetical G[enius de-]
fended *with* great *and* solid [Learning]
and Exemplary Piety; *exce[llent Quali-]
fications for a compleat* Paraph[rast. As]
ought Mr. Goodridge, *for his [Learning,]*
Piety *in promoting more* Correc[t]

The Preface.

[M]usick, *to be passed without a just Comendation.*

What might be said of the Use and [e]xcellency of Psalmody, *is so exhaust[ed] by* Dr. Woodford, Mr. Goodridge *[an]d* Dr. Ford, *as to supersede any thing [I] can say.* The Question only recurrs [no]w, *Is* Psalmody *a real* Part of Di[v]ine Worship, or is it not? If not, 'tis [no] matter whether* David's Psalms, *or [on]ly* Arbitrary Spiritual Philadelphian [H]ymns, *be sung; whether any, or none [at] all. If it be* a Part of Divine Ser[v]ice, *how comes it to pass that our* Ec[c]lesiastical Representatives *have not [t]hought* Uniformity in singing of Psalms [a]s beautiful, and as valuable, as in any [o]ther Part of the Publick Service? Why [n]ot in the Poetical, as well as in the [P]rose-Version? This would take the [c]hoice of them out of the* Parish-Clerk's [P]ower, *and make it the* Priest's Business, *[w]hose Discretion might be farther relied [o]n in it. Admit the Translation of* Stern[h]old *and* Hopkins *was rejected by the*

Con-

The Preface.

Convocation *or* Commissioners *of* Edward *the Sixth, as appearing too mean; that could not preclude a more agreeable* One. *And though it might seem a very hard Work, which few of the* Clergy *(though the fittest for it) durst undertake; yet, since at this time there are* several Versions of the Psalms *extant, why may not some* One, *or a choice* Collection out of All, *be made by Learned and Judicious* Persons, *skill'd in* Divinity *and* Poetry *too, appointed for that purpose, in a* Convocation? *Why may not such a* Committee *examine them severely as to* Clearness of Sense, Purity and Decency of Language, Agreeableness of Stile, Orthodoxy of Doctrine, Suitableness to the Original Text, *and* Smoothness and Musicalness of Numbers? *And may not these, after such an* Examination, *be approved by the* Convocation, *as the whole* Liturgy *formerly was, and so be recommended by them to the* Three Estates in Parliament, *and to* His Majesty *as* Head of the Church:

and

d *ſo receive a* Juſt *and* Legal San-
ion, *and become one Part of our* Pub-
k Unity *and* Uniformity ? *Would*
h *an Action bring them under a* Præ-
unire, *merely becauſe it was not parti-
larly commanded by* His Majeſty ? *I
 iy, perhaps, be. too fond of my own
 oughts ; but I conclude, this Piece of
 niformity would give leſs Offence to*
iſſenters *of all ſorts, than ſome other
 ings which are yet* juſtly *ſtood upon ;
  they are not about Laying down the*
ſt Tranſlation of the Bible : *The niceſt*
etenders to Conſcience *would have nothing to object to pure* Scripture-Forms :
or would they, when commanded *under*
Penalty *to ſing* David's Pſalms, of the
ſt Verſion, *complain of* the Miſchief
Impoſitions.
This is ſuch a Point of Uniformity,
all Churches, our own only except-
, *agree in : The* Scots *have* theirs ; *the*
utch *and* French, theirs ; *the laſt, in-
ed, corrected by Mr.* Conrart , *the
 andart of their Language having been
              much*

The Preface.

much alter'd by the Academy, *since* Marot *and* Beza *translated them; yet their Work being still good and* intelligible, *Monsieur* Conrart's *has taken only among* particular Persons, *without any* Intrenchment *upon the* general Harmony. *The* Lutherans *too keep up this* Uniformity; *though, besides* David's Psalms, *they have about* 750 Spiritual Songs *and* Hymns, *Stated, and Occasional. And who knows, but now that* Singing of Psalms by Rule *grows so much in Fashion, this Settlement might somewhat temper and cicatrate the* Humour of Separation *in other Matters?*

If such a thing should be thought fit, there is no doubt but that, of particular Versions, the best *ought to be chosen:* Of all in general, the best particular Psalms; *for one* Man's Spirit *might be raised, where* another *droop'd; and* Men *would commonly* perform best, *where they were* most affected *by the Matter. But to enjoin* Unity *or* Uniformity *in a worse* Translation, *where a* better *might be had,*

or

The Preface.

r to cull out meaner Performances, *where, out of our present Variety of Choice,* excellent Things *might be drawn, would dash us upon the same Rock again; and the next Age might complain, that* the Names *of our* Psalmographers *were alter'd indeed, but the* Defects *continued: This is a Failure which* a Convocation, *assisted by the good Spirit of God, could not easily fall under the* Suspicion *of.*

That I, as now an Ancient Presbyter *of the* Church *of* England, *might contribute my poor* Offering *to the Adorning of this part of* Sacred Worship, *I put this into your Hands,* Most Reverend, Right Reverend, *and* Reverend Fathers *and* Brethren! *A Work of some* Pains *and* Care; *and on which my most serious Thoughts were for a considerable time engag'd.* God's Honour, *and the* Church's Service, *was my* End; *and his* Grace, *earnestly and humbly implor'd, both in the* Beginning *and* Continuance *of the Work, my* Assistance. *The* Original *was my* Text; *the* Polyglot Bible *and* Criticks, *my* Interpreters,

ters, *where needful; and the*
Tranflation *of the* Reading P
that called the Bishops Bible, an
in our common Bibles, *my Co*
Though *I have not tied my felf*
tioufly to any, as not to ufe my
ment fometimes; and in fome
ftem the Current of Paraphrasts,
Writers *on that* Divine Book.
larly, I have adhered to thofe
tions made of feveral Paffages
Infpir'd Pen-men *of the* New T
whom to quit for over-nice and
zing Criticks, *I think abfurd and*
I have, in general, made the
Coherence *fo plain, that this*
perhaps may be as ferviceable t
Commentator.

The Meafures *I have ufed ar*
neither fo hard, nor fo harfh as
thought: The Rhymes *are e*
double, *fometimes more; fuch b*
unforced; more pleafant, and mo
I have generally avoided the C
Confonants, *as* Unmufical. *A*

twice Tranflated, some thrice; by that Means sometimes taking in those different Senses of particular Texts, of which 'tis hard to fix the best; Paraphrasing some lofty Pfalms more fully, and using higher Expreffions than a single Verfion could have admitted of. Hence every Pfalm has one Tranflation so close and plain, as may be sung in the plaineft Country-Congregations; and yet I have used such Variety of Meafures, as may answer all the Tunes in Playford's Edition: And that the Work might be the more compleat, I have given all such of Mr. Sandys's Meafures, with their Tunes in Two Parts, which could not be sung by the common Notes. The whole, indeed, may be an entire Body of Church-Mufick: No Old Tune is loft, several New are added; and the Words so fitted, as to be more agreeable both to the Dutch, French and Englifh Tunes, as sung in any of our Churches, than any former Verfion has been.

I have

The Preface.

I have generally followed the Stile of the Original, *rising and falling with* That. *The* Measures *of* Chearful Psalms *are fitted to* Chearful Tunes: *Those more* Melancholick, *to* Slow Tunes, *and of a sadder* Air. *The* Repetitions *in the* Hebrew *are so charming, that I could not but think they would be very* beautiful *in* English; *as particularly, in the* 118th Psalm. *I have industriously avoided both* Obsolete *and* New-fangled Words; *I have* invented *none, nor used any harsh* Transpositions *of* Words: *Though I doubt not, but, after all my Care, many* Mistakes *may have escaped me, which whosoever will* charitably *point out, will lay the* greatest Obligation *upon me. That we might use* Doxologies *as well to the* Singing, *as the* Reading Psalms, *I have suited* One *to every* Measure, *through the whole* Book. *A* Right Reverend Prelate *of our* Church *did me the Honour to read the whole over very carefully; whose* Encouragement *was a great*

Motive

The Preface.

Motive *to this* Publication. *If it be* acceptable *to others, and* bleſs'd *by* God, *as to promote his* Honour, *I have my* End: *And,*

Non nobis, Domine; non nobis:
Sed Nomini Tuo da Gloriam.

Advertisement.

THat this Verſion of the *Pſalms* may be the more uſefull to thoſe who delight in *Church-Muſick*, I have tranſlated them to ſuch variety of Meaſures, that there's no Tune in *Playford*'s Editions, either in the *Pſalms* themſelves, or in the *Hymns* before or after, to which there is not ſome particular Meaſure appropriated here: That the Compaſs of *Church-Muſick* might be the larger and more entertaining, I have tun'd ſome to Mr *Sandys*'s Meaſures, the Muſick of which was compos'd by that great Maſter Mr. *Laws*; for the private uſe of his pious Maſter *Charles* the Firſt of bleſſed Memory: The whole then preſents you with one Verſion of every *Pſalm* to be ſung in Common Tunes, if at leaſt we may call thoſe of the 113 and 148 *Pſalms* ſuch: and they are to be ſung to the *ſame* with thoſe of the *ſame denomination* in the old Verſion, unleſs where the Meaſures are different, and the Proper Tunes referr'd to. Such as are not in Mr. *Play-*

ford's Book, are here set down with the proper Notes from Mr. *Laws*'s and *Ravenscroft*'s; and the whole, if encourag'd, shall be re-printed with the Notes throughout. And that we may have a just Opportunity, at such a time as this, to remember that Faith into which we are Baptiz'd, in every part of Divine Worship, I have suited particular Doxologies to every particular Measure, in due Order, at the end of the Book, with what *Psalms* they refer to, besides some in the Body of the Version.

Benedicat Deus Operi & Authori.

The Tunes of the Psalms.

A Thousand Blessings crown his Head,
Whose Heart all impious Counsel flies,
And hates those Paths where Sinners tread,
Who God and all that's Good despise.

This serves indifferently for any Stanzas of Eight Syllables, which have no proper Tune of their own.

iv *The Tunes of the Psalms.*

For the 8th *Psalm.* 2d Metre.

LOrd, how Illustrious is thy sacred Name;

How blest, great God of Hosts, E--ter--nal King;

Whose Honours all the lower World proclaim,

Whose Honours all the Heav'nly Armies sing.

Psal. 11.

Psalm 15. 2d Metre.

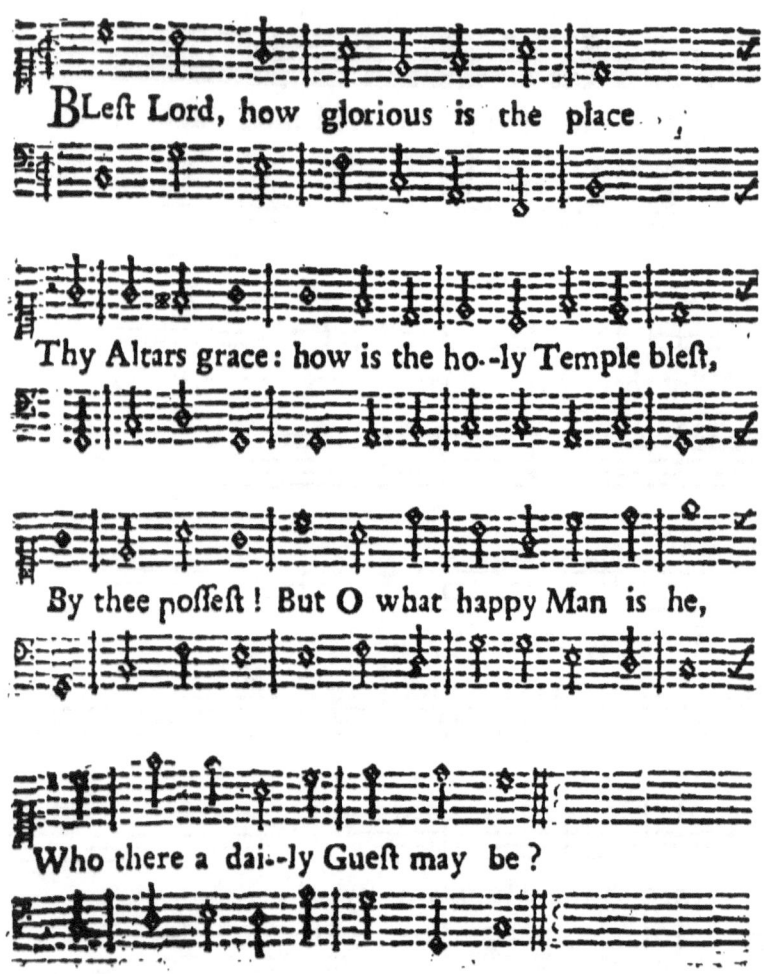

Blest Lord, how glorious is the place
Thy Altars grace: how is the ho--ly Temple blest,
By thee possest! But O what happy Man is he,
Who there a dai--ly Guest may be?

The Tunes of the Psalms. vij

Psalm 18, or 78.

HOW shall I praise my God, my King,

Thus ex—ta—sy'd with Joys and Love!

What worthy Hal—le—lu—jahs sing,

To his great Name who rules above?

Psal. 23.

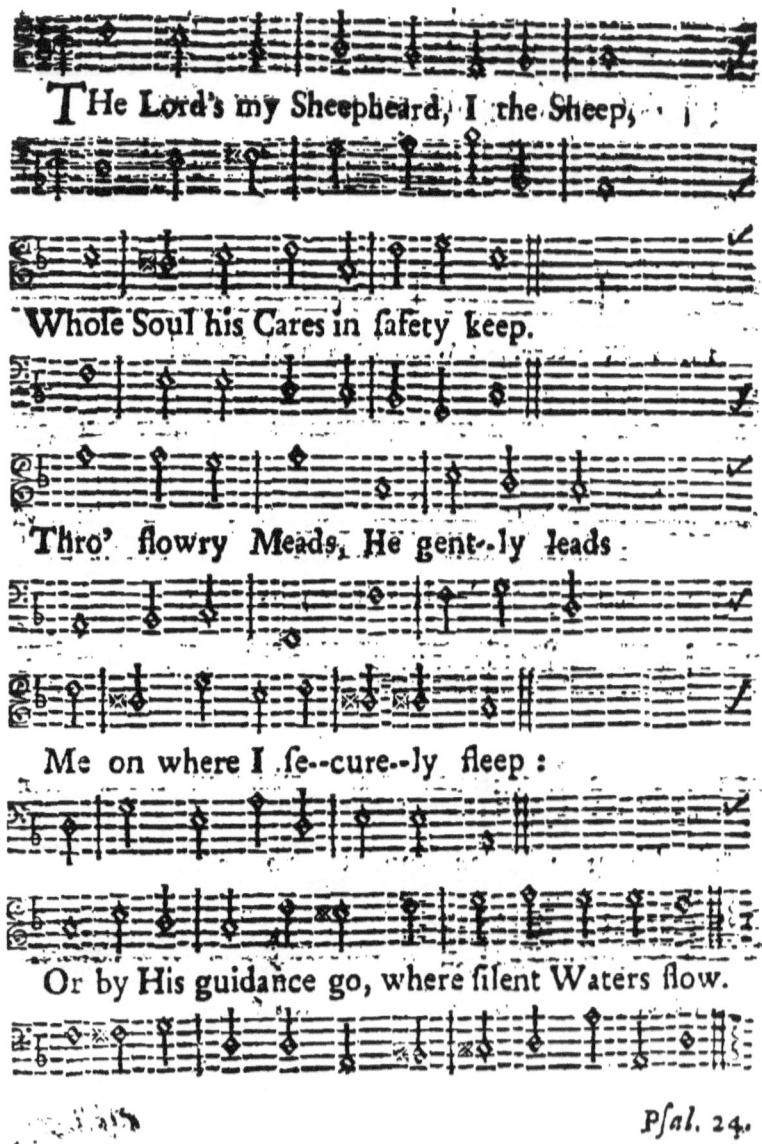

Psalm 24. 2d Metre.

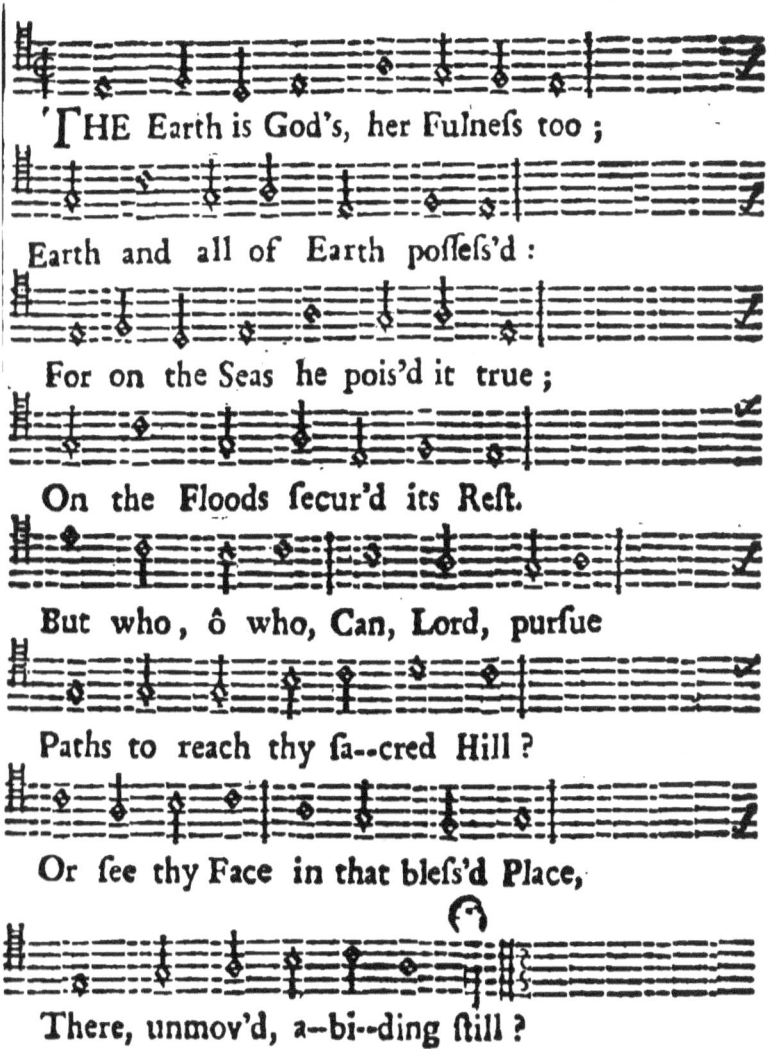

THE Earth is God's, her Fulness too;
Earth and all of Earth possess'd:
For on the Seas he pois'd it true;
On the Floods secur'd its Rest.
But who, ô who, Can, Lord, pursue
Paths to reach thy sa--cred Hill?
Or see thy Face in that bless'd Place,
There, unmov'd, a--bi--ding still?

Psal. 33.

Psalm 43. 3d Metre.

Judge me, my God; revenge my Cause

On cruel Hands, and faithless Hearts.

Save me from him who from the Laws

Of Truth, and so--ber Virtues starts:

The Tunes of the Psalms. xiij

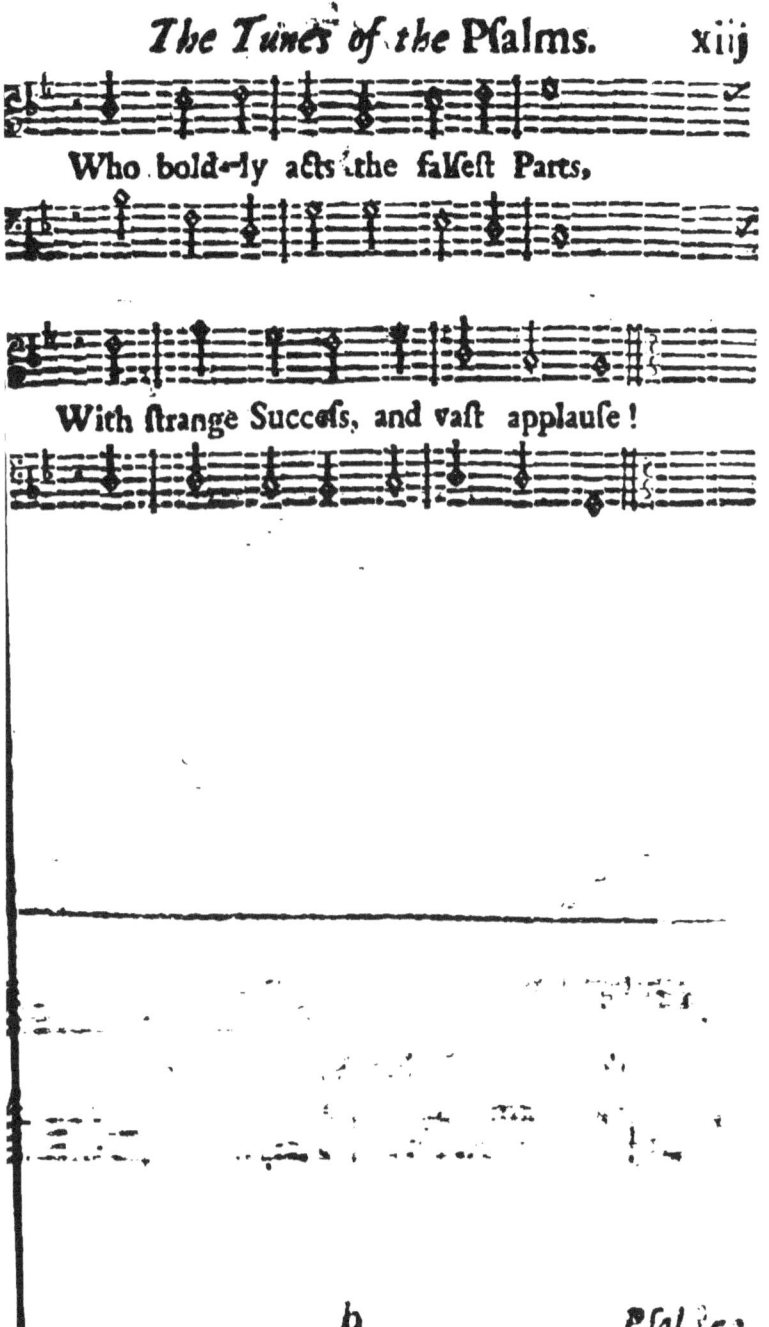

Who bold-ly acts the falsest Parts,

With strange Success, and vast applause!

b Psal. 53.

xiv   *The Tunes of the* Psalms.

Psalm 53. 2d Metre.

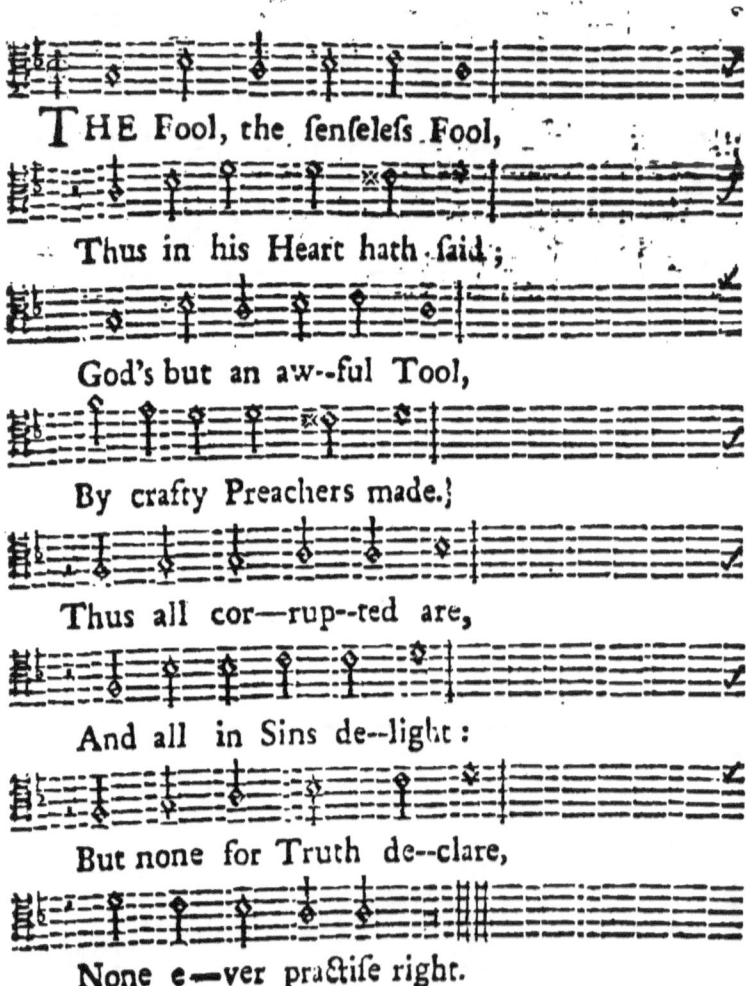

THE Fool, the senseless Fool,

Thus in his Heart hath said;

God's but an aw--ful Tool,

By crafty Preachers made.

Thus all cor—rup--ted are,

And all in Sins de--light:

But none for Truth de--clare,

None e—ver practise right.

The Tunes of the Psalms xv

Pſalm 58.   1ſt Metre.   *Pſalm* 72.
         Pſalm 106.

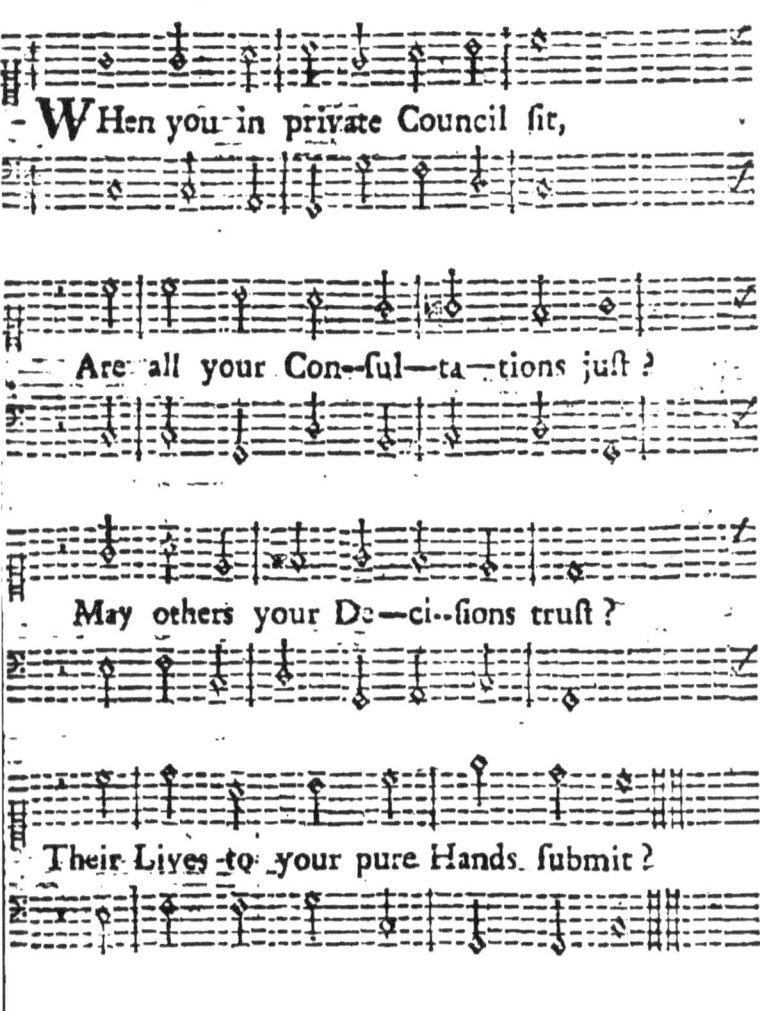

b 2   *Pſal.* 72.

xvi *The Tunes of the* Psalms.

Psalm 72. 2d Metre.

LOrd let the King thy Judgments find!

Enrich the Prince's Royal Mind,

— For Crowns and Governments design'd.

Then shall He sentence wisely give;

And

The Tunes of the Psalms: xvij

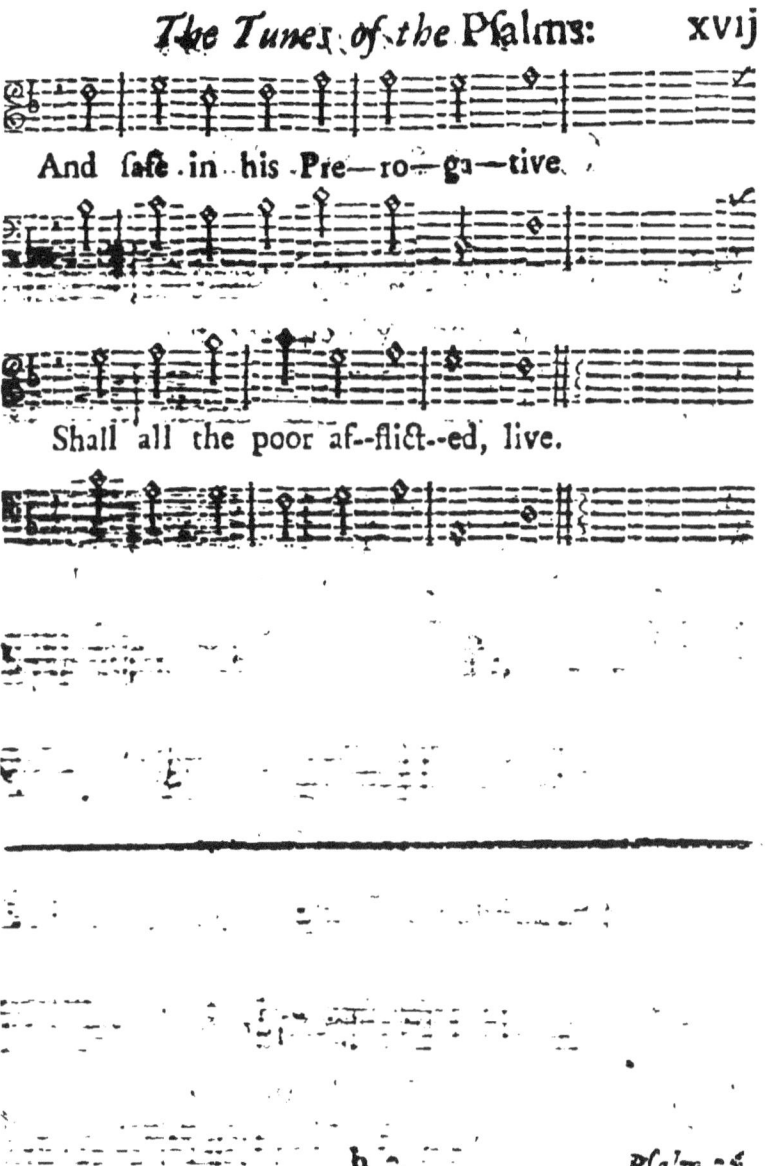

And safe in his Pre—ro—ga—tive,

Shall all the poor af--flict--ed, live.

Psalm 78

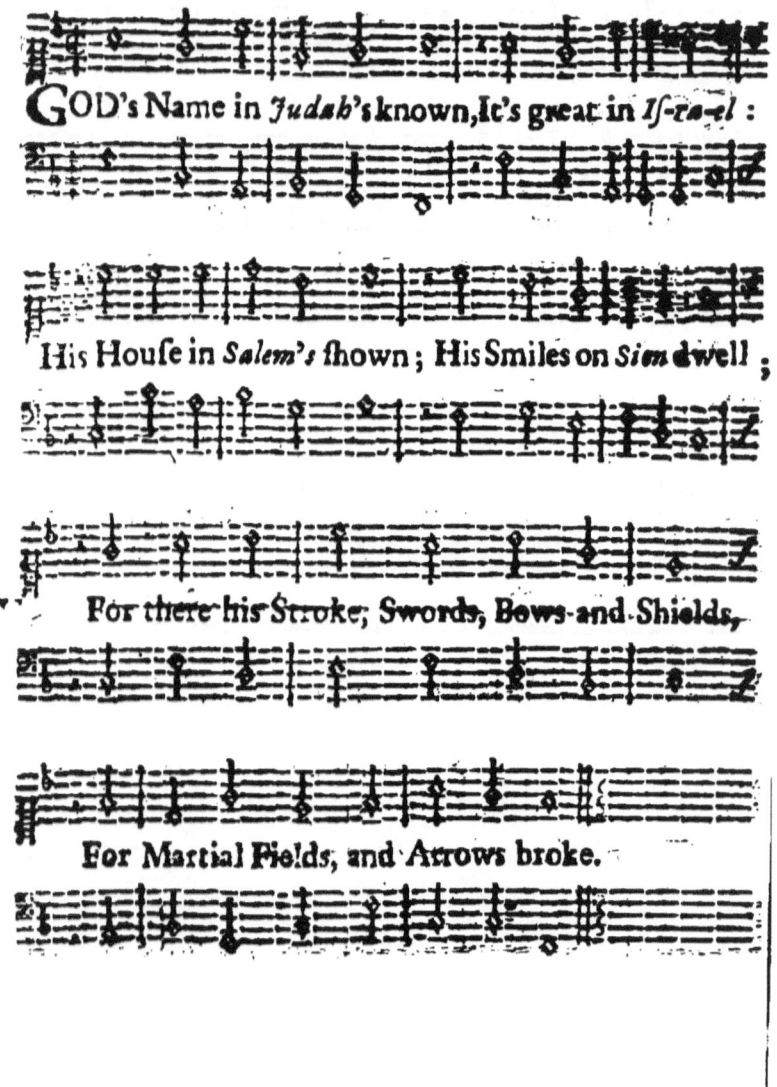

The Tunes of the Psalms. xix

Psalm 81. 1st Metre.

TO God, our Strength, your Voices raise!

Aloud the God of Ja—cob praise!

A Psalm toth' mer--ry Timbrel suit,

The pleasant Harp, or charming Lute.

Psal. 95.

The Tunes of the Psalms. xxi

Psalm 98. 2d Metre.

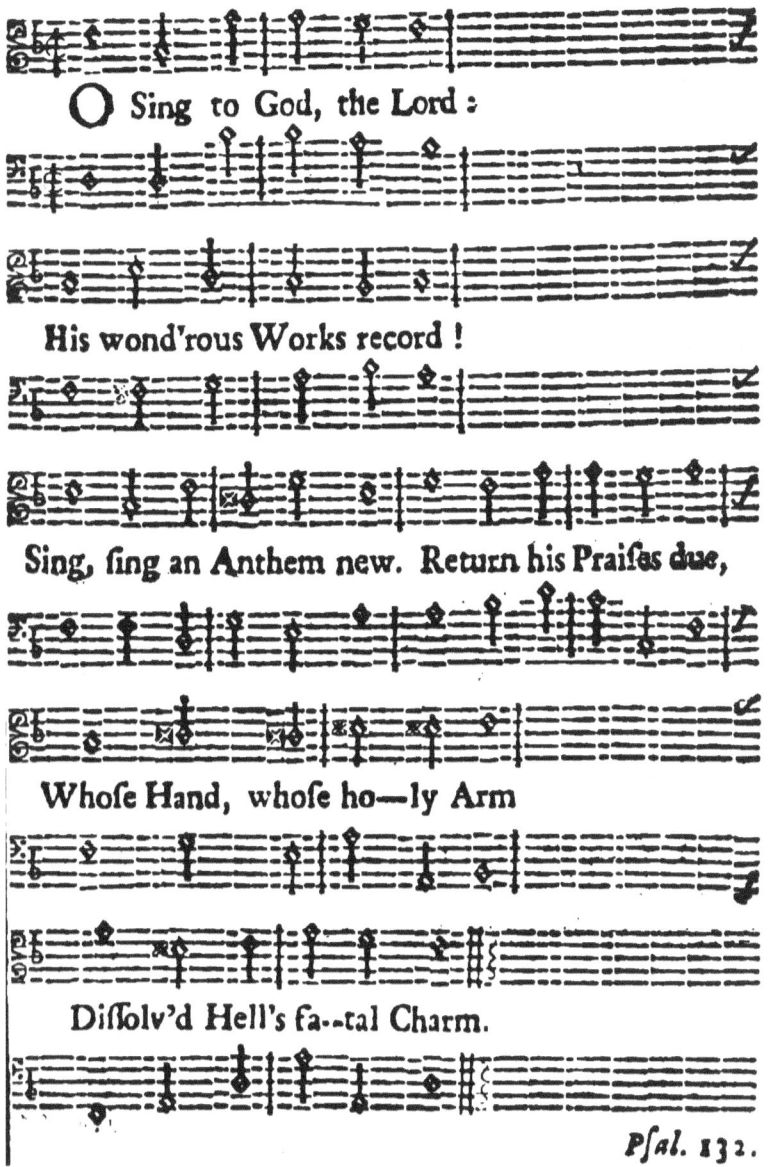

O Sing to God, the Lord:

His wond'rous Works record!

Sing, sing an Anthem new. Return his Praises due,

Whose Hand, whose ho—ly Arm

Dissolv'd Hell's fa--tal Charm.

Psal. 132.

xxij.   *The Tunes of the* Psalms.

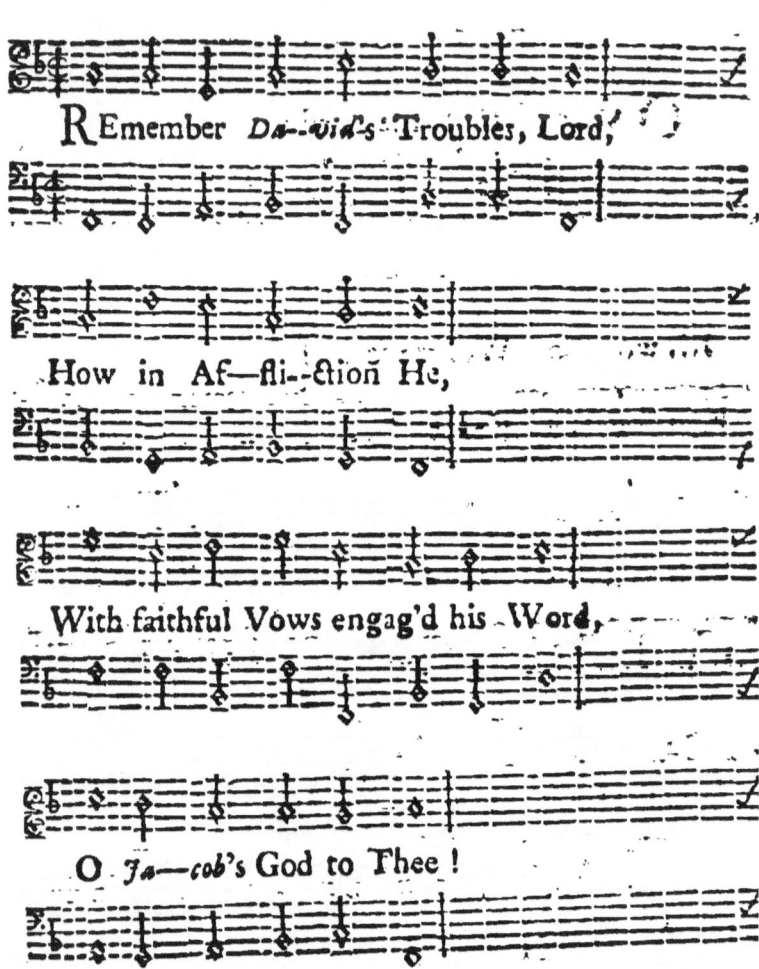

Woul

The Tunes of the Psalms. xxiij

High tho' my lof—ty Pa--lace rise,

With Ce—dars no——bly ceil'd.

And Beds with Golden Ca--no--pyes,

Would downy Slumbers yield.

E R.

ERRATA.

Page 7. line 20. for *Too*, read *As*. p. 12. l. 6. f. *the*, r. *thy*. p. 35. l. 4. f. *gain*, r. *claim*. p. 46. l. 23. f. *Those*, r. *Whose*. p. 51. l. 1. after *Truth* and *Mercy*, dele *s*. p. 64. l. 2. r. *the Voice*. p. 89, l. 1. r. *out-shine*. l. 17. f. *the*, r. *thy*. p. 90. l. 31. f. *the*, r. *thy*. p. 103. l. 21. r. *thou'dst*. p. 104. l. 27. r. *sacrifice*. p. 108. l. 18. f. *the*, r. *thy*. p. 142. l. 13. f. *thy*, r. *the*. p. 183. l. 28. f. *the*, r. *thy*. p. 185. l. 22. r. *sweet*. l. ult. f. *on*, r. *in*. p. 209. l. 5. r. *Skies*. p. 218. l. 23. r. *bring*. p. 222. l. 20. f. *the*, r. *thy*. p. 231. l. ult. r. *Wrath's* &c. d., p. 232. l. 23. r. *betray'd*. p. 234. l. 12. f. *the*, r. *tho'*. p. 238. r. *Part 5th. Metre 5th*. p. 240. l. 1. r. *quickly*. p. 265. l. 4. r. *And me with*. p. 266. l. 7. r. *Thy Law's the Truth*. p. 267. l. 11. d. ; p. 292. l. 7. r. *cheer*. p. 295. l. 20. d. *the*. p. 296. l. 29. r. *Thoughts*. p. 297. l. 17. f. *my*, r. *thy*. p. 298. l. 1. f. *then*, r. *them*. p. 309. l. 6. r. *Seed*.

DAVID's PSALMS PARAPHRAS'D,

IN ENGLISH METRE;

Agreeably to the TUNES commonly Sung in CHURCHES, &c.

Pſal. 1. *as the* 100th; *or Mr.* Sandys's 3d.

A Thouſand Bleſſings crown his Head,
 Whoſe Heart all impious Counſel flies;
And hates thoſe Paths where Sinners tread,
 Who God, and all that's good, deſpiſe.

But in his great Creator's Laws
 He ſpends his happy Days and Nights;
And thence, by Meditation, draws
 Both what inſtructs, and what delights.

All his Deſigns are juſt, and bleſs'd;
 His Hopes, and ev'ry Action thrives:
And when his mould'ring Clay's at reſt,
 His fragrant Memory ſurvives.

So fruitful Trees, near gentle Streams,
  Their Burthens to Perfection bring,
Unhurt by Summer's scorching Beams,
  And flourish with a constant Spring.

4 But the lost Sinner toils in vain,
  With faithless Joys to please his Mind;
His Roots, his Fruits, his cursed Gain,
  All fly like Chaff before the Wind.

5, 6 Let the last dreadful Trumpet sound,
  The Just, his Head undaunted rears;
While Woes the sinful Soul confound,
  With Terrours rack'd, and torn with Fears.

His Own, their mighty Master knows;
  And loves, and keeps, and wisely guides:
But Man, who sins, through various Woes,
  To Hell's dark Pains, unminded, slides.

Another Metre, Psal. 1.

1 HAppy, thrice happy's he, whose Feet
    Ne'er took that cursed Way,
  Where Atheists and Blasphemers meet,
    And God and Truth betray;
  Who ne'er stood by, to countenance
    What bold Transgressors dare;
  Nor, that he might in Guilt advance,
    Assum'd the Scorner's Chair.

2 He spends his happy Days and Nights
    To search his Maker's Laws;
  And thence Instructions and Delights
    By Meditation draws.

3 Constantly looks his Actions o'er,
    Their Justice calmly tries;

And

And then on Mercy's boundless Store
    For good Success relies.

So Trees near gentle Rivers plac'd,
    Their Fruits in Season bear;
With Leaves unfading always grac'd,
    And flourish all the Year.
But off, like Chaff, God's angry Wind
    The Godless Croud shall bear;
No Place shall they in Judgment find,
    Nor with the Just appear.

For God, with Favour, kindly knows
    The Just, and all their Ways:
But Ruin where the Sinner goes,
    And sure Destruction sways.

PSAL. ij.

GOD's wise Decrees are fix'd, and strong,
    As his Eternal Throne:
Why then should Heathen Fools so long
    His sacred Power disown?
Vain are their Hopes, vain ev'ry Thought;
    And all their Words are vain:
For what God's mighty Hands have wrought,
    God's mighty Hands maintain.

2 Weak Kings with flatt'ring Slaves combine,
    And fret with groundless Rage;
Against *their God* their Counsels join,
    Against *his Christ* engage.
3 Come, let us break their Bonds, *they say:*
    Throw off their slavish Yoke:
Why should we unknown Lords obey?
    Or unknown Pow'rs invoke?

4 But God, who, crown'd with Bliss, resides
    Above the lofty Skies,
Laughs at their Madness, and their Pride,
    And scorns their Policies.
5 From thundring Clouds his dreadful Voice,
    Distracts their trembling Souls:
And in his Wrath their Plots destroys,
    And thus their Rage controls.

6 Rave on, unhappy Fools! confound
    Your envious Thoughts in vain:
My King sits high, on *Sion* crown'd;
    And I'll his Crown maintain.

Part 2.

7 The Son, with Love, all Heavenly mild,
    His Awful Silence breaks;
And thus, to Pity reconcil'd,
    With gentle Language speaks:
Hear me, ah stupid World! declare
    Th' unchangeable Decree.
Thus my Eternal Father sware,
    Before Time's Birth, to Me.

Thou art my Son, begot by Me,
    On this Eternal Day:
8 Ask it, and I'll invest in Thee
    The whole Creation's Sway.
9 To Thee the World, when made, shall bow;
    Thee all its Host adore:
All Nations shall thy Rights allow,
    Thy Goodness all implore.

Thy Rod the Rebel Tribes shall feel,
    Thy Sceptre, forc'd, obey;
Crush'd by thy Hand, as harden'd Steel
    Would dash the mould'ring Clay.

PSAL. iij.

10 Be wise, ye Heav'n-born Kings; be wise
    All who on Earth command:
Adore your Lord with humble Eyes;
    With Awe before Him stand.

11 Joys, but with Fears alloy'd, express,
    And early Homage pay,
Lest in Rebellion's wild Excess
    You lose the perfect Way.
12 Bow, bow your Necks; for if his Wrath
    In angry Tempests rise,
Happy, ô happy's he, whose Faith
    On Him secur'd relies!

PSAL. iij.

1 HOW are my Foes, dear Lord, increas'd?
    What Crouds against me rise?
2 And to disturb my mournful Breast,
    A thousand Ways devise?
God is his only Help, *they cry*;
    On God his Hopes depend:
Yet see that God can Help deny,
    And leave his sinking Friend!

Yet Thou, Lord, art my Shield, my Praise,
    My Strength: And when to Thee
My Voice in humble Vows I raise,
    Thy Goodness answers me.
Safely I sleep, and safely wake;
    In thy Protection sure:
No gath'ring Host my Heart can shake,
    Nor my Defeat procure.

Rise then, my God, and save me now!
    And as thy Anger broke
My Rebels Teeth; and as they bow
    Beneath thy dreadful Stroke.

B 3

8 So send thy saving Health, and Grace;
 Let all thy Blessings flow:
And still to *Israel*'s faithful Race
 Thy promis'd Favour show!

PSAL. iv.

1 O Righteous God, whose Justice freed
   My Innocence of old;
 O let my present Pray'rs succeed,
   Thy Help my Cause uphold!
2 Vain Men, who by a fond Mistake,
   My solid Faith disgrace;
 And Vanities your Shelter make,
   And empty Lyes embrace:

3 See how God singles out the Just,
   His own peculiar Choice!
 See how my God rewards my Trust,
   And hears my suppliant Voice!
4 Fear then, ô fear Him! sin no more!
   Your own false Hearts survey;
 Examine all your Actions o'er,
   Your secret Crimes display.

5 Pardon, with silent Tears, intreat;
   And for an Off'ring give
 An upright Heart, without Deceit;
   And on his Promise live!
6 Mean Souls Earth's low Delights advance,
   And fading Wealth embrace.
 But grant us, Lord, thy Countenance,
   And thy Enlight'ning Grace!

7 So shall more Bliss my Heart enlarge,
   My Breast more Joys contain,
 Than theirs whom Wines and Oils o'er-charge,
   And who in Plenty reign.

PSAL. V.

3 No Terrours then shall break my Rest,
    No Fears disturb my Sleep,
While me thy pow'rful Arms invest,
    And safe from Dangers keep.

PSAL. V.

1 LORD, hear me from thy bless'd Abode,
    My Meditations weigh:
2 Attend my Cries, my King, my God,
    When I devoutly pray!
3 To Thee I raise my Morning-cries,
    To Thee my Prayers direct;
And with my longing Heart and Eyes,
    Thy kind Returns expect.

4 Thy Frowns on wicked Workers light;
    Thou hat'st Iniquity:
5 No Fools can bear thy angry Sight,
    Nor Sinners dwell with Thee.
6 Thy Wrath shall lying Lips consume,
    And those who thirst for Blood;
Or on deceitful Arts presume,
    Too rarely understood.

7 But to thy Courts, dear Lord, I'll go,
    Safe in thy Mercies store;
And tow'rd thy sacred Altars bow,
    And in thy Fear adore.
8 O lead me in thy righteous Way,
    To scape my watchful Foes:
To me thy Wisdom's Rules display,
    Thy happy Paths disclose!

9 My Foes in Fraud and Falshood deal,
    Their inward Parts are vile;
Their Throats devouring Graves conceal,
    Their flatt'ring Tongues beguile.

10 Destroy

10 Deſtroy them, Lord! in their own Arts,
   The Rebel Crew confound:
11 So Joys from merry faithful Hearts,
   In laſting Hymns ſhall ſound.

12 For, Lord, thy Favour on the Juſt
   In mighty Streams deſcends:
   Thy Goodneſs all who on Thee truſt,
   Like ſome firm Shield, defends.

PSAL. vj.

1 Rebuke me not in Anger, Lord;
   Nor in thy Wrath correct:
2 Health to my aking Bones afford;
   My wretched State reſpect!
3 My Soul quite faints: But oh! how long
   Muſt I no Anſwer have!
4 O turn! ô free my Soul from Wrong!
   My Soul in Mercy ſave!

5 In Death none thinks of Thee; no Praiſe,
   No Thanks our Graves diſcloſe:
   And, oh! my Strength, dear Lord, decays,
   Quite ſpent with waſting Woes!
6 All Night my Eaſleſs Bed with Tears,
   With Tears my Couch o'er-flows;
7 My Sight quite dim with Age appears,
   Through my prevailing Foes.

But ſee one Beam of chearful Light!
   Be gone, ye ſinful Crew!
8 My Prayers are in my Maker's Sight;
   And all my Tears in view:
9 Bluſh then, miſtaken Fools! for ſhame;
   For God has heard my Cries:
10 Be gone! for in his Mighty Name
   My Strength, my Safety lies.

PSAL.

PSAL. vij.

1 IN Thee, my Lord, I firmly trust;
  My Foe, dear God! control!
2 Lest, Lion-like, with Force unjust,
  He tear my helpless Soul.
3 If e'er against my Prince, if e'er
  My very Thoughts rebell'd;
  If I his Crown unjustly wear,
  Or e'er against him swell'd:

4 If e'er I War for Peace repay'd:
  Nay, if my Filial Care
  My King, my Foe unjustly made,
  Did never kindly spare;
5 Then let my bloodiest Foes prevail,
  And hurl my Glories down;
  My Life with due Success assail,
  And spurn my envy'd Crown.

6 But since I'm innocent, and from
  Such Imputations free,
  O now to my Assistance come,
  Redeem and rescue me!
  O rouze thy Fury, Lord! and break
  My Adversaries Rage!
  Rouze it, and in thy Judgment speak,
  And for my Rights engage!

7 So shall the Multitude surround
  Thy Courts with grateful Praise:
  Rise then, with awful Glories crown'd,
  And thy Tribunal raise.
8 O judge the Nations round, and me,
  By thy impartial Laws;
  Then clear'd my Innocence shall be,
  And vindicate my Cause.

Part 2.

9 Let Sin, and sinful Workers die,
    The Just more firmly stand:
The Hearts and Reins severely try,
    And righteous things command.
10 For God's my Shield; that God, whose Grace
    The Heart sincere protects;
11 He's just, and on the sinful Race
    His daily Wrath reflects.

12 If still his Sins the Sinner loves,
    His Sword he fiercely whets;
And oft his deadly Bow-string proves,
    His Bow as often sets.
13 Death's Instruments are all prepar'd,
    His Arrows pointed right
At such who dare, though kindly spar'd,
    Against their Maker fight.

14 The Wretch, big with Iniquity,
    And Lyes, and Mischief, goes;
The monstrous Birth brought forth, we see,
    With Hellish Pangs and Throws.
15 He plots, and is himself ensnar'd
    In Nets himself had spread;
His Pains and Rage recoiling hard
    On his contriving Head.

17 I'll praise the Lord; high as his Fame,
    My lofty Praise shall fly:
I'll sing to his Immortal Name,
    Who ever lives on high.

PSAL.

PSAL. viij.

1 GReat Lord of Lords! how swift thy Name
    Through ev'ry Climate flies!
Thy spreading Praise, thy glorious Fame,
    Surmounts the lofty Skies.
2 Thy Strength in Babes and Sucklings shines,
    To quell thy senseless Foes;
To crush the Rebel-World's Designs,
    And all their Rage expose.
3 When I the Sky's vast Arch survey,
    Rais'd by thy curious Hand;
How Moon and Stars thy Rules obey,
    And fix'd, in Order stand.
4 Lord, how has Man thy Thoughts possess'd!
    Lost Man thy Smiles obtain'd!
Who sinn'd, yet, with a Saviour bless'd,
    New Hopes of Mercy gain'd!
5 Though He, our Lives to purchase, took
    Less than an Angel's State,
All Graces in his God-like Look
    With humble Greatness sate.
6 To Him the whole Creation yields,
    And at his Foot-stool bow:
7 The Herds, which trace the Woods and Fields,
    His Sov'reign Rights allow.
8 To Him the feather'd Hosts resign,
    And his Commands obey.
And Fish, which through the Ocean's Brine
    Divide their wond'rous Way.
9 How swift, great Lord of Lords, thy Name
    Through ev'ry Climate flies;
O how thy Praise, thy glorious Fame
    Surmounts the lofty Skies!

Anoth

Another Metre, as Mr. Sandys's 17th.

1 Lord, how Illustrious is thy Sacred Name!
  How bless'd, great God of Hosts, Eternal King!
Whose Honours all the lower World proclaim!
  Whose Honours all the Heav'nly Armies sing!

2 Yet when the Foes, blind with malicious Rage,
  Affront thy Honours, or thy Name defie,
Poor Babes, weak Infants, on thy Part engage,
  And quickly make the boasting Monsters fly.
More Strength, more Truth, from Infant-Language (flows,
  Than haughty Learning, or presuming Pride.
The meanest Wretch, by thy best influence, grows
  A faithful Preacher, a victorious Guide.

3 When I survey the never-resting Skies,
  Whose moving Arch thy curious Fingers spread;
When to the Changing Moon I raise my Eyes,
  The Stars with inexhausted Brightness fed;

4 Lord, what's poor Man, or Man's polluted Race,
  So pity'd yet, so kindly own'd by thee?
How could he hope for such unbounded Grace,
  That for his sake, God should Incarnate be?

5 Yet God, for our lov'd sakes, our Nature took;
  Beneath Himself, beneath his Angels found:
Tho God-like Beauties grac'd his Heav'nly Look;
  His Sacred Head Majestick Glories crown'd.

6 Where-e'er He mov'd, submissive Nature bow'd;
  His Handy-works their great Creator knew:
And to adore his Feet, th' impatient Croud
  On the swift Wings of just Obedience flew.

7 Before

7 Before Him savage Brutes their Fierceness laid:
   On Him rough Lions fawn'd, and Panthers gaz'd:
Weak Sheep with hungry Wolves all fearless play'd;
   And with fierce Tygers Kine securely graz'd.

8 On lofty Trees, around his Glorious Head,
   With strange Delight the feather'd Chorus hung;
O'er Him their fanning Pinions gently spread,
   And in their native Tunes his Praises sung.

When o'er the Seas their King triumphant pass'd,
   Beneath his Feet the Billows silent lay;
The finny Herd his wondrous Foot-steps trac'd,
   And with their Silver Scales describ'd his Way.

9 Thy Honours thus the Lower World proclaim,
   Thy Honours thus all Nature's Armies sing.
Lord, how illustrious is thy Sacred Name!
   How bless'd, great Lord of Hosts, Eternal King!

PSAL. ix. *As the First.*

1 I'LL praise the Lord with Heart and Voice;
    His great, his wondrous Actions praise:
2 In Thee, O highest God, rejoice;
    Thy Name in Songs Triumphant raise.

3 My Foes shall turn their Backs, and fall,
    And sink before thy Glorious Face;
4 Thy righteous Bar has judg'd 'em all,
    And now my Cause obtains the place.

5 Thy Hand o'erturns the Nation round,
    Thy Hand the sinful World subdues;
Their Names Eternal Bars confound,
    And dark Forgetfulness pursues.

6 O Enemy, presume no more
    To lay huge Towns and Countries waste;
Thy Rage our burning Cities bore,
    Thy Rage their very Names defac'd.

7 But our Eternal God appears,
    His Bar prepar'd for Judgment stands;
8 The World His righteous Sentence hears,
    His wise Decrees, and just Commands.

9 The Lord, their Refuge, saves the Poor,
    With mighty Cares and Woes oppress'd:
10 His Saints live in His Help secure,
    And in his constant Presence bless'd.

Part 2.

11 To *Sion*'s God your Praises sing,
    His Acts through all the World declare!
12 When He his Quest for Blood shall bring,
    He'll grant the Poor's accepted Prayer.

13 Thou who my Soul from Death couldst raise,
    My Suff'rings, Lord, in Mercy view:
14 I'll then thy Name in *Sion* praise,
    And Joys in thy Salvation shew.

15 In their own Pits the Gentiles fall,
    Their own strong Nets their Feet have caught
16 Their own false Hearts have trap'd 'em all:
    So wisely God's Designs are wrought.

17 The Wicked all shall sink, and those
    Whose Heath'nish Souls their God forget:
18 But Suff'rers sha'n't for ever lose
    Their Hopes, or all in Darkness set.

PSAL. x.

19 Rise, Lord; ô let not Men prevail;
   But rise, and judge the Nations round!
20 Till all their Hearts with Terrour fail;
   Not Gods, but Men, and mortal found.

PSAL. XI.

1 WHY, Lord, ô why so far from me,
      In my afflicted State?
2 When Sin and haughty Pride agree,
      And all our Woes create?
3 O let their Arts themselves ensnare
      Who boast of Crimes they love,
   Who bless the Covetous, and dare,
      What God abhors, approve!

4 His God the prosp'rous Sinner scorns,
      God ne'er his Thoughts employs;
5 The World beneath his Greatness mourns,
      Which all Her Peace destroys.
   Thy Judgments, Lord, exalted far
      Above his Sense appear;
   Which makes him scorn his Foes in War,
      And puff at Dangers near.

6 His Heart concludes, I'm great; no Ill
      Can change my certain State:
7 His Mouth Fraud, Lyes and Curses fill;
      His Tongue, mischievous Hate.
8 Close in his Lurking-holes he lies,
      To kill the Innocent;
   Blood revels in his furious Eyes,
      On their Destruction bent.

9 He like some Lion Couchant lies,
      To seize the trembling Prey;
   And would God's holy Saints surprize,
      And tear their Souls away.

A thou-

A thousand Traps and Snares he sets
  Where harmless Vertue goes;
And to the Tangled in his Nets
  No Truth nor Mercy shows.

Part 2.

10 Sometimes the Wicked hangs his Head,
    And feigns Humility;
  That, by his harmless Air mis-led,
    The Meek may fall, and die.
11 God, if there's any God, he says,
    Forgets what Mortals do;
  He can't discern our crafty Ways,
    Our secret Actions view.

12 Up, Lord! stretch out thy pow'rful Hand,
    Afflicted Souls to save!
13 For why should Fools against thee stand?
    Thy dreadful Vengeance brave?
  Why should they cry, God minds it not?
14   O let thy piercing Sight
  Look through their dark mischievous Plot:
    Re-pay their secret Spite!

  On Thee the Poor for Help depend;
    To Thee sad Orphans fly.
15 Break wicked Arms, their Malice end,
    And Sin it self shall die.
16 The Lord for ever reigns; his Arms
    Our Land from Gentiles freed:
17 He hears the Meek, their Courage warms,
    And makes their Prayers succeed.

18 He helps the Fatherless and Poor,
    And quells the Sinner's Rage,
  Lest they, our Ruins to procure,
    Should all their Force engage.

PSAL. xj.

IN God my Hope securely stands,
    Why then should Wretches cry?
Fly! fly to Hills, or foreign Lands!
    Like Birds affrighted fly.
See how the Wicked bend their Bows,
    And Nock their Arrows sure!
That they with unexpected Blows,
    May Death to thine procure.

And since Hopes best Foundations are
    By wicked Hands destroy'd,
Oh, how sha'l Men of Justice fare!
    Or how their Force avoid?
God in his Holy Temple sits
    Enthron'd above the Sky,
And all the Faults weak Man commits,
    His pierceing Eye-lids try.

He proves the Just, but hates all those,
    Who Sin and Rapine love;
On them Snares, Flames and Sulphur throws,
    And Terrors from above.
For God, who's infinitely Just,
    In Justice takes Delight:
And Upright Men may safely trust
    In His reviving Sight.

Another Metre, as Mr. Sandys's *4th.*

MY Faith is fix'd on **God** most High,
    Why then should Fools to vex me cry,
      As Birds afraid,
      By Noises made,
    Hence to the Mountains fly!

2 For loe! the Wicked bend their Bows,
  Their Arrows on the strings dispose,
    At Men upright
    In Woes dark Night,
  They make their deadly Blows.

3 Ill Men, by Force and Art, have thrown
  The Governments Foundations down.
    Where then, ô where
    Can those appear,
  Who Truth and Justice own?

4 God in his Holy Temple reigns,
  The Lord enthron'd on High remains,
    And with His Eyes
    Severely tries
  What Sins the Soul retains.

5 Hee'l try and vindicate the Just,
  But His Eternal Vengeance must
    With Death pursue
    That Impious Crew
  Who dare in Rapine trust.

6 Thick Snares, hot Flames, and Sulphur shall,
  Like dismal Storms on Sinners fall;
    Strange Terrors will
    Their Fancies fill,
  And Fears confound them all.

7 The righteous God in Actions Right
  Has ever fix'd his whole Delight;
    Onely the Man
    Who's Righteous can
  Procure his favouring sight.

PSAL. xij.

O Help me Lord, for Goodness now,
    And Truth from Earth are flown!
None Honesty nor Mercy show,
    They'r all Deceiful grown.
All double Hearts and Tongues employ,
    When with their Friends they speak;
But God will Lying-lips destroy,
    And haughty Boasters break.

Who say, Come let our Tongues be free,
    Our Words at Random fly;
And when we use that Liberty,
    What Lord shall ask us why?
But to relieve their misery
    To hear the Needy's cry,
I'le rise, says God, and set him free
    From Scorn and Cruelty.

And, Lord, Thy Promises are pure
    As Silver oft refin'd,
And will thy happy Saints secure
    From Men to Vice enclin'd.
The Wicked proudly stalks and swells,
    But when Exalted high
Grief on each Humane visage dwells,
    And Blushes Crimson Dye.

PSAL. xiij.

LOst in Oblivion, Lord, shall I
    No more behold thy Face?
Must all my Thoughts distracted ly,
    And Woes my Heart embrace.
Still shall my Foes my strength assail,
    And still above me rise?

3 Lord, hear me! and e're Death prevail
    Unclose my failing Eyes!

4 O never let my haughty Foes
    Presume they've conquer'd me!
If they my smallest Trip disclose,
    They'l all Triumphant be.
5 But in thy mercy, Lord, I trust,
    Thy saving Health adore.
6 And sing to Thee whose Bounty must
    My doubting Soul restore.

PSAL. xiv.

1 THe wicked Fool's misguided Heart
    The World's great God denies;
Hence all from Ways of Virtue start,
    And horrid Crimes devise.
2 God from above the World surveys,
    And Humane Actions reads,
To see who common Sense obeys,
    And God, or Goodness heeds.

3 But all from God's pure Ways decline,
    And in his Nostrils stink,
None, None at all on Truth's Divine,
    Or sober Virtues think.
" Their Throats like gaping Graves appear,   [Ex
    " Their oily Tongues deceive,   Septua-
" Their Lips more dealy Poisons bear,   ginta.
    " Then biting Aspies leave.

" Their Mouths with bitter Curses stor'd,
    " Their Feet to Murders fly,
" Destruction all their Paths afford,
    " And certain Misery.
" No Ways of Charity, or Peace,
    " Their Pride, or Malice knows,
                             " And

" And they as still their Crimes encrease,
" No Fear of God disclose.

But can the Sons of Sin so loose
    Their Understanding power,
That they like Bread my Saints abuse,
    And all at once devour.
To God no Sense can make them pray:
    Tho' where no Ground appears
Their Souls a thousand Terrors sway,
    And causless senseless Fears.

But God who loves the Righteous Race,
    Among the Just remains,
And while Ill Men their Hope disgrace,
    He still their Hope sustains.
Oh, whence shall *Israe.*'s safety rise?
    If God their mournful State
Restore, in Them the kind surprize
    Will boundless Joys create.

PSAL. XV.

HOw blest, how glorious is the Place,
    Where thy great Name resides!
How blest the Man whom there thy Grace
    From impious Crouds divides!
But, Lord, what Gifts can fix him there?
    What wondrous Virtues raise
His Soul to love thy House, and there
    To sing thy daily Praise.

He only can with Hopes be blest
    Of that Cœlestial State,
Who hides no Envy in his Breast
    Nor deadly lurking Hate:
But all his Thoughts are fix'd and true,
    And all his Actions right.

Faith to his Word is always due,
    His Lips in Truth delight.

No Falshood e'er perverts his Heart,
    No Lyes defile his Tongue;
3 Nor dares he, with malicious Art,
    Contrive his Neighbour's Wrong.
He scorns those Tales by Malice rais'd,
    To blast his fragrant Name;
And all those senseless Scandals blaz'd
    Against his rising Fame.

Part 2.

4 That harden'd Wretch, who proudly slights
    His great Creator's Laws;
Whose Wit against his Maker fights,
    And backs a Godless Cause;
That vile, that despicable Slave
    His nobler Thoughts despise.
But smiles the Good shall always have,
    And Kindness in his Eyes.

No Loss, no Gain his Justice bows,
    His Words Assurance speak;
He'll ne'er his Oaths, nor sacred Vows,
    Nor just Engagements break.
5 Boundless and wide his Bounty flows,
    And vile Extortion hates.
Large as Men's Wants his Mercy grows,
    And all their Wealth creates.

He loves the Innocent, and strives
    Their Vertues to protect;
From him no Bribe can buy their Lives,
    Nor Falshood gain Respect.
Thus shall he reach thy holy Place,
    There grow, and flourish there:

And in the Glories of thy Face
    No Loss nor Dangers fear.

Another Metre, as Mr. Sandys's 7th.

Bless'd Lord, how glorious is the Place
    Thy Altars grace!
How is that holy Temple bless'd,
    By Thee possess'd!
But, ô, what happy Man is he
Who there a daily Guest may be!

He's only of that Bliss secure
    Whose Life is pure,
Who never lets Contagious Sin
    Prevail within;
For Right and Justice only cares,
And from his Heart the Truth declares.

He'll never slander, never lye;
    Nor will his Eye
With Malice, or an envious View,
    His Friend pursue;
Nor to his Neighbour's Hurt proceed,
Or break his Peace by Word or Deed.

He will, if Men in Sin delight,
    Abhor their Sight;
And with a just Contempt despise
    Their shameless Lyes.
But Rev'rence and Respect afford
To such as love and fear the Lord.

If to his Neighbour's Profit e'er
    He kindly swear,
Though to himself a Prejudice
    From thence may rise;
Falshood on him shall ne'er prevail;
His Gain, but not his Faith, may fail.

5 He'll

5 He'll, if Extortion rais'd it, hate
       A vaſt Eſtate;
  And won't, for Bribes, quit the Defence
       Of Innocence.
  The Man whoſe Life is thus approv'd,
  Shall ne'er by Fears or Pains be mov'd.

PSAL. xvj. *As the Firſt.*

1 PReſerve me, Lord, who truſt in Thee!
2   To God my thankful Heart has ſaid,
  Thou art my Lord, but canſt not be
     More bleſs'd by my Submiſſions made.

3 I, with unbounded Bliſs, delight
     In Saints, in ſuch as Goodneſs mind:
4 But Sorrows multiply'd ſhall light
     On Men to other Gods inclin'd.

  I'll ne'er, though kindly call'd, partake
     Of their deteſted Sacrifice;
  Nor Mention of their Idols make,
     They never from my Lips ſhall riſe.

5 My God's my bleſs'd Inheritance,
     My Right his mighty Arm ſuſtains:
6 My Lines on pleaſant Parts advance;
     For me a goodly Lot remains.

Part 2.

7 My Thanks I'll to my Teacher ſhow,
     I nightly feel his gentle Hand;
8 He's ever fix'd before me, ſo
     I ſtill unmov'd, unſhaken ſtand.

PSAL. xvij.

My Heart hence springs with rising Joys,
  My Tongue's with glorious Praises bless'd:
Though Death my Mortal State destroys,
  My Flesh in certain Hope shall rest.

o The Grave shall soon my Flesh resign,
  Death quit his Triumphs o'er my Soul.
Tombs sha'n't thy Holy One Confine,
  Nor Worms my mould'ring Corps control.

1 To me thy Grace new Life shall show;
  Lord, in thy Presence Joys abound;
With thee Eternal Pleasures flow,
  And lasting Bliss, with Glories crown'd.

PSAL. xvij.

HEar me, ô hear me, Lord?
  Accept my earnest Cry!
Thy Justice to his Pray'rs afford,
  Who hates Hypocrisie!
O weigh my Right, and let
  My Sentence come from Thee!
Thou try'st my Heart, thy Looks are set,
  By Night to visit me.

Yet thou hast found me pure
  When in thy Furnace try'd:
My Lips, by Resolutions sure,
  Are to thy Precepts ty'd.
Whate'r vile Sinners dare,
  I know thy Word's Divine:
And from destructive Paths, with Care,
  My wand'ring Feet confine.

Lord, all my Motions guide
  To tread thy sacred Way!

And never let my Foot-steps wide
From Paths of Vertue stray!
6   I only call to thee,
Who hear'st the Cries of thine:
Lord, bow thy gracious Ears to me,
And to my Words incline!

7   Thy wondrous Love disclose
To those who trust in thee;
And save them from the Rage of those
Who would their Ruin see!
8   Keep me as Eye-lids keep
And guard the tender Eye,
That I beneath thy Wings may sleep,
Beneath thy Shade may lie!

Part 2.

9   Save me from bloody Hands,
Who now inclose me round;
And all those cruel angry Bands,
Which would my Life confound!
10   Who, fat and haughty made,
Speak big with lofty Pride;
11 But Snares which in our Paths are laid,
With down-cast Looks can hide.

12   Who, like fierce Lions, would
Surprize the trembling Prey;
Or Lions Whelps, which, mad for Blood,
In Thickets lurking stay.
13   Rise, quell their Malice, Lord,
And break their Insolence!
From wicked Men, thy deadly Sword,
Be thou my Soul's Defence.

14   From Godless Brutes, employ'd
To scourge a careless Age;

Men who with Earthly Blessings cloy'd,
   Their Hearts on Earth engage ;
 Whose craving Bellies all
    The secret Treasures fill ;
Whose Sons are far, whose Lordships fall
   Down to their Children still.

15   So I in Righteousness
   Thy glorious Face shall see
Which, when I'm rais'd again, shall bless
   Me to Satiety.

PSAL. xviij. *as the* 100*th, or Mr.* Sandys's 9*th.*

1 HOW shall I praise my God, my King,
    Thus ecstasy'd with Joys and Love ?
  What worthy Hallelujahs sing
    To his great Name who rules above ?

  He, by a thousand sacred Bands,
    Has made my grateful Heart his own.
2 My Strength, my Rock, my Fort He stands,
    His Force in my Deliv'rance shown.

  My God, my solid Hope, my Shield,
    Against my fierce insulting Foes :
  Safe in his Strength I keep the Field,
    My Crown his mighty Arm bestows.

3 Him will I praise, to him I'll pray,
    And so from all my Foes be free,
4 Tho' Death's strong Chains should stop my Way,
    And Floods of Horrour compass me.

5 Hell's dismal Sorrows hedg'd me round,
    Death's cruel Chains oppos'd my Way ;
6 Yet my Distress his Mercy found,
    And from his Seat He heard me pray.

Part 2.

7 His Awful Nod my Cries receiv'd,
    Which all the World's Foundations shook,
And Mountains from their Bases heav'd,
    Unhing'd by his revenging Look.

8 Thick Smoak his kindling Furies rais'd,
    His Wrath the streaming Vapour show'd,
Devouring Flames before him blaz'd,
    And Bolts with living Sulphur glow'd.

9 He came, Heav'ns bending Arches groan'd,
    His Steps thick Darkness cover'd o'er;
10 Triumphant Flames their Lord inthron'd,
    On Wings of rapid Tempests bore.

11 Mysterious Gloom around him flow'd,
    And where he forc'd his wond'rous Way,
His Way Majestick Darkness show'd,
    And heavy Clouds obscur'd the Day.

12 But soon his fiery Wrath dispell'd
    The Clouds, the Clouds dissolv'd around;
And Drops to monst'rous Hail congeal'd,
    With burning Bolts, rak'd o'er the Ground.

13 The thund'ring Skies his Voice reveal'd,
    The Air return'd the dreadful Sound;
And Drops to monstrous Hail congeal'd,
    With burning Bolts, rak'd o'er the Ground.

14 Thick as his Hail his Arrows flew:
    Nor could his Foes their Force avoid,
While his sure Hand thick Lightnings threw,
    And all their scatter'd Hosts destroy'd.

Part 3.

5 Great God, when thy fierce Fury storm'd,
   Distracted Nature trembling lay;
And the unfathom'd Deep, deform'd
   Through horrid Ruptures, felt the Day.

The Seas old Parent Springs appear'd,
   And the great World's Foundations torn;
The tott'ring Hills their Doom's-day fear'd,
   By thy impetuous Wrath o'er-born.

6 For me yet were his Loves engag'd,
   His Brows with softer Glory shin'd;
He sav'd me from the Gulphs enrag'd,
   And all the greedy Floods combin'd.

7 His gracious Arm still rescues me
   From all my Foes insulting Hate,
That Arm which me alone can free,
   And their prevailing Force abate.

8 Their Spite my saddest Moments watch'd,
   But God was then my Guard, my Stay;
He lov'd, he lov'd my Soul, and snatch'd
   From hungry Jaws the fainting Prey.

9 My harmless Innocence he knows,
   And with his bounteous Love pursues;
0 For I his sacred Methods chose,
   Nor would his just Commands refuse.

Part 4.

1 God's Statutes still before me lay,
2 Nor durst I cast his Laws aside,
3 But with Him trod the perfect Way,
   And all my craving Lusts deny'd.

24 So God my Love with Love repay'd,
   Repay'd my righteous Innocence,
   And to my Hands thus guiltless made
   Hee'l still His kind Rewards dispense.

25 God's ever Just; where Mercy shines
   His Mercy meets the tender Heart,
   Where Man to perfect Deeds inclines,
   His Smiles a perfect meed impart.

26 Where the plain Heart sincerely moves,
   God's Blessings are unmix'd and plain,
   Where Man deceit and falshood loves,
   False Hopes, false Joys, are all his gain.

27 Thou shalt thy poor Afflicted raise,
   Bring down the Looks which proudly swell.
28 And make my Light more brightly blaze,
   And all my darker thoughts dispel.

29 By Thee with Godlike vigour arm'd
   Thro' rally'd Hosts I force my way,
   Scale lofty Walls, till all alarm'd
   My ever conquering Sword obey.

Part 5.

30 God's ways are perfect, try'd and pure
   His Word; His Strength a certain Shield.
31 What God but Ours can help secure?
   What Lord so firm a Shelter yield?

32 My God, my Arm with strength supplies,
   And makes my Ways and Counsels plain,
33 Through him my speed the Hart out-flies,
   And I set high securely reign.

34 H

34 He taught my unskill'd Arms the flight
    To throw the Spear and lift the Shield,
    To break steel Bows with ease, and fight
    The Duel, or the Marshall'd field.

35 Thro' Thee I'me safe and guarded sure,
    And Greatness gain, and kind support,
36 My Paths grow large, my Feet secure,
    My Foes my Conquering Armies sport.

37 My flying Foes I'le swiftly chase
    And seize, and soon confound them all:
38 Till in their Breasts my Shafts take place,
    And Dead beneath my feet they fall.

39 When numerous Armies take the Field
    With strength thy Spirit girds me round,
40 Thou make'st my fierce Opposers yield,
    Their humbled Necks to kiss the ground.

    Thro' Thee my Hands with ease destroy
    Those Crouds whose spite my Glory cross'd.
41 In vain to God for Help they cry,
    Their Prayers, their empty Cries are lost.

Part 6.

42 Thro' Thee my scatter'd Foes are blown
    Like Dust before the stormy Wind,
    Or like vile Dirt in streets are thrown,
    And I tread down their hated kind.

43 No more shall strife the Tribes divide,
    But I'le by join'd Agreement reign,
    And o're strange Heathen Lands preside,
    And Realms unknown shall drag my Chain.

44 They'l by my Name alarm'd obey,
    And Strangers smooth pretences make,
45 And humble Reverence seem to pay
    When all their strongest Frontiers quake.

46 Bless'd be my God! ô ever blest!
    My ever-living Rock! may He,
47 Whose saving Help my Foes deprest,
    More honour'd still, more glorious be!

48 Their Heads it's mark His Vengeance makes,
    And He the subject Nations leads,
Me from their cruel Envy takes,
    And sets me high above their Heads.

And tho' Man's heady Fury still
    Fly out, thy Arms my Safety bring;
49 And I before the Gentiles will
    Thy Praise, in grateful Anthems, sing.

50 To Kings He great Salvation gives;
    And sure of his protecting Grace
His *David*, his Anointed lives,
    And all his long succeeding Race.

PSAL, 19. *As the* 18*th.*

1 Look up obdurate Wretch! Survey
    The Heavens, the far extended Skyes:
See what those sacred Volumes lay,
    Before thy Unbelieving Eyes.

To prove our God's Existence, there
    A thousand starry Beauties shine,
A thousand glorious Marks appear,
    Of Providence and Love Divine.

2 If still thy sullen Silence dare
    Neglect thy great Creator's Praise,
  Yet wiser Nature's grateful Care
    His Being speaks, his Might displays.

  There, Days to Nights, and Nights to Days,
    Instructive Wisdom's Lectures read.
3 Yet to proclaim God's wondrous praise,
    They neither Voice nor Language need.

  Orders prodigious Eloquence,
    O're all the seeing World prevails;
  And with strong Truth, and weighty Sense,
    Their willing Eyes and Hearts assails.

4 Nor can Earth's darkest Corners be
    So far from Light or Sense remov'd,
  But they our God's Existence see,
    And Atheistic Lyes disprov'd.

Part 2.

  Above in open Skies He blest
5   The Place from whence the lightsom Sun
  Like some Illustrious Bridgroom drest;
    Or well-breath'd vigorous Youth should run.

6 Thro' every Point he swifty drives,
    And sheds his Influences round,
  And as He runs disperses Lives,
    His Heat's with vast Productions crown'd.

7 Yet tho' that radiant Star declare,
    So plain the Majesty Divine,
  Tho' Nature speak her Maker's care,
    And God in every Creature shine.

More happy we, to whom his Grace
  Imparts his Will, aud sacred Laws;
Where, through each Word, the Poor may trace
  His Works, and Him, their mighty Cause.

Thy Laws in full Perfection shine,
  Great God, thy Statutes firmly stand;
Those, sinful Thoughts to Good incline;
  These make the Simplest understand.

8 Thy Precepts right, thy Dictates pure,
    Give Joy, and clear the Cloudy Eyes;
9 Thy Worship ever shall endure,
    Thy Judgments all are just, and wise.

Part 3.

10 Honey we'd eat, and Gold we'd gain;
     That, for its Sweetness; this, its Price.
   But nobler Sweets thy Laws contain;
     More worth, thy Word's Divine Advice.

11 They warn my Soul when Danger's near,
     Dangers which Health and Lust create;
   And then conduct me safely where
     Rewards on just Obedience wait.

12 Yet who, ô ho'y God can know
     What Guilt his inmost Thoughts attends,
   Who weighs his Words, his Actions who?
     Or on their Innocence depends?

   Cleanse me, ô cleanse my Soul, my God,
     From Sins o'er-look'd, and Guilt unknown:
13 O let me not beneath the Load
     Of Madness or Presumption groan!

    So from great Guilt, great Errours, free,
14 I'll praise my strong Redeemer's Name,
    Till all my Thoughts and Words with Thee
    May Favour and Acceptance gain.

PSAL. xx. *As the* 12*th.*

1   WHen, press'd with weighty Cares,
       The Lord accept thy Prayers,
  Thee with his glorious Name defend!
2   May his Assisting-Grace
     Come from thy Holy Place;
  His Strength from *Sion*'s Hill descend!
3   O may thy Sacrifice
     Right from his Altars rise,
  Consum'd at once by Flames Divine!
4   He give thee wish'd Success,
     And all thy Counsels bless,
  While we in Thanks and Praise combine!

5   With Joys Triumphant we
     Thy great Salvation see:
  In God's great Name our Standards high,
     With humbly grateful Praise,
     And chearful Hands, we'll raise:
  May God to all thy Prayers reply!
6   He, from his holy Throne,
     Will his Anointed own;
  On him his God's Salvation flows:
     That Health and Safety strong,
     Which to our God belong,
  God's mighty Arm alone bestows.

7   Some in their Chariots most,
     And some in Horses boast;
  But we, in God's more pow'rful Name.

8   They, crush'd and broken all,
     In weighty Ruins fall,
  While we our Saviour's Strength proclaim:
     Through that we strongly rise,
     And with erected Eyes,
  The Spring of all our Strength adore.
9   O Thou, our God, our King,
     Accept the Vows we bring,
  When we thy needful He'p implore!

Another Metre. As the 100*th.*

1 THE Lord, in dang'rous Times receive
     Thy Pray'rs; his Name defend thee still
2 Thy Wants with holy Aids relieve,
     And help thee from his sacred Hill!

3 O may He all thy Vows record,
     Consume thy grateful Sacrifice:
4 Success to thy vast Thoughts afford,
     And bless each mighty Enterprize!

5 So, in his Health Triumphant, we
     Will raise our happy Standards high
  In God's great Name, while kindly he
     Shall to thy fervent Pray'rs reply:

6 Now, now I know the Lord his Health
     on his Anointed King bestows;
  Whose Strength, whose Happiness, and Wealth,
     From his Celestial Treasure flows.

7 Some trust in well-arm'd Chariots; some
     In Horses, and in Horse-men's Force:
  In God's more pow'rful Name we come;
     To him alone's our whole Recourse.

8 They

8 They quickly bend, and quickly fall;
　　We rise more high, and stronger stand;
9 Help, Lord! and when, distress'd, we call,
　　For us thy Royal Aids command!

PSAL. xxj.   *As the 100th.*

1 THE King shall in thy Might be glad,
　　And in thy saving Health rejoice,
2 Since he, bless'd Lord, his Wishes had,
　　And thou hast heard his humble Voice.

3 Thy Goodness all his Hopes prevents,
　　And crowns his Head with envy'd Gold:
4 He beg'd for Life; thy Love consents,
　　He long may live, and ne'er be old.

5 Thy great Salvation set him high,
　　With all Majestick Glory crown'd:
6 On him Eternal Blessings lie;
　　Thy Heav'nly Joys his Heart surround.

7 The King on God above relies,
　　And in his Mercy firmly stands:
8 No Foe beyond his Anger flies,
　　Nor scapes his long revenging Hands.

9 Lord, when thy dreadful Fury burns,
　　Its Flame their Stock at once consumes,
10 And all their Race on Earth o'erturns,
　　And all their wretched Pride intombs.

11 Against thee they conspir'd, and fram'd
　　Such Plots as no Effect could take.
12 O let them turn their Backs asham'd!
　　Thine Arrows sharp against them make!

13 Exalt

13 Exa't thy Might, thy G'ory, Lord;
　　Arife, exalt thy lofty Name,
　While we with Songs thy Might record,
　　And all thy wondrous Acts proclaim.

PSAL. xxij.

1 WHY, ô my God; my God, ô why
　　　Haft thou forfaken me!
　How long fo diftant from my Cry
　　Shall thy Salvation be!
2 To thee, my God, I cry by Day;
　　To thee by Night I cry:
　With Tears, with reftlefs Tears, I pray;
　　Yet, unregarded, die.

3 Yet Thou art holy, Lord, and pure;
　　With faithful Praife ador'd:
4 Our Father's Hopes in Thee were fure,
　　Thy He'p their Souls reftor'd.
5 On Thee they call'd, and hop'd in Thee,
　　Yet no Difgrace receiv'd:
　Thy Hand procur'd their Liberty,
　　And all their Wants reliev'd.

6 But I, a wretched Worm, the Name
　　Of Man in vain have born;
　By Men expos'd to common Shame,
　　And all the Vulgar's Scorn.
7 Their Heads, their Lips, when I appear,
　　With Scoffs difdainful move.
8 Let's fee, they cry, if God can hear,
　　If God his Caufe approve.

　God was his Hope, in God his Truft,
　　On God the Wretch rely'd:
　God, if He'll have him, ftrong y muft
　　Efpoufe his Darling's Side.

PSAL. xxij.

9 But from my Mother's Breasts and Womb,
    Thou wast my God, my Guide:
10 Thy careful Hand my youthful Bloom,
    My Infant Cries supply'd.

11 So on thy Grace I still depend,
    O never cast me by;
For daily Woes my Life attend,
    And no Assistant's nigh.

Part 2.

12 Against me Sinners fierce engage,
    And impious Arms prevail;
13 And me with Lions rampant Rage,
    And open Mouths, assail.
14 My Life runs off, like Winter-Streams;
    My Bones, disjointed, start:
As Wax before the Sun's hot Beams,
    So melts my careful Heart.

15 My Strength quite dries away, my Tongue
    Cleaves to my parching Jaws;
And I shall soon to Earth belong
    By Death's determin'd Laws.
16 For angry Dogs around me meet,
    And all the Godless Crew:
They pierce my bleeding Hands and Feet,
    And Wounds on Wounds renew.

17 Each Passenger may tell my Bones,
    While here I rack'd appear;
And gaze in Scorn, while deathful Groans
    My wasted Vitals tear.
18 My Robes my cruel Murd'rers seize,
    And carefully divide;
And for their Shares, their doubtful Pleas,
    Impartial Lots decide.

19 But

19 But leave me not, my Strength, my Lord!
    O fly to refcue me!
20 My helpleſs Soul, ô from the Sword,
    And bloody Dogs ſet free!
21 From Lions Mouths, and Brutiſh Might,
    O ſave, and hear my Prayer!
22 So I'll, in all thy Church's Sight,
    Thy Name, thy Praiſe declare.

Part 3.

23 O ye who fear the Lord, with Praiſe
    His happy Smiles implore!
  Ye faithful Seed, his Glories raiſe,
    His ſacred Name adore!
24 He ne'er deſpis'd, nor caſt aſide
    The Poor's afflicted Caſe;
  Nor hid his Face; but when I cry'd,
    Beſtow'd his wonted Grace.

25 To thee, my God, I'll lofty Praiſe
    In vaſt Aſſemblies ſing;
  My humbleſt Vows on holy Days,
    With juſt Devotion bring.
26 The Poor ſhall eat to Fulneſs there,
    Thy Saints thy Praiſes found;
  Their joyful Hearts with Heav'nly Cheer,
    And Life Eternal crown'd.

27 Earth's fartheſt Bounds to Thee ſhall bow,
    The World thy Grace proclaim:
  All Nations Thee their God ſhall know,
    And bear thy ſacred Name.
28 For God above the Nations reigns,
    And o'er the Word preſides:
  His Word their quiet State maintains,
    And Truth to all divides.

29 The

29 The Rich shall all his Rights allow,
    And just Obedience pay.
The Poor to him shall gladly bow,
    And his Commands obey.
Nay, those whose drooping Souls draw near
    The dark devouring Grave,
Shall at his Name reviv'd appear,
    And his Protection crave.

30 Their Seed their gracious God shall serve,
    And in his Family
Their happy States and Names preserve,
    And all his Goodness see
31 They shall his Righteousness to all
    Succeeding Ages show,
That those to come on God may call,
    And all his Wonders know.

Another Metre: As the 124th.

1 WHY, ô my God; ô why, my God, dost Thou
    Desert a Soul oppress'd with mighty Woe!
Thou, whose unbounded Mercies largely flow;
And ready Help, and kind Supports allow
To others, who beneath their Suff'rings bow!

2 Crush'd by thy weighty Wrath, my dreadful Cries,
    My flowing Tears, consume the chearful Light;
    My restless Groans disturb the silent Night:
Yet still my absent God his Smiles denies;
For Tears or Groans has neither Ears nor Eyes.

3 What! Can thy Wrath against a Godless Race
    Thy Nature change? or to thy Servants make
    Thy Promise fail? Can God himself forsake?
O, no! He's holy still: His wondrous Grace
The faithful Word with Praise and Thanks embrace.

4 On him our happy Fathers long believ'd;
  Their Faith in him, in him their Hopes were sure;
  Their Confidence in him from Shame secure.
5 His ready Arm their pressing Wants reliev'd;
  Their ancient Freedom, and their State retriev'd.

6 But I'm beneath a Man's exalted Name,
  A trampled Worm, a Wretch, forgot, forlorn;
  Expos'd to all th' insulting Vulgar's Scorn.
  My heavy Woes their scoffing Wits inflame,
  And think I merit greater Pains and Shame

7 See how they toss their Heads! the barb'rous Crew
  Shoot out their Tongues with pointed Flouts and
  (Unkind returns for all my sanguine tears!)(Jeers,
  With cruel Joys the Rout my Life pursue,
  And my unutterable Torments view.

8 God was th' Impostors Patron once, they cry;
  God was his Strength, his Friend, his Father too:
  Let's see what that Almighty Friend can do:
  Let's see his God, through the dividing Sky,
  On rapid Wings, to his Assistance fly!

9 Yet from my Mother's Breasts, and Virgin-womb,
  Wast thou my God, and I was only thine;
  My Birth, Conception, Nature, all Divine.
10 On Thee I trusted in my early Bloom:
  Thy Image in my Infant-Soul had Room.

  And can I doubt my God's immortal Love?
  Can Seas or Earth again, or can the Sky,
  Dissolv'd in one unshap'd Confusion, lie?
  Can groundless Hate pursue the spotless Dove?
  Or can unkind Oblivion reign above?

                                    11 Lord,

11 Lord, be not absent long! to thee alone
   My drooping Soul for sure Assistance flies;
   On Thee, for Help, my drooping Soul relies.
   My Griefs are nearer now, and stronger grown;
   My Foes unnumber'd, my Assistants none.

12 Not angry Bulls with more ungovern'd Rage,
   Curl'd Bulls of lofty *Basan*'s surly Breed;
13 Not hungry Lions rouz'd, with fiercer Speed
   Against the daring Hunters Spears engage,
   Than against me this blind malicious Age.

14 With cruel Spite they vex and wildly tear
   My mangled Body, and my wounded Mind;
   No sinewy Strength my loos'ning Joints can find.
   Woes swell my throbbing Heart, and deadly Care,
   And horrid Pangs approaching Death declare.

15 What Pray'rs, what Cries, what melting Tears can I,
   To cool Men's Rage, or ease my Torments, use?
   My Tongue its Cries, their Tears my Eyes refuse.
   And that thou, Lord, may'st cast thy Thunders by,
   I groan, I sweat, I bleed, and faint, and die.

16 To grieve me more, they pierce my Hands and Feet,
   My Hands, my bleeding Feet, are rudely torn;
   My dying Groans suppress'd by noisy Scorn.
   So greedy Dogs about the Carcase meet,
   And Passengers with surly Snarlings greet.

17 Stretch'd on this Cross, my Bones are all descry'd;
   Their Eyes, still dry, the stupid Vulgar raise,
   And, hard as Rocks, on all my Sorrows gaze.
18 My Robes among themselves my Guards divide;
   And with impartial Lots, their Claims decide.

19 But,

19 But, ô with Haste, my God, with Haste to me;
   Fly on thy own Salvation's Balmy Wings:
   From that alone my Strength and Safety springs.
   To give me Life, let thy Assistance be
   Swift as my own Obedience was to Thee!

20 And though my Foes with Dog-like Fury rave,
   My wretched Soul, deserted, Friendless, mourn,
   And all their Swords against my Bosom turn,
   Be thou but mine, their swords and teeth shall have
   A Check, and all their Malice find a Grave.

21 Though Men, as Rampant Lions fierce, would tear
   My trembling heart, tho they'd with force control
   With rabid Force distract my peaceful Soul;
   Be thou but mine, I'll live more free from Fear
   Than Mariners when Halcyon Calms appear.

22 Then to my faithful Brethren I'll declare
   Thy gracious Actions, and thy glorious Name;
   And in thy House thy wondrous Love proclaim.
23 O ye who in th'Almighty's Favour share,
   Now to his Court with grateful Songs repair!

   Ye who of *Israel*'s Privilege partake,
   By Faith united to the chosen Seed,
   To his bless'd Courts with grateful Songs proceed!
24 He ne'er would yet his praying Saints forsake,
   Nor to th' Oppress'd himself a Stranger make.

25 Thy Name I'll in the great Assemblies praise,
   And there, in publick, pay my Vows to Thee:
   There all thy Saints my Gratitude shall see:
   My Sacrifice their fainting Hope shall raise,
   And turn their Mourning to their Feasting-Days.

26 Then

26 Then thofe who feek their God, their God fhall fee;
   Their Hearts with no uncertain Tumours fwell,
   But in Eternal Joys and Pleafures dwell:
Where chang'd their happy Hymns of Praife fhall
To Angels Tunes, and Heav'nly Harmony. (be,

27 Thee fhall the blefs'd converted Nations know:
   Earth's utmoft Borders, deareft Lord, be thine:
   To Thee the fartheft Pagan Tribes incline.
To Thee fhall all th' en'ightned Nations flow,
And holy Rev'rence and Devotion fhow.

28 For God's the King, and o'er the Nations reigns:
29   The Rich, the Mighty to his Sceptre bow:
   His Government the naked Poor allow.
   Their God to them his Kindnefs ftill retains,
   And gives them Life, and then their Lives main•
                       (tains.
30 From them fhall an immortal Race defcend,
   To God devoted, and from God be nam'd;
   For facred Rites and ho'y Virtues fam'd:
31 Who downward fhall the gladfom Tidings fend,
And his great Acts to future Heirs extend.

To God the Father, and to God the Son,
   And God the Holy Ghoft, Almighty Three,
   One only God, one Glorious Trinity!
As fhall be, is, and was e'er Time begun,
Be lafting Glories paid, and Homage done.

PSAL. xxiij. *As the 100th.*

1 AMidft a Thoufand Wants and Woes,
    My Soul on God for He'p relies:
My Griefs his pitying Wifdom knows;
   My Wants his pitying Love fupplies.

2 He

2 He like a Shepheard gently leads,
 My Soul thro' Truths delightful Ways:
My Foot sure by his Conduct treads,
 And ne're from Paths of Wisdom strays.

3 As grassy Meads, and wholesom Streams,
 New Health on sickly Flocks bestow,
So in thy Favours quickning Beams
 I sweetly live, and kindly grow.

4 Thro' Death's dark shades I fearless move,
 By Thee, dear God, secur'd from Harms;
Thy very Rod demonstrates Love,
 Thy Staff supports my wearied Arms.

5 What tho' an envious World should frown
 On all my chief Delights? from Thee
Sweet Wine and Oil my Bowl shall crown,
 And boundless Plenty compass me.

6 In Thee, my God, I'me always blest.
 On Thee my Hopes, my Joys depend.
Then in thy House I'le fix my Rest,
 My Life in lasting Praises spend.

Another Metre, as Mr. Sandys's 10*th.*

1 THE Lord's my Sheepherd, I the Sheep,
 Those Soul his Cares in safety keep.
  Through flowery Meads,
  He gently leads
Me on where I securely sleep:
  Or by His guidance go,
  Where silent Waters flow.

3 His Loves, his constant Loves refin'd,
 The Errors of my wand'ring Mind:

For

PSAL. xxiij.

For his Name's fake,
He brought me back,
When I from Virtue's paths declin'd.
And to his righteous Ways,
Confines my fleeting Days.

4 I now no Fears or Danger know,
Tho' thro' Death's gloomy fhades I go;
Since there with me,
My God will be.
From Thee alone my Comforts flow,
Which to me, ever Lord,
Thy Rod, thy Staff afford.

5 Thou wilt for Me before my Foes,
A Table nobly ſtor'd difpoſe,
Oils largely fhed,
Around my Head.
And till the purple Juice o're-flows,
Thy endleſs Bounty will,
My Bowl divinely fill.

6 Goodneſs and Mercy both fhall be,
A Portion a'l my Life for me:
And then my Reſt,
Supremely bleſt,
Within thy ſacred Houſe fhall be;
Where, to my God and King,
I'le endleſs Praiſes ſing.

PSAL. xxjv.

1 THis Earth, the World, their Hoſts, and Store,
To God above belong,
2 Who rais'd it on the Seas, and o're
The Waters built it ſtrong.
3 Yet fix'd in one ſelected place
His own Immortal Name:

But ô, what Man can find such grace,
   Dear Lord, to reach the same!

What happy Man divinely blest
   Attend thy Altars there,
Or of a Seat secure possest
   Before thy Face appear?
4 He, whose pure Hands are free from Blood,
   From all Corruptions free,
Whose honest Heart, sincerely good,
   Abhors Hypocrisy.

Who ne're in Thoughts, or Actions vain,
   His active Soul employ'd,
Nor falsly swore, nor liv'd in pain
   To make his Promise void.
5 To such a Man God's goodness will,
   Unfading Blessings give,
Reward him well, and let him still,
   On his Salvation live.

6 Such, with unweary'd Dilligence,
   Seek God's Immortal Name,
And *Israelites* by Faith commence,
   And *Israel*'s portion claim.
7 Yee Doors, yee Gates Eternal high,
   Your glorious Arches raise,
Then shall the King of Majesty,
   Come in with lofty praise.

8 O who'es that great that glorious King?
   It's God, the mighty Lord,
Whose Might his happy Servants sing,
   And wondrous Wars record.
9 Yee Doors, yee Gates, Eternal high
   Your glorious Arches raise.
Then shall the King of Majesty,
   Come in with lofty praise.

10 O who's that great, that glorious King?
　　It's God, the mighty Lord
Of Hosts; whose Praise his Subjects sing,
　　Whose Honours all record.

Another Metre : As Da Pacem Domine.

1 THE Earth is God's, her Fulness too;
　　　Earth, and all of Earth possess'd:
2 For on the Seas he pois'd it true;
　　On the Floods secur'd its Rest,
3　　　But who, ô who
　　　Can, Lord, pursue
　Paths to reach thy sacred Hill?
　　　Or see thy Face
　　　In that bless'd Place,
　There, unmov'd, abiding still?

4 He, only he, whose Hands are clean,
　　He who purifies his Heart;
Whose Soul is neither proud, nor vain,
　　Nor can from his Oaths depart.
5　　　All Blessings he
　　　From God shall see,
　And his Saviour's Righteousness:
6　　　Such, such are they
　　　Who ev'ry Way
　After *Jacob*'s Maker press.

Lift up your Heads, ye sacred Gates!
　　Doors Eternal, open wide!
Then shall the King of glorious State
　　Through your Ports triumphant ride.
　　　O who is He
　　　Whose Majestie
　Your Angelick Anthems sing?
　　　The Lord of Might
　　　Supream in Fight;
　He's our Great, our Glorious King.

D　　　　　　9 Lift

9 Lift up your Heads, ye sacred Gates;
  Doors Eternal, open wide;
 Then shall the King of glorious State
  Through your Ports triumphant ride.
10 O who is He
   Whose Majestie
  Your Angelick Anthems sing?
   The Lord, whose Sway
   All Hosts obey:
 He's our Great, our Glorious King.

PSAL. XXV.

1 I Lord, to thee my Heart dispose;
2   My God, I trust in thee!
 O save me from insulting Foes,
   And Shame, and Infamy!
3 Let wilful Sinners sink with Shame,
   But keep thy Servants free:
4 And let thy Faith my Heart inflame,
   Reveal thy Paths to me;

5 O let thy Truth direct my Ways,
   To me Salvation give;
 To me, dear Lord, who all my Days
   In sacred Longings live!
6 Thy never-ending Mercies, Lord,
   Thy Bowels, Lord, re-call!
7 My youthful Crimes, my Sins abhorr'd,
   Forgive, forget them all!

  O, for thy tender Mercy's sake,
   With Favour think on me!
8 The blindest Sinners God will make
   His righteous Paths to see.
9 He makes the Meek with Prudence move;
   The Humble kindly draws:

PSAL. xxvj.

10 His Ways all Truths and Mercies prove
   To those who keep his Laws.

Part 2.

11 For thy Name sake, a Sinner spare,
    With weighty Guilt oppress'd:
12 To him who fears thee, Lord, declare,
    Thy Paths with Safety bless'd!
13 His Hand on happy Ground shall build,
    His Race the Land shall hold;
13 T' his Soul, with holy Secrets fill'd,
    Will God his Grace unfold.

15 To Thee I look, dear Lord, my Feet
    From subtile Snares retrieve:
16 My Sorrows, Lord, with Mercy meet;
    With Love my Woes relieve.
17 Increasing Woes distress my Soul;
    O kindly rescue it!
18 My Sorrows and my Pains controul,
    And all my Sins remit!

19 Help from my num'rous Foes I crave,
    Who hate me wrongfullie.
20 My Soul from all Confusion save,
    Because I trust in Thee.
21 Truth, Justice, I'll as Guards esteem,
    And on thy Favours wait:
22 But, Lord, thy holy Church redeem
    From its afflicted State!

PSAL. xxvj.

1 Judge, Lord; assert my Cause; for I
    Have trod the perfect Way:
  I trust in Thee; no Dangers nigh
    Can make my Hopes decay.

2 Prove me, my God; examine well,
 My Reins, and search my Heart:
3 My Eyes on all thy Mercies dwel;
 From Truth I'll ne'er depart.

4 The Lyer's Seat my Thoughts abhor;
 My Soul hates Hypocrites:
5 Ne'er joins with wicked Councils, nor
 In impious Ways delights.
6 I'll wash my Hands in Innocence,
 And grateful Off'rings bring:
7 Of Thee declare my humble Sense,
 And all thy Wonders sing.

8 Lord, I have lov'd thy Temples while
 In them thy Glories dwell:
9 O don't my Life to Sinners vile,
 Nor bloody Murth'rers fell!
10 Whose Hands to any Mischief move,
 Who love large Bribes to see:
11 So I'll in all that's good improve:
 O save, ô pity me!

12 I'll to the Paths of Righteousness
 My ready Steps confine;
 And stand where thy great Name, to bless
 Assembling Saints, combine.

PSAL. xxvij.

1 THE Lord's my Light, my Health; Can I
 Poor changing Mortals fear?
 His Smiles my Life and Strength supply;
 And can I faint appear?
2 When wicked Men, my spiteful Foes,
 To eat me up design'd,
 They trip'd, and fell, but never rose,
 With Malice deadly blind.

What though huge Hosts beset me round?
  My Heart no Fear can know:
Though War's Alarms about me sound,
  My Faith shall stronger grow.
One Grant, to keep his House Divine,
  From God I long to hear;
To see his sacred Beauties shine,
  And serve his Altars there.

He me in dang'rous Times shall hide
  Within his secret Place;
A Rest, a Rock for me provide;
  My Head with Honours grace
Above my Foes, which press me round;
  While mighty Off'rings I
Shall bring with Joys triumphant sound,
  And praise my God most High.

Part 2.

Thy Ears, Lord, to my Cries afford,
  And hear, and pity me!
To seek Thee thou command'st me, Lord,
  I'll seek, dear Lord, to Thee.
O never, never hide thy Face
  In Anger, Lord, from me:
My Help of old, ô let thy Grace
  My Guard, my Safety be!

Though off by cruel Parents thrown,
  My God will own me still.
To save me from my Foes, make known
  To me thy righteous Will;
O give me not, dear Lord, a Prey
  To barb'rous Enemies!
Who Snares for me by Falshood lay,
  And hunt my Soul with Lyes.

13 Lord, of thy wond'rous Goodness sure,
   My fainting Soul reviv'd,
Of thy refreshing Love secure
   While here on Earth I liv'd.
14 Wait then on God with Courage bold,
   And he'll exalt thy State:
Thy Heart, with Strength renew'd, uphold;
   On him ô humbly wait!

PSAL. xxviij.

1 TO Thee, my Rock, my Lord, I cry:
      Thy Answer, Lord, I crave,
  Lest, by thy Silence ruin'd, I
      Too soon approach the Grave.
2 Hear his Petitions when to Thee
      Thy lowly Servant prays;
  When toward thy Seat of Mercy he
      His Hands shall humbly raise.

3 O leave me not with impious Men,
      With wicked Workers, who
  Speak friendliest to their Neighbours when
      They plot their Overthrow.
4 On their own wicked Heads at last
      Their black Designs return:
  And let 'em all, beneath the Blast
      Of self-sown Mischief, mourn.

5 Since they God's mighty Works despise,
      And what his Hands have wrought,
  Let Ruin all their Works surprize,
      To swift Destruction brought!
6 O bless'd, ô bless'd be God, who hears
      His praying Servant's Voice;
7 My Might, my Shield from all my Fears,
      In whom my Thoughts rejoice!

To

To Him, whose Help my Faith requites,
    I'll joyful Praises sing;
Whose Strength, and whose Salvation fights
    For his Anointed King.
O save, ô bless thy People, Lord,
    Thy old Inheritance;
And their Salvation, by thy Word,
    From Age to Age advance!

PSAL. xxix.

1. BRing to the Lord, ye Sons of Might,
    A grateful Sacrifice:
In his unbounded Strength delight,
    And to his Glories rise!
2. Rise to his Glory, praise his Name,
    His sacred Name alone:
Bow, bow to Him, his Praise proclaim
    Before his Awful Throne!

3. See how his dreadful Lightnings break!
    Heark how his Thunder rolls!
The Lord from o'er the Water speaks,
    And all the Deep controls.
4. Vast is the Force, the Brightness great,
    Which on his Voice attend:
5. Flames shot from his Imperial Seat,
    The lofty Cedars rend.

6. He makes the frighted Mountains trip,
    Like Heifers o'er the Field;
Old *Libanus* and *Hermon* skip
    When Clouds their Thunder yield.
7. Wrap'd in a Thousand Flames, it roars,
8.   And makes the Desart shake.
The barren Sands, and distant Shoars,
    Before his Thunder quake.

9 His Terrours make the trembling Deer
    Their Young unperfect cast;
And Forests bare and stripp'd appear,
    As with a Winter's Blast.
10 The Lord, on Clouds enthron'd on high,
    Reigns an Eternal King;
And all his glorious Majesty
    In Heav'ns bright Temples sing.

11 The Lord, with unresisted Might,
    Will guard his Churches round:
His Blessings on their Heads shall light,
    With Peace and Plenty crown'd.

Another Metre: As the 112*th.*

1 COme! to the Lord a Sacrifice
    Of fattest Rams from *Bashan* bring:
To Him let mighty Princes rise,
2 His Might, his wondrous Glories sing;
    Just Honours to their Lord allow,
    And in his sacred Temple bow.

3 Heark how the Lord, from Clouds above,
    In Cracks of dreadful Thunder speaks!
4 With horrid Force his Thunders move,
    His Voice with dismal Glory breaks:
5 Down fall the lofty Cedars torn,
    With its tempestuous Force o'er-born.

6 The Hills their strong Foundations leave,
    The rooted Hills before him shake;
Before his Voice the Mountains cleave,
    And *Libanus* and *Hermon* shake:
    And Earth as sudden Motion yie'ds,
    As Heifers tripping o'er the Fields.

7 His Voice shoots out with pointed Flames,
8   And shocks the Desarts all around :
  Its Force the trembling Wild proclaims,
9   And at his Thunders awful sound.
       The Forest-Herds, and trembling Deer,
       Cast out their Young, unform'd, for Fear.

  His Lightnings strip the Forests round ;
10   His Might the swelling Floods restrains :
  All in his House his Praises sound,
    And He a King Eternal reigns.
11   That God who His with Strength endues,
       And all the Sweets of Peace pursues.

PSAL. xxx.

TO Thee, my God, with Heart and Voice,
    I'll Praises sing to Thee,
Who hast not made my Foes rejoice,
    But hast exalted me.
I cry'd, my Lord, my God, to Thee,
    And Health thy Mercy gave.
My Life from Death's sharp Pains set free,
    And from the loathsom Grave.

Sing to the Lord, ye Meek! with Praise
    His sacred Name adore :
His Wrath but one short Moment stays,
    His Favours Life restore.
One Night may pass in Griefs and Tears,
    One melancholy Night ;
But Joy, with Golden Wings, appears
    Before the dawning Light.

Once, bless'd with Peace, I boasting said,
    I ne'er should fall, nor move :
Thou, Lord, my Hill so strong hadst made
    By thy surrounding Love.

Thy Face withdrawn, a Thousand Cares
    Disturb'd my tortur'd Breast :
8 Then I to God, with hearty Prayers,
    And fervent Cries, address'd.

9 What Honours can my Blood to Thee,
    My Death what Trophies raise?
Can mould'ring Dust thy Glories see,
    Thy Truth or Goodness praise?
10 Hear, Lord, and pity him who mourns;
    To my Assistance fly!
11 Thy Love my Tears to dancing turns;
    My sable Weeds to Joy.

12 To Thee, my Lord, my God, I'll sing;
    My Tongue shall praise thy Name:
My Harp on ev'ry tuneful String,
    Thy Deathless Praise proclaim.

PSAL. xxxj.

1 IN Thee, dear Lord, I trust: my Soul
    From all Confusion free!
With Justice all my Foes control,
    And still de'iver me!
2 To me thy gracious Ears incline,
    And to my Rescue fly!
Be thou my Guard, with Strength Divine;
    My Rock, and Fortress high!

3 Thou art my Rock, my Fortress Thou:
    O, for thy Mercy's sake,
For thy great Name, direct me now
    The safest Ways to take!
4 From secret Nets withdraw my Feet,
    O Thou, my Strength esteem'd!
5 I to thy Hands my Soul commit,
    Lord, by thy Truth redeem'd!

6 I hate vain lying Men, but in
    God's Mercy sure rejoice,
7 Who has my deep Affliction seen,
    And heard my mournful Voice.
8 Me to my Foes he ne're betray'd,
    But set my Feet at large.
9 O with thy Mercies undelay'd
    My present Woes discharge!

Part 2.

My Eyes, my Mind, my Bowels all,
    Beneath thy Anger waste,
10 My Spirits with my Sufferings fall,
    My Years in Sighs are past.
My strength with Sins huge weight opprest,
    My putrid Bones decay.
11 Foes, Neighbours, such as know me best,
    With my Disasters play.

To them a Laughing-stock, a Scorn,
    A Bug-bear I appear,
And those who meet a Wretch forlorn,
    Draw back their Heads for fear.
12 Me they, like Men long dead, forgot,
    Or threw like Potsherds by,
13 While cruel Censures were my Lot,
    And barbarous Emnity.

Fear sinks my Soul, while mighty Men
    Against my Life combine;
14 Yet said I to my Saviour then
    Thou still, dear Lord, art mine.
15 My Times are Thine, ô rescue me,
    From persecuting Foes,
16 And, that I may thy Mecies see,
    Thy saving Smiles disclose!

17 Preserve me, Lord, from Shame, who call,
    And thy Assistance crave!
But let confounded Sinners fall
    Down to the silent Grave!
18 So shall those wretched Fools be hush'd,
    Whose proud Contempt and Scorn,
That good Men might be throughly crush'd,
    Could lying Lips suborn.

Part 3.

19 Oh, what vast Good's reserv'd for those
    Who fear thy sacred Name!
What Good for them thy Loves dispose,
    Thy mighty Works proclaim.
20 Thou from the Proud thy Saints shalt hide,
    Within thy secret Place;
And in thy House a Rest provide,
    From brawling Tongues Disgrace.

21 O bless'd be God, whose Mercies wrought
    Such wondrous Things for me!
Who from a well fenc'd City brought
    Me out, and set me free!
22 I said in haste, No more shall I
    Before my God appear;
Yet, Lord, thou heard'st my Pray'r; my Cry
    Obtain'd thy gracious Ear.

23 O love the Lord, ye Saints! the Lord
    His faithful Servants keeps;
But off at once the Proud, abhor'd,
    His equal Vengeance sweeps.
24 Take Courage then, and God to you
    More Courage still shall send,
Whose Hearts are to his Service true,
    And on his Truth depend.

PSAL.

PSAL. xxxij.

Thrice happy's he whose Sin's past o'er,
    Whose Errours Mercies hide;
Whose Crimes his God imputes no more;
    Whose Soul's sincere, and try'd.
But I, unpardon'd, speechless lay,
    My aking Bones decay'd;
And through long Night, and tedious Day,
    One dismal Roaring made.

Me thy severe afflicting Hand
    All Day, all Night chastis'd;
My fainting Spirits were at a stand,
    Like Brooks by Drought surpriz'd.
At last I all my Crimes display'd,
    My wretched Sins confess'd:
To God I'll own my Guilt, I said;
    And God my Guilt releas'd.

Now Saints to thee, when thou 'lt be found,
    shall in their Pray'rs complain;
And though Woes deluge all around,
    Themselves untouch'd remain.
By thee I'm hid from mighty Woes,
    From pressing Ills secur'd;
And all my chearful Musick flows
    From Liberty assur'd.

Come to me all who'd fain be bless'd,
    And I'll your Souls instruct;
And in the blissful Ways of Rest
    With careful Eyes conduct
O don't like Mules or Horses move,
    Whose Brutish Furies will,
Unreign'd, uncurb'd, unruly prove,
    And balk their Riders Skill.

10 Great Sorrows on the Wicked fall;
　　The Juſt with Mercy's crown'd.
11 Ye Juſt in God rejoice, and all
　　Whoſe Hearts are right and ſound.

PSAL. xxxiij. *As the* 100*th.*

1 YE Righteous, in the Lord rejoice:
　　From you how comely Praiſe appears?
2 With Lute and Harp's melodious Voice
　　O reach the Great *Jehovah*'s Ears!

3 Sing to his Praiſe a Song that's new;
　　His Praiſe with Art and Courage ſing:
4 For all his ſacred Words are true,
　　His Faith approv'd in ev'ry thing.

5 Judgment and Juſtice gain his Love,
　　O'er Earth his wondrous Mercies flow;
6 The Skies, and all the Hoſts above,
　　His Active Word and Spirit ſhow.

7 He makes the Seas like Mountains ſwell,
　　And ſinks unfathom'd Deeps below.
8 Let Earth it ſelf, and all who dwell
　　On Earth, their mighty Maker know!

9 He ſpoke, and ſtreight this mighty All
　　Broke from vaſt Nothing's fruitful Womb;
　And did, at his commanding Call,
　　Shape, Order, Beauty, Strength aſſume.

10 God makes the Gentiles Counſels vain,
　　And breaks the Nations fond Deſigns:
11 But firm his own Reſolves remain,
　　And paſs all Time's extended Lines.

Part 2.

12 O bless'd, thrice bless'd that happy Land,
  Where God has Fix'd his glorious Name!
 Where He assumes the chief Command,
  And lays his own peculiar Claim.

13 God from his holy Heav'n look'd down,
  And Man's weak Race and Actions view'd;
14 His Eyes, from his Imperial Throne,
  Survey'd the careless Multitude.

15 He forms their Hearts, their Tempers guides,
  And all their various Actions weighs.
16 No prudent Prince in Crouds confides,
  Or mighty Hosts, or empty Praise.

17 In vain for Courage, Strength, or Flight,
  He on his foaming Steed relies:
18 The Good alone God's guarding Sight
  With Help and Mercy both supplies.

19 From Death's strong Arms He sets them free,
  In Famine He their Wants relieves.
20 On Him our Souls attend, and He
  To us his Shield's Assistance gives.

21 His Name's our Confidence and Fear,
  By which we all our Hopes excite.
22 O, as our Faith's in Thee sincere,
  On us, Lord, let thy Mercy light!

Another Metre: As Mr. Sandys's 34th.

1 YE Righteous in the Lord, rejoice:
  Its sweet when with a chearful Voice
   The Just his Praises sing.

2 O let no Tongue or Hand be mute,
But with Voice, and Harp, and Lute,
  Praise our Immortal King!

3 With skilful Notes advance his Praise,
With loudest Joys his Glory raise;
  Let all your Songs be new!
4 For all God's Promises are right,
Performance is his whole Delight,
  And all his Works are true.

5 He Righteousness and Judgment loves,
With spreading Wings his Mercy moves
  O'er all the spacious Earth.
6 God by his Word stretch'd out the Skies,
And bade their num'rous Armies rise;
  That Word was all their Birth.

7 At his Command those Waters rose,
Which now the rolling Seas compose;
  And Heaps on Heaps were thrown:
Unfathom'd Whirl-pools, dang'rous Deeps
His Subterraneous Treasure keeps
  In hollow Vaults; unknown.

8 His Name let all the Nations fear:
With Awe let all the World appear
  Before its Maker's Face!
9 He spoke, the solid Earth was made:
He gave the Word, it fix'd and stay'd
  In its appointed Place.

10 God baffles all the deep Designs,
The subtile Plots, and crafty Mines,
  Which Heathens closely frame.
11 But all his own Designs are sure,
His Thoughts and all his Ways endure;
  From Age to Age the same.

Part

Part 2.

2 Happy's the Nation, happy sure,
  Which God will to himself secure,
      His own Inheritance.
3 He sits above the lofty Skies,
  From thence o'er all Mankind his Eyes,
      His piercing Eyes advance.

4 All Men He from his Throne surveys;
5 He frames their Hearts; and all their Ways
      His Thoughts severely try.
6 No prudent Kings on Crouds depend:
  The Men who mighty Strength pretend,
      On Strength in vain rely.

7 A Horse, though fleeter than the Wind,
  And, by his Make, for War design'd,
      His Rider can't secure.
8 God views his Saints with gentler Eyes,
  And all his Mercy's kind Supplies
      Are to the Faithful sure.

9 From Death the fainting Souls he saves:
  In Famine, what their Hunger craves,
      His careful Hands provide.
10 Our Souls on Him with Patience wait:
  He, as a Shield, secures our State;
      And is our Help and Guide.

11 In Him shall all our Hearts rejoice;
  His holy Name's our happy Choice,
      On which our Hopes may rest.
12 O Father, as we trust in Thee,
  So let thy faithful Servants be
      With thy Compassion bless'd!

PSAL. xxxiv.

1 I'LL ever bless God's mighty Name,
  My Mouth shall sound his Praise:
2 In God my Soul its Boast proclaim,
  His Love in Anthems raise.
  The meek and humble Souls shall hear
  Of my exalted State:
  Thy Loves, which so immense appear,
  Shall all their Joys create.

3 O hear my Lot; rejoice with me,
  My Saviour magnifie!
  Let's to exalt his Name agree,
  And raise his Glories high.
4 I sought the Lord, He heard my Case,
  And all my Fears redress'd:
5 And others too, without Disgrace,
  With Love and Life were bless'd.

6 I in my deep Affliction pray'd,
  And God receiv'd my Pray'r;
  And free from all Afflictions made,
  And all perplexing Care.
7 Bright Angels happy Saints surround,
  And threat'ning Ills divert.
8 See, taste how good the Lord! how crown'd
  With Bliss the faithful Heart!

9 O fear, ô fear the Lord, ye Saints!
  For such no Wants surprize.
10 The Lion's Whe'p with Hunger faints,
  And, spent with fasting, dies.
  But those who seek the Lord, with all
  That's good or sweet are stor'd:
11 Come then, ye Children, hear my Call;
  And learn to fear the Lord!

Part 2.

2 Who's he who loves long Life, and fain
    Would see delightful Days?
3 Thy Lips from all that's ill refrain,
    Thy Tongue from guileful Ways.
4 Ill Works of ev'ry kind decline,
    What's good and vertuous do;
And Love and Peace with Flames Divine,
    And constant Care, pursue!

5 God on the Just hath fix'd his Eyes;
    His Ears their Pray'rs attend:
6 His Frowns against the Wicked rise,
    Their Lives from Earth to rend.
7 To good Men's Pray'rs He Favour shows,
    And sets them safe from Harms;
8 But loves the broken Heart, and those
    Whose Souls Repentance warms.

9 A Thousand Ills the Good surround,
    But God their Force dispels;
10 And keeps their Bones and Entrails sound,
    And all their Bruises heals.
11 Ill Men their in-born Malice kills,
    And those who hate the Just;
12 While God his own with Goodness fills,
    Who on his Mercy trust.

PSAL, xxxv.

Lord, plead my Cause, my Battels fight,
    With such as strive with me!
Rise, take the *Shield,* defend my Right;
    My mighty Guardian be!
Put on thy dreadful Arms, oppose
    My Persecutors Rage!

> To me thy Saving Health disclose,
> And for my Soul engage!

4 Let such as hunt my Soul, with Shame
> Their own Confusion see;
5 With Scorn their Dastard Flight proclaim,
> Who Mischief brew for me:
6 Like flying Chaff, let Angels Force
> Disperse their angry Crew!
Their slipp'ry Ways be dark, their Course
> Angelick Arms pursue!

7 For, unprovok'd, their Pits they made;
> For me they laid their Snare:
O let such Woes their Hearts invade,
> As unsuspected are;
8 O let the Nets for mine design'd,
> Their own Destruction prove!
While flowing Joys my raptur'd Mind
> With kind Salvation move.

Part 2.

9 O let my Bones his Praise dec'are,
> Who gives the Poor distress'd,
10 From savage Foes, and deadly Care,
> And bloody Tyrants, Rest!
11 False Witnesses against me rise,
> And unknown Crimes object;
12 With Ill, for Good, my Death devise,
> And on my Soul reflect.

13 Yet when on sickly Beds they groan'd,
> I fasted, mourn'd and pray'd;
Their Pains with kind Concernment own'd,
> To Heart their Sorrows lay'd.
14 If Mother, Brother, or my Friend,
> My dearer Self, had dy'd,

PSAL. XXXV.

No farther could my Griefs extend,
    My Love no more be try'd.

15 But when I fail'd, the Croud my Woes
    With barb'rous Joy survey'd;
The Rabble grew my sawcy Foes,
    And us'd the flouting Trade.
16 With Men of double Hearts combin'd
    The witty scornful Crew:
And at my Life, with Hate refin'd,
    And gnashing Fury, flew.

17 And canst thou this with Patience see?
    O save my helpless Soul!
My Darling from their Jaws to free,
    Their Lion-Force control.
18 So where the great Assemblies are,
    I'll celebrate thy Name;
And where the valiant Bands repair,
    Thy lofty Praise proclaim.

Part 3.

19 Let not my Foes rejoice; uncheck'd,
    My Causeless Haters smile;
20 Who Wars with peaceful Men project;
    Whose study'd Words beguile.
21 They gap'd, and cry'd, Aha, Aha!
    Our Eyes his Downfall see.
22 Thou seest; ô don't in Silence stay,
    O stay not long from me!

23 Awake! arise! to judge my Cause,
    My God, my Lord, descend!
24 O clear me by thy righteous Laws,
    And from Reproach defend!
25 O let not scornful Sinners say,
    We have our Heart's Delight:

Nor let them proudly boast, Aha!
    We have devour'd him quite.

26 Let Shame and Blushes those pursue,
    Who at my Harms rejoice;
And Horrour and Disgrace subdue
    The proud insulting Voice.
27 But those who love my righteous Ways,
    With chearful Spirits sing:
God loves his Servants Peace; ô praise,
    O praise our mighty King!

28 So shall my Tongue with chearful Air
    Thy righteous Acts proclaim;
Thy Justice ev'ry Day declare,
    And praise thy glorious Name.

PSAL. xxxvj.

1 WHen th' horrid Acts of impious Fools
    My sober Censures try
My Heart concludes by Reason's Rules,
    Such Brutes a God deny,
2 Their Consciences no Terrours wound,
    But Sin's their who'e Delight;
Till all their dark Intendments found,
    A gen'ral Hate excite.

3 Their Ta'k's deceitful, all in vain,
    And off their Vertue's thrown:
4 Vile Thoughts their very Beds contain,
    In viler Actions shown.
5 Thy Mercy, Lord. in Heav'n commands,
    Thy Truth surmounts the Skies:
6 Thy Righteousness like Mountains stands;
    Thy Judgments dark and wise

Like some unfathomable Deeps,
 Unbounded Wealth inclose:
And Man and Beast thy Favour keeps,
 And Health on all bestows.
7 What Worth thy Mercies, Lord, contain!
 Beneath thy sacred Wings
How safe the Sons of Men remain
 At Lov's immortal Springs!

8 They're with o'erflowing Mercies fill'd,
 And drink delightful Streams,
From those Eternal Springs distill'd;
 And feel thy gracious Beams.
9 From thee Life's lasting Fountains flow;
 Thy Light affords us Light:
10 O Goodness then, and Justice show
 To those whose Hearts are right!

11 From wicked Pride, Lord, set me free,
 My tott'ring State restore!
12 Till such as work Iniquity
 Sink, fall, and rise no more!

PSAL. xxxvij.

1 FRet not, nor for great wicked Men
 Thy self of Peace deprive:
Nor swell with secret Envy when
 The wicked Workers thrive.
2 See how green Grass and Herbage dies,
 And painted Flow'rs decay!
More swift the Sinner's Glory flies,
 And sooner fades than they.

3 Do good, and trust in God, and live;
 And Faith and Truth defend:
4 Delight in him, he'll largely give,
 And all thy Pray'rs attend.

5 Walk

5 Walk upright, on his Grace recline,
    For his Performance stay:
6 He'll make thy righteous Counsels shine
    Bright as the Cloudless Day.

7 On God with faithful Silence wait,
    But ne'er for Sinners grieve;
Nor wicked Men, in all their State,
    Secure, or fix'd believe:
8 But Wrath and wrathful Hate refrain,
    Lest Sin on thee prevail;
9 For Godly Men the World shall gain,
    But Sinners sink and fail.

10 Wait but a while, the Sinner's Race
    Destroy'd, no more shall be:
Yea, thou shalt search to find his Place,
    And not his Dwelling see.
11 The lowly Hearts shall seize the Earth
    For their Inheritance;
There live, and with delightful Mirth,
    Abundant Peace advance.

12 Sinners, with gnashing Teeth, and Rage,
    Against the Just combine:
13 God's scornful Smiles their Falls presage;
    He sees their Days decline.
14 Against the Poor and Righteous, fierce
    Their Bows and Swords they try:
15 But their own Hearts their Swords shall pierce,
    Their Bows in Splinters fly.

Part 2.

16 On pious Men, their humbler State
    More true Content bestows,
Than Sinners find when all their State,
    With Pride and Plenty flows.

For God's A'mighty Arm sustains,
    And strongly guards his own;
While broke the Sinner's Force remains,
    His cruel Hopes o'erthrown.

God knows the good Man's Ways, and makes
    His Heritage endure:
In spiteful Days from Scandal takes,
    In Famine feeds them sure.
His sinful Foes fly, like the Fat
    Of Lambs, in Fumes, away;
Those faithless Brutes, who borrow that
    They ne'er design to pay.

The Just compassionately give,
    And all their Race is bless'd;
And when the Sinners fall, they live
    Of all the World possess'd.
God's mighty Hand their Steps directs,
    Their Ways their Maker please:
They stumble, but their God protects
    And holds them up with Ease.

Young have I been, and now am old,
    But never yet could see
The righteous Man to Ruin fold,
    Or his Posterity.
I ne'er God's holy Saints have known,
    Deserted quite, complain;
Nor oft their wretched Children thrown,
    Nor beg their Bread in vain.

Part 3.

Good Men are pitiful and Kind,
    And all their Seed are bless'd:
Cease then from Sin, and bend thy Mind
    To Good, and live at Rest.

28 The Juſt, the Merciful, the Free,
    God's ſacred Arms embrace,
And ſuch in Safety keep, but he
    Cuts off the Sinner's Race.

29 This Earth to pious Men belongs,
    Where many Years they live:
30 Their Lips in Wiſdom ſpeak, their Tongues
    A righteous Sentence give.
31 God's Statutes in their Hearts you'll find,
    Their Steps are firm and ſure ;
32 Though wicked Men their Fall deſign'd,
    Or would their Deaths procure.

33 Yet God in cruel Hands will ne'er
    His faithful Friends forſake ;
Nor Goodneſs, like a Judge ſevere,
    His Anger's Object make.
34 Wait then on God, obſerve his Ways ;
    And ſo, exa'ted high,
On Earth thou'lt ſee delightful Days,
    And impious Wretches die.

35 I've ſeen a Sinner, Great, and ſpread
    His Boughs, like Laurels, round ;
36 Yet ſoon he vaniſh'd, quickly fled,
    Nor could his Place be found.
37 Obſerve the good, the perfect Man,
    How down in Peace he lies ;
38 While the vile Wretch, beneath the Ban
    Of weighty Curſes, dies.

39 God, who Salvation to the Juſt,
    And Might in Danger ſends,
40 From Sinners, ſuch as in him truſt,
    Sets free, aſſiſts, defends.

PSAL. xxxviij.

IN Fury, Lord, rebuke me not,
    Nor in thy Wrath chastise!
2 Thy Arrows through my Sides are shot,
    On me thy Terrour lies:
3 Thy Anger makes my Flesh decay,
    Sins make my Bones to waste;
4 On me a damning Weight they lay,
    And o'er my Head are pass'd.

5 My Sins make e'ery gaping Wound
    With foul Corruption flow;
6 My Vigour-cutting Pains confound,
    And I all mourning go.
7 My Loins with horrid Pains are torn,
    My Carcase mortify'd;
8 My throbbing Heart with Sighs o'er-born,
    My roaring Cries divide.

9 Yet, Lord, to Thee are all my Pray'rs,
    To Thee my Sighs are known.
10 My Strength decays, my Heart despairs,
    My Sight and Eyes are gone.
11 My Friends, my dear Companions once,
    My Wounds at distance view;
My Kindred all my Doom pronounce,
    And cruel Strangeness shew.

Part 2.

12 My Foes, who seek my Hurt, for me
    Their subtile Snare have set;
Their Tongues are all to Mischief free,
    Their Studies, all Deceit:
13 But I was deaf and dumb, nor could
    Their cruel Words deny;

15 But hop'd my God, my Saviour would
    On my Behalf reply.

16 I said, My God wou'd soon rebuke
    My Foes insulting Pride,
Who Pleasure in my Stumbling took,
    And all my Hopes defy'd.
17 Too near, indeed, my Fall appear'd,
    My Woes before my Face;
18 I knew my Trespasses, and fear'd
    My wretched guilty Case.

But now my Sins, and guilty Fears,
    I'l in thy Presence lay,
Till Sorrows and repenting Tears
    Shall wash my Guilt away.
19 My Causeless Foes in Might increase,
    And in their Multitude:
20 Ungrateful! who disturb'd my Peace
    Because I Good pursu'd.

21 Then 'eave me not, my God, my Lord;
    Nor stay too long from me:
22 But haste, thy ready Aids afford,
    And my Salvation be.

PSAL. xxxix.

1 I Said, When wicked Men were by,
    I'd watch my sinful Ways;
For oft my Words at random fly,
    My Tongue, unguarded, strays.
2 So I a while in Silence stood,
    And curb'd my hasty Tongue:
Nay, I forbore to talk of Good,
    Till Sorrow grew too strong.

3 My Heart within my Bosom glow'd,
　　　Sad Thoughts inflam'd my Breast;
At last my Words in Torrents flow'd,
　　　And thus my Thoughts express'd:
4 My final Doom, Lord, let me know,
　　　How far my Days extend,
That I may all my Time bestow
　　　To weigh my latest End.

5 Loe! Thou hast made my Days a Span,
　　　A Point, compar'd with Thee:
And all the wretched Race of Man
　　　Is empty Vanity.
6 Man, as a Shadow, vainly moves,
　　　And spends himself in vain;
In vain that useless Wealth improves,
　　　Which unknown Heirs may gain.

Part 2.

7 On whom then, Lord, should I rely?
　　　My Hopes are all in Thee:
8 Save me from all my Sins, that I
　　　No Scorn to Fools may be!
9 The Strokes on me thy Hands had laid
　　　I humbly silent bear:
10 O cure the Wounds thy Strokes have made,
　　　And ease my wasting Fear!

11 When us for Sin thy Hands correct,
　　　Our broken Beauties lie
Like Cloth which fretting Moths affect,
　　　And prove we're Vanity.
12 O view my Tears, attend my Cry,
　　　My Supplications hear;
For like a Stranger here am I,
　　　As all my Fathers were.

13 O spare a while! my Suff'rings ease,
My failing Faith restore,
E'er Death my fainting Spirits seize,
And I appear no more!

To Father, Holy Ghost, and Son,
One sacred Trinity,
Who fram'd this Universe, alone,
Eternal Glories be.

PSAL. xl.

1 With longing Expectation I
For God's Compassion stay'd;
Who bow'd his Ear, and heard my Cry,
When I submissly pray'd:
2 He rais'd me from the dismal Pit,
And from the miry Clay;
And on a Rock secur'd my Feet,
And then prepar'd my Way.
3 Then to my Mouth new Songs he gave,
New Songs of sacred Praise:
This all shall see, and fear, and have
Just Grounds their Faith to raise.
4 His Head a Thousand Blessings crown,
Whose Trust on God relies;
Who scorns the Sinner's haughty Frown,
And Men inur'd to Lyes.
5 Would I, my Lord, my God, pretend
Thy wondrous Acts to show,
Thy Thoughts for us, thy Acts transcend
Whate'er I think or know.
6 When Off'rings fail'd, thy Wisdom fram'd
A Body fit for me
By Thee were no Burnt-Off'rings claim'd,
To purge Iniquity.

7 Then

7 Then said I, Loe! I come! Thy Book
    My Name and Work describes:
8 To do thy Will, my God, I took
    My Flesh from Jacob's Tribes.
Thy Laws, which I in Heart embrace,
    Flow from my grateful Tongue.
9 Thou know'st, Lord, how I preach thy Grace
    To all the list'ning Throng.

Part 2.

10 My Tongue thy Righteousness reveals,
    And thy Salvation shows;
My Heart thy Mercy ne'er conceals,
    My Lips thy Truth disclose.
11 Thy Servant never, never from
    Thy Pity, Lord, exclude:
To save me let thy Goodness come,
    And all thy Truth be show'd!

12 For Ills, beyond all Numbers gone,
    My wretched Heart surround:
My Trespasses, too weighty grown,
    My failing Sight confound.
More than my Hairs my Sins appear,
    And break my fainting Heart:
13 To free me, Lord, from all my Fear,
    Thy winged Aid impart.

14 Let Shame and Blushes on them fall,
    Who hunt my Life with Hate:
Let dark Confusion seize them all,
    Who for my Ruins wait.
15 That black Disgrace, design'd for me,
    On their own Heads return,
Who laugh, and proudly flout, to see
    Thy wretched Servant mourn.

16 Let those who love and seek thy Name,
  With live'y Briskness rais'd,
Sing all to thee; and all proclaim,
  The Lord, the Lord be prais'd!
17 But, Lord, I'm poor, in Sorrows lost;
  On me some Thoughts bestow:
Nor let thy Help to me be cross'd,
  Nor thy Assistance slow!

PSAL. xlj.

1 THrice happy he, whose tender Care
    The needy Poor supplies;
  The Lord will to his Help repair,
    When greatest Dangers rise.
2 He shall be safely kept alive,
    And prosper'd here below;
  And the malicious Hate survive
    Of his designing Foe.

3 When on his Sick-Bed faint he lies,
    The Lord will raise his Head;
  In sharpest Pains, some Means devise
    To ease his restless Bed.
4 Lord, pity! heal my Soul, I said,
    Too long in Sins employ'd!
5 My Foes, with Curses, wish'd me dead;
    My very Name destroy'd.

6 If they pretend to visit me,
    Their whole Discourse is Lyes;
  Their publick Talk's Iniquity,
    Which there their Hearts devise.
7 My Hurt, with hollow Whispers, all
    My spiteful Foes contrive:
8 God's Plagues, they cry, upon him fall;
    He can't his Plague survive.

9 Nay,

PSAL. xlij.

9 Nay, he my Confident: My Friend,
  Who was my daily Guest,
 Cou'd all his fubtile Counfels bend
  Againſt his Maſter's Breaſt.
10 In Mercy raife me, Lord, again,
  And I'll their Deeds requite.
11 I fee thy Love, thy Hands reſtrain
  My Foes' triumphant Spite.

12 I'll walk in my Integrity,
  Thy Strength my Heart fupports;
 And all my Happinefs fhall be
  To tread thy facred Courts.
13 O bleſs'd be *Iſrael's* God! his Praife
  Through laſting Ages fing:
 With loud Amens the Glories raife
  Of *Jacob's* mighty King!

PSAL. xlij.

1 AS Harts, by Thirſt and Heat oppreſs'd,
   Pant for the cooling Streams,
  So pants my Breaſt, dear God, till bleſs'd
   With thy reviving Beams.
2 My thirſty Soul to God would fly,
   The living God be near:
  O when fhall I, Lord, happily,
   Before thy Face appear!

3 By Night Tears wafh'd my reſtlefs Bed,
   By Day my Cheeks o'erflow'd;
  On Tears I fed, while Scorners faid,
   Where's now his boaſted God?
4 When that fweet Blifs, of old poſſeſs'd,
   My ferious Thought re-calls,
  In my fad Breaſt, my Soul, oppreſs'd,
   Beneath its Burthen falls.

E 5   Then

Then I, with mighty Numbers proud,
　　To God's bless'd Temple went;
And all the Croud, with Songs aloud,
　　To Him their Praises sent.
5 But now, alas! Those Days are past,
　　Those blissful Minutes gone!
Yet where so fast, with Sorrow's Blast,
　　Is all my Courage flown!

Why droops my Soul so much? O why
　　Dost thou disturb my Breast?
My Faith on high to God shall fly,
　　And on his Bosom rest.

Part 2.

6 Near *Hermon*'s Caves, and *Jordan*'s Flows,
　　While I thus banish'd live,
Against my Woes tormenting Throws,
　　Dear Lord, I vainly strive.
7 Deeps call to Deeps, and from their Source
　　Thy treasur'd Tempests blow;
And in their Course, with mighty Force,
　　The mighty Waters flow;

8 All break on me: yet, Lord, I find
　　Thy Mercies still by Day;
To praise my Mind by Night's inclin'd,
　　Or I devoutly pray.
9 I'll say to God, my Rock, O why
　　Am I rejected so?
O why must I thus groaning lie,
　　Beneath my angry Foe?

10 My wounded Heart with Scorn they view;
　　And with Reproaches fly,
And Scoffs anew, my Soul pursue;
　　And, Where's his God? they cry.

PSAL. xilij.

11 Yet why, my Soul, dejected so
    In my despairing Breast?
What weighty Blow, what dreadful Woe
    Thus breaks thy ancient Rest?

Hope yet in God, in Patience wait
    On Him, my Hea'th, my God;
I yet his State shall celebrate,
    And spread his Works abroad.

PSAL. xliij.

BY Men of Blood beset, distress'd
    By all the treach'rous Crew,
My Pray'rs to pitying Heav'n address'd,
    For Life and Safety sue:
O Thou, just God, assert my Cause,
    My sinking Cause maintain;
And, try'd by thy impartial Laws,
    Let me thy Smiles re-gain.

2 Thy Strength, dear God, is all my Stay;
    Why, from thy Presence thrown,
Must I, despairing all the Day,
    Beneath Oppression groan?
3 O yet thy Truth, thy Favour lend,
    My wandring Steps to guide,
Till I thy holy Mount ascend,
    And near thy House reside.

4 There I'll before thine A'tars bow,
    And chearful Anthems sing:
Thy Praise, bless'd God, my Harp shall shew
    On ev'ry tuneful String.
5 Why so dejected then, my Soul,
    Within my wounded Breast?
Why shou'd Despair thy Thoughts control?
    Or break thy ancient Rest?

Trust yet in God! I shall my Part
　　Still in his Love obtain:
And God within my grateful Heart,
　　Enthron'd in Joys, shall reign.

Another Metre. As the old 130th.

1 JUdge me, Lord; revenge my Cause
　　On those who Mercy hate!
From deceitful, cruel Jaws
　　O save my sinking State!
2 All my Strength descends from thee;
　　Why then must I, unbless'd,
Thus a constant Mourner be,
　　By barb'rous Foes oppress'd?

3 Send thy Truth, ô send thy Light,
　　And let them guide me still;
To thy House conduct me right,
　　And to thy holy Hill!
4 I'll to God's pure Altars go,
　　the God of all my Joy;
And his Praises there to show,
　　My tuneful Harp employ.

5 Why, my Soul, then why depress'd?
　　Why thus disturb'd within?
On that God securely rest,
　　Who oft thy Help has been.
Fear not, droop not; I shall yet
　　His Health with Praises see:
He's my God, and can'd forget
　　My kind Defence to be.

Another

Another Metre, as Mr. Sandys's *22th.*

JUdge me, my God; revenge my Cause
   On cruel Hands, and faithless Hearts.
Save me from him who from the Laws
   Of Truth, and sober Virtues, starts,
   Who boldly acts the falsest Parts,
With strange Success, and vast Applause!

Thou art my God alone; from Thee
   My Strength, and Help, and Hopes descend:
Why then must I rejected be?
   Why thus beneath Oppressions bend?
   On thee so long in vain attend,
From bloody Foes to set me free?

O send thy Truth, thy saving Light,
   To be my constant, faithful Guides;
To 'ead me to that sacred Height,
   Where thy illustrious Name resides,
   Where thy Illustrious House abides,
With thy immortal Glories bright.

Then I'll to God's pure Altars go,
   That God who all my Joy creates,
To whom I all my Pleasures owe,
   On whom my Soul, reviving, waits.
   My Lord, my God, in whose bless'd Gates
His Praise my tuneful Harp shall show.

Why then cast down, my Soul? ô why
   Thus vex'd in my uneasie Breast?
To God for Help and Safety fly,
   On his Divine Assistance rest,
   For with my God's Salvation bless'd,
I yet shall sound his Praises high.

PSAL.

PSAL. xliv.

1 Lord, oft we've heard our Fathers tell
  Thy wondrous Works of Old;
2 How by thy Hand the Gentiles fell,
  And we their Countries hold.
3 Them their own Swords could ne'er advance,
  Nor Native Valour save:
  Thy Arm, thy Love, thy Countenance
  Their Lands and Safety gave.

4 Thou art my King: Salvation, Lord,
  For *Jacob*'s Seed command:
5 We'll crush our Foes if thou afford
  Thy kind assisting Hand.
  Their Heads, in thy Almighty Name,
  We'll quickly trample o'er;
6 And I'll my Bow's Defence disclaim,
  And trust my Sword no more.

7 Thou only sav'st us from our Foes,
  And break'st their Hearts with Shame:
8 Each Day we'll with thy Glory close,
  And ever praise thy Name.
9 But thou hast cast us off, and we
  A strange Disgrace endure:
  Thy Aids no more our Armies see,
  Nor can thy Help procure.

10 Before their Foes the Dastards fly,
   And we are spoil'd with Ease:
11 Like scatter'd Sheep, dispers'd we lie,
   Where-e'er the Gentiles please.
12 Thou hast thy wretched People sold,
   Yet not advanc'd thy Gain:
13 And us in Scorn our Neighbours hold,
   And treat with proud Disdain.

PSAL. xliv.

Part 2.

14 We are the Gentiles By-word now,
    At us each shakes his Head:
15 And while we suffer Shame, my Brow.
    A Thousand Blushes spread.
16 My Shame from Men's foul Blasphemies,
    And black Reproaches, grows,
The Barb'rous Acts, and shameless Lyes
    Of our revengeful Foes.

17 Yet though we're thus with Woes oppress'd,
    We can't our God forget;
But in thy Covenant we rest,
    Thy Truth before us set.
18 Our Hearts have ne'er declin'd from Thee,
    But to thy Judgments true,
19 Though we the Dragon's Fury see,
    And Death our Steps pursue.

20 Had we forgot God's glorious Name,
    Or Idol-Gods ador'd,
21 Wou'd not our God have found the same,
    Our secret Thoughts explor'd?
22 For Thee we 'ere kill'd all Day; like Sheep,
    To Slaughter deem'd for Thee.
23 Wake, Lord; ô rise, no longer sleep,
    No distant Stranger be!

24 Why, Lord, are all our Woes despis'd?
    Why hid thy lightsom Face?
25 While we with Sorrow's Dust disguis'd,
    The Earth, forlorn, embrace.
26 O rise! with thy Almighty Aid
    Our sinking State retrieve!
Our Souls, to Sorrow Captives made,
    With Mercy, Lord, relieve!

PSAL. xlv.

1 Warm'd by a Beam of sacred Light,
    I'll sing a lofty Song;
The Streins, my busie Thoughts indite,
    To our bless'd King belong.
And though the Pen-man's nimble Hand
    Flies swiftly o'er his Scrowl,
More swiftly, and with more Command,
    My Tongue attends my Soul.

2 Fair be the Sons of Humane Race;
    Thou, Lord, art fairer found:
Thy Lips distil Celestial Grace,
    With God's due Blessings crown'd.

3 Ride on thou Prince of wondrous Might,
    Gird on thy dreadful Sword,
With Majesty, and glorious Light,
    And Truth's All-conqu'ring Word.

4 May Love and Righteousness attend
    Thee with assur'd Success:
Thy dreadful Arms all Fame transcend,
    And all thy Foes depress.

5 Before thy Pointed Arrows all,
    Thy Foes shall spread the Field;
And at thy Foot-steps wounded fall,
    And to their Conqu'ror yield.

Part 2.

6 Thy Throne, ô God Eternal, stands,
    And Right thy Sceptre crowns;
Bright Justice fils thy righteous Hands,
    Sin dies beneath thy Frowns.
Mov'd with thy Gifts, and Acts Divine,
    Thy God anoints thy Head;

Thy

Thy Joys thy Fellows Joys out-ſhines,
  On Thee in plenty ſhed.

Myrrh, Aloes, and Caſſia ſweet
  From all thy Garments flow;
And round thy Iv'ry Palace meet,
  And all thy Motions ſhow.
Kings Royal Daughters, richly dreſs'd,
  Among thy Maidens ſtand:
The Queen, with Golden Crowns oppreſs'd,
  Waits at her Sov'reign's Hand.

Hear me, great Queen, my Words receive
  With humbly prudent Care:
Thy Fondneſs of thy Fathers leave,
  And of thy Country's Air.
So ſhall the King his boundleſs Love
  To thy bright Charms allow;
For He's the Lord, He reigns above;
  To Him ô humbly bow.

Part 3.

Then ſhall the *Tyrian* Dames reſort
  With Gifts, fair Queen, to thee:
The wealthy Men ſhall make their Court
  To awful Majeſty.
Rich Robes the Royal Princeſs wears,
  But richer far her Mind;
An inward Heav'nly Treaſure bears,
  By Love and Grace refin'd.

Her they, to ſee her King, adorn
  With all th' Embroid'rer's Art;
Her Train's by Royal Virgins born,
  Who ſhare her Joys and Heart.
Pleaſures around their Boſoms play,
  Their Eyes ſoft Loves create,

When,

When, to attend their Monarch, they
On their great Miſtreſs wait.

16 For Fathers, Sons, thy Court adorn,
A gallant, ſprightly Train:
Brave Youths, to Crowns and Sceptres born,
And o'er the Nations reign.
17 Thy Praiſe, ô thou Immortal King,
I'll ever thus proclaim;
And all the joyful World ſhall ſing
Thy Godlike Acts, and Name.

Another Metre: As the 113*th.*

1 TOuch'd with a Beam of Love Divine,
My Heart, my Head, my Tongue combine
To bleſs the World's Incarnate King.
No nimble Pen-man's flying Hand
More ſwiftly can his Quill command,
Than I my Saviour's Glory ſing.
2 How wondrous bright, how Heav'nly fair,
Dear Lord, thy Godlike Beauties are!
Thy Lips Eternal Sweets diſtil.
Hence, by thy mighty Father bleſs'd,
Thy humble, but capacious Breaſt,
All Heav'n's immenſe Endowments fill.

3 Gird on thy Thigh, moſt mighty Lord,
Gird on thy dreadful, glitt'ring Sword;
And with Majeſtick Honours crown'd,
4 In proſp'rous State triumphant ride;
Truth, Meekneſs, Juſtice guard thy Side.
Thy Arm with Terrours brac'd around,
5 Each Bow then drawn, each Arrow loos'd
By the Right Hand, to Conqueſt us'd,
Shall pierce thy ſtubborn-hearted Foes:
And all the trembling World ſhall meet,
To caſt themſelves beneath thy Feet,
O'er-aw'd by thy reſiſtleſs Blows.   6 T

6 Thy Throne, bless'd God, for ever stands;
   A righteous Sceptre fills thy Hands:
     To Thee the suppliant Nations bow.
7 The vertuous Soul thy Favour gains,
   Thy Frown the wicked World restrains,
     And Sinners fly thy threatning Brow.
   Hence God, thy God, with Joys around,
   Above thy Mates, thy Heart has crown'd;
     His Balmy Joys thy Passions warm.
8 Thy Robes with noblest Odours flow,
   Which from thy lofty Palace blow;
     And Sweets thy pleas'd Attendants charm.

Part 2.

9 Among thy Maids of Honour, wait
   Fair Virgins, all of Royal State,
     Like bigger Stars i' th' Galaxy.
   And at thy Hand enthron'd is seen
   Thy charmingly victorious Queen;
     Her Crown pure Gold, but purer she.
10 Hear me, illustrious Queen! forget
   Thy native Land's and Father's Seat;
     And for thy King, thy Kindred quit:
11 So shall he love thy Beauties more,
   And thou his Deity adore,
     And to his Heav'nly Will submit.

12 Nor shall thy Beauties slighted lie,
   Thy Service in Oblivion die;
     But through the farthest Regions fam'd:
   To thee shall *Tyrian* Dames resort;
   And wealthy Princes make their Court
     To thee, by thy Renown inflam'd.
13 Fair are thy Eyes, but fairer far
   Thy Soul; a Thousand Beauties there
     Thy Diamonds and Rubies stain,

14 When

14 When in Embroider'd Robes they bring
    Thy Majesty to meet thy King,
      Attended with thy Virgin-Train.

15 Bless'd by the ravish'd Croud, they'll move;
   Bless'd by thy King's exalted Love,
     Thou'lt in his Starry Palace reign.
16 For thy old Stock, a lovely Race
   Of Princely Youths thy Marriage grace,
     And Royal Crowns and Empires gain.
17 The Name, great King, I'll celebrate:
   Thy Majesty, and glorious State,
     I'll sing in never-dying Verse.
   The World shall thy bright Throne adore,
   The Suppliant World thy Grace implore;
     Thy Spousals bless, and praise rehearse.

PSAL. xlvj.

1 GOD is our Hope, our Strength, our Aid,
     When greatest Danger's near:
2 Whence, for those dreadful Changes made
     On Earth, we scorn to fear.
  Though Mountains, torn from ev'ry Shoar,
     Into the Seas be hurl'd;
3 And swelling Waves, with threatning Roar,
     Assault the trembling World.

4 Yet near God's House, and those fair Walls
     Which round his City go,
  Refreshing Springs, with gentler Falls,
     And easie Windings, flow.
5 God in his House resides; no Force,
     No Strength his Walls can move:
  God guards it; Malice can't divorce
     It from his earliest Love.

6 Whe

When he in dreadful Thunder spoke,
    The frighted Nations heard;
The Kingdoms felt the fatal Stroke,
    And Earth dissolv'd appear'd.
With us the Lord of Hosts remains,
    To us his Care extends:
With us the God of *Jacob* reigns,
    And all our Coast defends.

Come, see the mighty Works which He
    Through all the World has wrought;
What wondrous Desolations He
    On ev'ry Land has brought!
He makes the Noise of Battels cease,
    And breaks the Spears and Bows;
And to the Flames, to keep the Peace,
    The ratling Chariot throws.

0 Be still! with humble Silence know
    I'm God, and only I:
To me the Nations round shall bow,
    And raise my Glories high.
1 With us the Lord of Hosts remains,
    His Care to us extends:
With us the God of *Jacob* reigns,
    And us from Ills defends.

PSAL. xlvij.

With Hands and Hearts accod,
    All People, praise the Lord:
With Triumph's Voice, in him rejoice,
    His wondrous Name record!
For He, the Lord most High,
    With dreadful Majesty;
A Monarch reigns, and Earth restrains
    With his commanding Eye.

3   He makes the People all
       Beneath our Empire fall:
The Nations meet, to kiss our Feet,
       And us their Masters call.
4   But us He chose, that we
       His Heritage might be:
His Favours grace the faithful Race,
       Whose Wealth He loves to see.

5   Our Lord's gone up on high,
       With Trumpets toward the Sky.
6 Sing Praises, sing, to our great King;
       With Songs and Praises vye!
7   With Understanding raise
       Earth's mighty Monarch's Praise,
8 Whose sacred Throne the Nations own;
       Whose Will the World obeys.

9   To God, his Servants now,
       With neighb'ring Princes bow;
While He, though high, continually
       Defends our Earth below.

PSAL. xlviij.

1 GReat is our Lord, and greatly prais'd
       In *Sion*'s sacred Hill:
On which immortal Buildings rais'd,
       That glorious Mountain fill.
2 Fair is it's Sight, the Pleasures vast,
       It gives to distant Lands;
And on its Northern Quarters plac'd,
       God's holy Temple stands.

3 God in her Palaces is great,
       A certain Refuge known;
4 And angry Kings, who fiercely met,
       Are off as swiftly gone.

5 The

They saw, admir'd, and terrify'd;
   From thence distracted flew:
Fear seiz'd 'em all; and o'er their Pride,
   Pangs, as of Child-birth, drew.

Though mighty Navies, close combin'd,
   For our Destruction meet,
He breaks them with his stormy Wind,
   And scatters all the Fleet.
Oft have we heard, and oft have seen,
   In thy bless'd Residence,
How Thou, great God of Hosts, hast been
   Thy City's strong Defence.

Secur'd by Thee, it ne'er decays;
   And in thy Temple we
Thy Everlasting Mercies praise,
   And sing, dear Lord, to Thee.
o Great is thy Name, thy Praises great
   Through all the World resound:
Thy Name with Righteousness compleat,
   Thy Hand with Justice crown'd.

1 Let *Sion*'s Mount rejoice and sing,
   And *Judah*'s Daughters dance;
Such Blessings, Lord, thy Judgments bring,
   So much their Peace advance.
2 Walk *Sion* round; quite round her go,
   Her Bulwark's Numbers find;
Her Battlements and Ramparts know,
   Her stately Buildings mind.

Then let unborn Posterity
   Your wondrous Records have;
For God's our God for ever, He
   Our Souls from Death shall save.

Another

Another Metre: As the 112*th.*

1 OUR Lord is great, and greatly prais'd
   From Salem's Walls, and Sion's Hills;
2 That sacred Mount, which nobly rais'd,
   Our happy Land with Glory fills;
     That Temple guilds her Northern sides,
     Where God, the King of Kings, resides.

3 God in her Palaces is known;
   A strong Defence, and Refuge sure.
4 See how th' assembling Kings are flown!
   Nor could the glorious Sight endure:
5   They saw, and what they saw, admir'd;
     But off, on Terrour's Wings, retir'd.

6 They felt such horrid Pangs and Throws,
   As Women in their Child-birth feel:
  By Land they met God's angry Blows,
7 By Sea their shatter'd Navies reel.
     By furious Eastern Tempests toss'd,
     Till all their Strength and Pride are lost.

8 Within God's holy City we
   Have seen what oft we'd heard of old:
  The Lord of Hosts her Strength will be,
   His Hand her lasting Walls uphold.
9   Thy ancient Love and Kindness, Lord,
     We in thy holy House record.

10 Thy Name Earth's utmost Borders know:
    As far, great God, thy Praises fly,
   Thy Hands Eternal Justice show:
     Let Sion's Mount then cheerfully,
     Let Judah's Virgin-Daughters sing
     The Judgments of their glorious King.

12 Walk

2 Walk *Sion*'s Rounds, her Towers defcribe;
    Obferve how ftrong her Bulwarks are:
The Palaces of *Judah*'s Tribe,
    Let thofe to come with theirs compare;
    They'll read God here: and only He
    So good, fo fure a Guide cou'd be.

PSAL. xlix.

ALL People, Nations all, which o'er
    The World your Tribes extend;
The High, the Low, the Rich, the Poor;
    My facred Songs, attend:
My Mouth fhall Wifdom fpeak, my Heart
    Of Knowledge meditate:
My Harp myfterious Truths impart,
    And Things of ancient weight.

Why fhould I fear in dangerous days,
    By finful Men diftrefs'd,
Who on their Lands, and crafty Ways,
    And mighty Treafures reft?
Yet all their Wealth, and all their Store
    Can't one loft Soul redeem:
Nor God, to bate their finful Score,
    Their largeft Gifts efteem.

9 Nay, though they live a Thoufand Years
    The Grave's expected Prey,
Such Price a Soul's Redemption bears,
    As they can ne'er repay.
They fee the Wife and Fools muft die,
    And all that Wealth defcend
To unknown Heirs, which foolifh'y
    They thought no Time could fpend.

Part 2.

11 They vainly thought their Seats secure
 From Time's consuming Hands;
 Their Names and Memories endure
 On all their purchas'd Lands.
12 Yet Man in Honour can't remain,
 But, like the Beast, must fa'l:
13 And, though their Heirs their Wit maintain,
 Their Ways are foolish all.

14 Death feeds on them, as Sheep; the Just
 Shall soon their Force subdue:
 Their Graves, soon fill'd with crumbling Dust,
 Their fading Natures shew.
15 But God sha'l save my Soul from Hell,
 His Hand will mine support.
16 Then fear not Men, whose Wea'th may swell;
 Nor Sin exalted court.

17 For when Death comes, they'll leave behind
 Their Wealth and Glories too;
18 Tho' while they liv'd they pleas'd their Minds,
 As common Mortals do.
19 Men who enrich themselves below,
 A mighty Name may gain;
 But quickly to the Dead they go,
 And Light no more obtain.

20 Man, when to Honours rais'd, if he
 The Ways of Wisdom slight,
 Involv'd like Thoughtless Beasts must be
 In everlasting Night.

PSAL. l.

Vain Hypocrites and Atheists, bow
  To new Alarms your careless Ears:
The Lord, the Great *Jehovah*, now
  To plead Religions Cause appears.

From East to West, from Shoar to Shoar,
  The dreadful Summons swiftly rolls:
His Voice, in Thunder's dismal Roar,
  At once the frighted World controls.

Our God shines from his chosen place,
  With Majesty and Terrours crown'd:
He comes! devouring Flames his Face,
  His Steps impetuous Storms surround.

To hear his Judgment pass'd, he calls
  The Heavens above, and Earth below;
That where his righteous Sentence falls,
  The World, all satisfy'd, may know.

Go, call my Saints together; those
  Who in my Laws delight, and o'er
Their Sacrifice my Covenant chose,
  And there to me devoutly swore.

The Summons pass'd, the Lord alone,
  As Judge, the great Tribunal holds:
Bright Angels make his Justice known,
  While He Eternal Truth unfolds.

Part 2.

Hear me, my People; *Israel*, hear!
  With thee the Case I'll calmly plead:
Loe! I, the Lord of Hosts, appear;
  Thy mighty God, thy Sov'reign Head!

8 Did I e'r call for Sacrifice?
    Or of thy sparing Hand complain?
  Or bid that constant Steams should rise,
    From bleeding Bullocks, duly slain?

9 Poor Trifles all! Thy solemn Feasts,
    Thy Bullocks, and thy Goats, I scorn:
10 The Forest-Herds are mine, the Beasts,
    Which on a Thousand Hills are born.

11 The feather'd Host, the Fowls, are mine;
    And all the Droves which graze the Fields:
12 If hungry, I'd not ask of thine;
    To me the World its Plenty yields.

13 Think'st thou the Flesh of Bulls I'd eat,
    Or Goats? or drink their streaming Gore?
14 No: Give me Praise, my Praise repeat;
    My Grace, with Vows perform'd, implore:

15 Then in the Times of Danger cry
    To Me, to me thy Griefs display;
  And thou, when I to save thee fly,
    Just Honours to my Name shalt pay.

Part 3.

16 Then to the Wicked thus: And how
    Dar'st thou to preach my Laws presume?
  With what strange Impudence canst thou
    My Covenant in thy Lips assume?

17 Thou hat'st all sacred Discipline,
    Behind thy Back my Words are thrown:
18 Thy Thoughts with crafty Thieves combine,
    And make th' Adult'rer's Lot thy own.

Thy Mouth is all engag'd in Ill;
  Thy Tongue deceitful Lyes contrives;
Thy Brethren, thy malicious Skill,
  Thy Mother's Sons of Fame deprives.

Thus haft thou done, while silent I
  Thy senseless Crimes with Patience view'd:
And thou, with wondrous Policy,
  Couldst me just like thy self conclude.

But now before thy mournful Eyes
  I'll set thy Sins, thy Crimes dispose:
My Wisdom shall thy Soul surprize,
  And all thy foolish Arts disclose.

Consider this, ô ye who dare
  Forget your mighty God, lest He
Your Souls with utmost Fury tear,
  And none your fainting Souls can free.

That Man who offers Praise, alone
  Due Glory to my Name can raise:
And I'll my Saving Health make known
  To him who wisely guides his Ways.

Another Metre, to the old proper Tune.

Wake drowzy World! no more let Sleep surprize
  The heavy Lids of thy Lethargick Eyes.
Hark; thy Creator calls! awake! awake!
He comes! See how the Dead their Graves forsake!
Before his Face the fatal Trumpet sounding,
And all his Angel-Guards his Throne surrounding.

From East to West the dreadful Summons roll,
And shake the Southern and the Northern Pole.

Nature in cold faint Sweats diffolving lies;
A fudden Heat melts down the folding Skies;
　And Seas and Earth, torn from their old Foundation,
　Are all o'erturn'd in one great Defolation.

2 That God who long in *Sion*'s Glory reign'd,
　Whofe Prefence long her happy State maintain'd,
3 Mov'd by our Crimes, no more can Silence hold;
　His Menaces in difmal Flames are roll'd:
　　Black Clouds from ev'ry piercing Eye defend him;
　　And dreadful Storms, with Thunder's Roar, attend
　　　　　　　　　　　　　　　　　　　　(him.
4 Hark, how he calls! Earth, Sea, and Air, and Sky,
　Before his Frowns, in empty Vapours fly:
　The new-cloath'd Bones for their old Mates enquire,
　And flutt'ring Souls to their own Homes retire.
　　Then God his Silence breaks, his Angels hearing,
　　With Adorations at his Bar appearing.

5 Go fly, fwift Angel-Bands: go fetch me thofe
　Whofe Follies durft my juft Commands oppofe:
　But gently home thofe holy Souls convey,
　Who would my Laws, with upright Thoughts, obey;
　　Who in blefs'd Covenants, for their Salvation,
　　Depend on me by folemn Dedication.

6 Hear Me, my bright Eternal Throne; and you,
　Blefs'd Guards, my Judgments and my Juftice view
　I'll no unrighteous Judges Part affume;
　My Lips on none fhall pafs a private Doom:
　　My very Foes this Honour fha'n't deny me;
　　And even Souls condemn'd fhall juftifie me.

7 Hear Me, ô ye of *Ifrael*'s faithful Race;
　His Sons by Nature, and his Sons by Grace:
　I am thy God, ô *Ifrael*, only thine;
　And all, thy felf, thy Strength, and Hopes, are mine

I'l

I'll plead my Cauſe with thee: ô, ſpeak ſincerely!
If e'er I dealt with thee, or thine, ſeverely!

8 Tell me: Did ever I thy S'ackneſs chide?
  Or bid thee greater Gifts, or more, provide?
  Did I complain when Incenſe rarely fum'd,
  And ſcarce one Lamb my holy Day conſum'd?
  Did I ever for Sacrifice reprove thee?
  Or to external coſtly Worſhip move thee?

9 For me, thy Bullocks ſafe their Stalls may hold;
  Of Goats or Kids I'll never rob thy Fold.
80 What ſhould I ask of thee? The ſpacious Field,
  Hils,Foreſts,Woods, to me their Stores muſt yield.
11 Mine are the Fowls about woods,lakes & fountains;
  And all the Cattel on a Thouſand Mountains.

12 If Hunger's Force my Nature could invade,
  Canſt thou believe I'd beg the Creature's Aid?
13 That I the Fleſh of *Baſhan*'s Bulls would eat?
  Or Goats rank Blood would make a Heav'nly Treat?
  Can He who owns the World, and all its Plenty,
  Or He who fills *this All*, himſelf be empty?

14 But if th' ſhould'ſt bring a grateful Sacrifice,
  Let humble Praiſe, with holy Incenſe riſe.
15 Thy Vows, made in Affliction, juſtly pay;
16 And to thy God in deep Afflictions pray;
  And I'll ſoon change thy melancholick Story,
  And thy Deliv'rance ſhall advance my Glory.

17 But to the Wicked, God in Anger turns,
  And thus at him his jealous Fury burns:
18 Thou whoſe black Soul Divine Inſtruction hates,
  In whom my Word no Reverence creates: (them:
    Know thou, my Laws are Life to thoſe who chuſe
    But, ô, how dare thy wretched Lips abuſe them?

How dar'st thou th' Office of a Priest assume?
Or in my Cov'nant read thy dismal Doom?
No Thieves commended, in my Laws appear;
Nor canst thou find Adult'rers pardon'd there:
 Yet with Adulterers and Thieves thy Sentence,
 Thy Words, thy Life, agree, without Repentance.

19 All Hellish Arts thy Lips, thy Tongue pollute;
Lyes are their Product, Falshood all their Fruit.
Thy Talk, thy Neighbor and thy Friend blasphemes;
20 Thy Mother's Sons are all thy scornful Themes:
 Its thy whole Study, thy affected Fashion,
 To spread vile Scandals with Deliberation.

21 Thus hast thou done, and I in Silence still
Ne'er broke thy Rest, and never cross'd thy Will:
So my Existence was at last deny'd;
Or mine, at least, by thy vile Nature try'd;
 Like some mean Idol, to the World presented:
 And against me, all bold Affronts invented.

But now my Anger's rouz'd, thy Actions all,
Before my Sight, in horrid Order fall.
See how they stand before thy trembling Eyes;
And in thy Face thy guilty Conscience flies.
 No Sleep, no Rest, nor Quiet now befriend thee;
 But Hellish never-ceasing Woes attend thee.

22 O ye who God forget, my Speeches weigh,
 Lest you become my uncheck'd Fury's Prey!
23 Praise to your Maker's Glory sai fice;
 Be your Words holy, and your Actions wise:
 So may your Bliss obtain a long Duration,
 And all be crown'd with my Divine Salvation.

PSAL.

PSAL. lj.

1 MErcy! ô Mercy! Lord, to me
     Extend thy Mercy's Store!
 Let me thy pard'ning Mercy see,
     To clear my sinful Score.
2 Wash me from my Iniquity,
     And purge me, Lord, from Sin;
3 For I my Folly throughly see,
     It racks my Breast within.

 I see, I see my Crimes when Sleeps
     Should seal my weary'd Eyes:
 Me still awake my Conscience keeps,
     Or frightful Dreams surprize.
 If I with noisie Pleasures try
     To ease my tortur'd Soul,
 Black Lust and Blood are ever by,
     And all my Joys control.

4 To thee alone I've sin'd, to thee,
     And trespass'd in thy Sight;
 That justify'd thy Words might be,
     And all thy Dealings right.
5 Loe, I at first was shap'd in Sin,
     In Sin at first conceiv'd;
 To that I've since a Captive been,
     By Hellish Arts deceiv'd.

6 Thou look'st for inward Truth; to me
     Thy secret Wisdom show:
7 Purge thou my Soul, my Soul shall be
     More white than Northern Snow.
8 O let me once again the Voice
     Of Joy and Gladness hear;
 And let these broken Bones rejoice,
     Which now thy Vengeance bear!

Part 2.

9 From all my sinful Actions past
    O turn thy angry Face!
10 Make me a Heart that's clean at last,
    A Mind renew'd by Grace!
11 Cast me not wholly off, nor take
    Thy sacred Gifts from me:
12 Restore thy Saving Health, and make
    My Spirit large and free!

13 Then I the sinning World shall teach
    To tread thy perfect Way;
Conversion and Repentance preach
    To such as loosely stray.
14 Save me from Guilt of Blood; to me
    Thy kind Salvation bring,
And then my Tongue, from Fetters free,
    Thy righteous Acts shall sing.

15 Unseal my Lips, and then my Tongue
    Shall celebrate thy Praise;
Thy Praise shall be my constant Song,
    As in my fairer Days.
16 God wo'n't for costly Offrings call,
    Nor ask for Sacrifice;
Else should a Thousand Oxen fall,
    And Incense daily rise.

17 No: God demands a nobler Part;
    The Heart's his Sacrifice:
A wounded Soul, a bleeding Heart,
    His Mercy can't despise.
18 O now at last thy Favour show
    To thy selected Place:
Thy Church, now despicably low,
    With lofty Walls embrace!

19 Then

19 Then shall a righteous Sacrifice
  With thee Acceptance gain:
And humble Hearts and lifted Eyes
  Thy Altars Flames maintain.

Another Metre, to the old proper Tune.

1 ROus'd from a deadly, sinful Dream,
    With guilty Pangs of Conscience torn,
  I prostrate here, without one Beam
    Of Comfort, lie, a Wretch forlorn.
  Mercy to me, ô Mercy shew;
    A Wretch thy Mercy, Lord, implores:
  On me ô let thy Mercies flow,
    And wash out all my guilty Scores!

  O wash, ô cleanse my Conscience, Lord,
    From Falshood, Lust and Cruelty;
3 For now I all my Guilt record,
    And only dismal Objects see-
  Lord, how it racks my Soul! how strong
    Guilt's terrible Convulsion moves!
  What Chains of Woes it drags along!
    How bitter Sin's Remembrance proves!

4 Against Thee, Thee alone, I've sin'd,
    And boldly trespass'd in thy sight;
  That I thy righteous Truth might find,
    Thy Judgment pure, thy Sentence right.
5 Shap'd in Iniquity at first,
    At first in Sin and Guilt conceiv'd;
  I was originally curs'd,
    My Soul of Innocence bereav'd.

  Hence sprung the fatal Fruit, and Hell
    With Ease my native Proneness won,
  My careless Pride, unguarded, fell,
    With shameless actual Guilt undone.

6 If inward Truth, Lord, pleases Thee,
    O let my Heart thy Wisdom know:
7 Wash, purge me through, and I shall be
    More white, more pure than Northern Snow.

8 So shall I feel thy Beams again,
    Thy Loves shall fill my pardon'd Soul.
  My Bones, long justly rack'd with Pain,
    With Balmy Joys be sound and whole.

To Father, Holy Ghost, and Son,
  One bless'd, one glorious Trinity,
On whom our Hopes depend alone,
  Eternal Praise and Glory be.

Part 2.

9 From all my Crimes, Lord, turn thy Face,
    No more my cancell'd Errours view.
  O change my Heart, and, by thy Grace,
    My Mind with Heav'nly Thoughts renew!
11 Cast me not off, nor from my Breast
    Thy sacred Influence remove;
12 But, with the saving Pleasures bless'd,
    In Good my forward Soul improve.

13 Then Sinners I'll bring home to thee;
    Transgressors shall thy Laws esteem.
14 From Blood, dear Saviour, rescue me;
    My Soul from Crimson Guilt redeem!
15 If thou, bless'd Lord, my Lips unseal,
    My Tongue, thy sacred Name shall raise;
  Thy Love, my flowing Songs reveal!
    My Mouth thy righteous Judgments praise.

16 No bloody Sacrifice with thee,
    No Fumes from steaming Altars rais'd,
  Prevail; else, num'rous Herds, for me,
    Had on a Thousand Altars blaz'd.

PSAL. lij.

17 A Soul with Sense of Sin depress'd,
    Is Lord, thy noblest Sacrifice:
  A broken Heart, a contrite Breast,
    Thy tender Mercies ne'er despise.

18 Lord, in thy Love thy Church defend,
    Its ruin'd Hopes and Walls repair;
19 So shall our favour'd Vows ascend,
    With righteous and accepted Pray'r.

To Father, Holy Ghost, and Son,
  One bless'd, one glorious Trinity,
On whom our Hopes depend alone,
  Eternal Praise and Glory be.

PSAL. lij.

1 AND canst thou, vilest Wretch, of thy
    Prevailing Malice boast?
  Think'st thou God's Mercies e'er can die?
    His boundless Love be lost?
2 We know thy Tongue the Razor's Edge
    Out-cuts with sharpest Lyes:
  We know thy Heart, Hell's certain Pledge,
    Can only Frauds devise.

3 Mischief thy very Soul approves,
    But honest Actions hates:
  Thy Tongue no Truth or Justice loves,
    But Lyes on Lyes creates.
  Thy Tongue, base Wretch, such Language speaks,
    As may the Just devour:
4 But God thy cruel Pride shall break,
    By his resistless Pow'r.

  He'll tear thee out, and from thy place
    Root out thy hated Name
5 The Just shall see thy strange Disgrace,
    And thus expose thy Shame: Loe!

PSAL. liij.

"Loe! here's the Man, who, lofty grown,
  "His God regarded not;
"But could his favouring Hand disown,
  "And God himself forgot.

"5 But of his mighty Wealth he'd boast,
  "With vast Possessions bless'd:
"In impious Arts he trusted most,
  "In Malice fix'd his Rest.
"See where he lies, forgot, forlorn,
  "By all the World despis'd:
"His Name, his shatter'd Fortunes torn,
  "His Life by Hell surpriz'd.

7 But like a thriving Olive, I
  In God's bless'd House shall stand;
  And on the Mercies sure relie
  Of his unchanging Hand.
8 Through thee I scap'd th' intended Blow,
  And I'll adore thy Name;
  And with thy Saints thy Mercies show,
  Thy gracious Acts proclaim.

PSAL. liij.

1 GOD, in his Heart, the Fool denies,
  Such Fools the wretched World are grown:
Corrupt, defil'd, seduc'd with Lyes;
  Not one for sober Practice known.

2 God, from his lofty Seat, survey'd
  The World, and all their Actions view'd
To see if any duly pray'd,
  Or Wisdom's Lectures understood.

3 But all were now Apostates, a'l
  Corrupt at once, and filthy grown;
Not one would on his Maker call,
  Not one to practise Good was known.

4 Is all their Sense so lost in Sin,
   That they, like Bread, my Saints devour?
In all their Talk, God ne'er comes in;
   They ne'er invoke, nor own his Pow'r.

5 Yet now with groundless Fears they fly,
   Their Strength God's weighty Anger breaks,
With Shame thy fierce Besiegers die;
   God's angry Scorn their Downfall speaks.

6 O whence may *Israel's* Safety spring!
   If God his banish'd Tribes restore,
Then *Israel* shall triumphant sing,
   And *Jacob's* Race despond no more.

Another Metre: As the Complaint of a Sinner.

1 THE Fool, the senseless Fool,
   Thus in his Heart hath said;
God's but an awful Tool,
   By crafty Preachers made.
Thus all corrupted are,
   And all in Sins delight:
But none for Truth declare,
   None ever practise Right.

2 God, from the lofty Sky,
   Look'd down on Earth below,
To see what Man would try
   His God to seek or know.
3 But all Apostates there,
   They're vile and filthy all:
None good on Earth appear,
   Nor on their Maker call.

4 But have the Wretches lost
   Their Apprehensions quite,

   Against my Saints to boast,
     And with their God to fight?
   Dare they my *Israel*'s Seed,
     Like common Bread, devour?
   And on my People feed,
     And scorn my saving Pow'r?

5 Fear shall their Hearts surprize,
     A senseless, groundless Fear:
   And all thy Enemies,
     Who durst in Arms appear,
   Shall crush'd and scatter'd lie
     By God's revenging Hand;
   And all, confounded, die,
     Despis'd by God's Command.

6 Oh, when shall *Israel*'s Wealth
     From *Sion*'s Mount proceed!
   When shall their Saviour's Health
     Redeem his Captive Seed!
   When that bless'd Time appear,
     Poor *Israel* shall rejoice;
   And *Jacob*, freed from Fears,
     Exalt his chearful Voice.

PSAL. liv.

1 ME, Lord, with wondrous Might,
     By thy great Name relieve!
2 O in my Pray'rs, dear Lord delight;
     My flowing Words receive!
3   For cruel Stranger, here
     Against me fiercely rise;
   They hunt my Life, who have no Fear
     Of God before their Eyes.

4   But see; my God, for me,
     Among my Friends appears!

He'll crush my Foes: His Truth shall be
    The End of all my Fears.
To Thee, with Sacrifice,
    I'll then devoutly pray:
Thy Name shall in my Praises be;
    It's good thy Praise to pay.

God has my Saviour been,
    From all my Griefs and Woes:
Through him my longing Eyes have seen
    My Wish on all my Foes.

PSAL. lv.

Lord, hear my Pray'rs! ô never turn
    From him who prays to Thee!
When I in Words distracted mourn,
    O hear! ô answer me!
Free me from cruel Foes, from those
    Who would oppress me quite;
Who me with impious Lyes oppose,
    And prosecute with Spite.

My Heart bleeds with its inward Wounds,
    Death's Terrours round me fall;
Fear, Trembling, Horrour, Woe confounds
    My Thoughts and Actions all.
I cry'd, Oh, who swift Wings will give,
    Swift as the Doves, to me?
Then would I fly away, and live
    Where I some Rest might see.

I'd wander far, and, in my Flight,
    Some lonesom Desart find,
Where I might soon in Safety light,
    From ev'ry stormy Wind!
Lord, to confound their plotting Brains,
    Their Tongues and Hearts divide;

For Strife within the City reigns,
    And cruel Thieves reside.

Part 2.

10 Such, Day and Night, their Walls surround;
    Within are Sins and Woes:
11 All Mischief in their Streets are found,
    And Fraud and Falshood grows.
12 Had Foes profess'd procur'd my Shame,
    I then had Patience held:
Had Enemies despis'd my Name,
    I h'd soon my self conceal'd.

13 But it was he, my trusted Guide,
    My Bosom's Partner made,
In closest Bonds of Friendship ty'd,
    My private Thoughts betray'd.
14 Oft with a charming sweet Consent,
    Each other's Souls we read:
Oft to the Temple jointly went,
    By like Devotions led.

15 O let the treach'rous Brute, alive,
    To Hell's dark Womb descend!
Who could with Hellish Art contrive
    To kill his kindest Friend!
16 For me, to God, the Lord, I'll cry;
    My God shall rescue me:
17 Each Night, each Noon, each Morning, I
    His suppliant Slave will be.

Part 3.

18 He'll hear my Pray'rs, my Life redeem
    From Wars, on me design'd:
And though too strong my Foes might seem,
    My God was always kind.

PSAL. lvj.

19 That God who ever lives shall hear,
    And humble all their Pride
Who ne'er were shock'd on Earth with Fear
    And therefore God defy'd.

20 They Wars with Men of Peace began,
    And all Agreements broke:
And Spite through all their Counsels ran,
    Howe'er they soft'y spoke.
21 Not Oil nor Butter smoother flow'd,
    Than their deceitful Words;
Yet Villains ne'er more Malice show'd,
    Nor fought with sharper Swords.

22 Thy Cares then on thy Master cast,
    His Hand shall set thee free:
He'll always hold the Righteous fast,
    No Time their Change shall see.
23 The Bloody and Deceitful shall
    Untimely sink, and die,
And in the Pit's Destruction fall:
    But I'll on God rely.

PSAL. lvj.

1 TO me thy Mercy, Lord, extend,
    For Men wou'd me devour;
Against me all their Forces bend,
    And press me ev'ry Hour.
2 Each Day my cruel greedy Foes
    Design'd to swallow me;
And Armies which my Soul oppose,
    Would my Destruction see.

3 When-e'er I fear, I'll trust in Thee,
4   Thy faithful Word I'll praise:
Nor will I fear what Hurt to me
    Poor mortal Man can raise.

5 Each Day they wreſt my Words; to work
    My Fall their Thoughts are bent:
6 They meet, they trace my Steps, they lurk
    Againſt my Life intent.

7 But ſhall they always ſcape in Sin?
    In Wrath deſtroy them all!
8 Thou know'ſt my dang'rous Flights; haſt ſeen
    My Tears, which daily fall:
O let them ever in thy Sight,
    In Books recorded, lie.
9 But all my Foes ſhall turn to Flight
    When I to God ſhall cry.

   I know't; for God's my Patron dear,
10   Through Him his Truth I'll ſhew:
11 I'll truſt in God, and nothing fear
    Which mortal Men can do.
12 To Thee, dear God, my Vows are made;
    To Thee my Praiſe I'll pay,
13 Who ſav'd'ſt me from Death's gloomy Shade
    When I in Danger lay.

And ſtill I hope, through God, my Feet
    Shall ever firmly ſtand:
My Steps thy ſaving Favours meet,
    And I poſſeſs the Land.

PSAL. lvij.

1 MErcy to me, Lord, Mercy ſhow;
    My Soul depends on Thee:
Thy Wings, till off this Danger blow,
    Shall my Protection be.
2 To God I'll cry, to God moſt High,
    Who all my Wiſhes ſends:
3 Who me from his ſuperior Sky,
    From barbarous Men defends.

4 His Truth and Mercy God applies,
    To save my drooping Soul,
Which now with raging Lions lies,
    Who would devour it whole.
I ly with fiery Men, whose Words
    Like Spears and Darts appear,
Whose piercing Tongues than sharpest Swords,
    A greater sharpness bear.

5 Lord, raise thy self, exalt thy Name,
    Above the lofty Skies,
And o're this Earths enlightned Frame,
    Lord, lift thy glorious Eyes.
6 My Soul with sorrow sunk, dismaid
    At fatal Nets prepar'd.
But now my Foes in Pit-falls made
    For me, themselves are snar'd.

7 My Heart, dear Lord's prepar'd, my Heart
    Is fix'd, thy Praise to sing.
8 Awake my Pride, my charming Art,
    To praise thy gracious King.
9 Awake my Lute, my Harp awake,
    And I'le prevent the Day:
To God's great Name new Anthems make,
    And to his Glory play.

10 His Name, his wondrous Works, will I
    Among the Nations praise,
11 And in my Songs above the Sky,
    His Truth and Mercy raise.
12 Lord, raise thy self, exalt thy Name,
    Above the lofty Skies,
And o're this Earth's enlightned Frame,
    O lift thy glorious Eyes!

Psalm lviij. *As the* 100, *or, as Mr.* Sandys's 14.

1 WHen you in private Council sit,
  Are all your Consultations just?
  May others your Decisions trust?
Their Lives to your pure Hands submit?

2 No wretched Men! your tainted Hearts
  Iniquities alone pursue,
  Earth groans so long opprest by you,
Your bloody Hands, and faithless Arts.

3 I long the wicked Race have known,
  All Lyers from the Breasts and Womb.
  Lyes in their Infant-Souls have room,
In Lyes their Elder years are grown.

4 Poor harmless things compar'd with these
  Black poisonous Toads, and Serpents are,
  Nor can the deafest Asp compare,
With their hard-hearted Policies.

5 Asps scorn the curious Charmer's Arts,
  And all his Magic Cant defy,
  These won't admit the Sufferer's cry,
No Tears can move their stubborn Hearts.

Part 2.

6 Lord, break their Teeth, their dreadful Jaws,
  Who, with a brutish Force enrag'd,
  Against weak Innocence engag'd,
Confound the Poor and Righteous Cause.

7 As sliding Waters sink and fail,
  So let their Malice quickly dy:
  And when they let their Arrows fly,
Let neither Bows nor Shafts prevail.

8 Let

8 Let them, like Snails, when melting, waste;
   Or like untimely Births decay,
9   And to thy stormy Wrath give way
As Thorns before a fiery blast.

10 The Righteous then shall droop no more,
   But God's all-righteous Vengeance view,
   And all the Paths of Joy pursue,
And wash their Feet in impious gore.

11 Then all the World convinc'd shall say,
   " The Just are well rewarded now,
   " A God at last we must allow,
" A God the lower World to sway.

Or thus,

1 WHen you in private Councils sit,
    Are all your Counsels just?
May Men to you their lives commit,
    Or your Decisions trust?
2 No wretched Men! your tainted Hearts
    Iniquity pursue,
Your bloody Hands, and faithless Arts,
    Make Earth her Groans renew.

3 I long their impious Race have known,
    How from the Womb they ly'd,
Their Infant Years, to Falshood prone,
    Their Elder Age supply'd.
4 Poor harmless things compar'd with these
    Black poisonous Serpents are,
With their hard-hearted Policies,
    Deaf Adders can't compare.

5 Adders defy the Charmer's Arts,
    And all his Cant defy:
And these with unrelenting Hearts,
    Throw off the Sufferer's cry.

6 Lord, break their Teeth, their dreadful Jaws,
 With brutish force enrag'd,
Against the Poor's afflicted Cause,
 And Innocence engag'd.

7 As sliding Waters sink and fall,
 So let their Malice dy,
Nor let their shiver'd Bows prevail,
 Or broken Arrows fly.
8 Let them, like Snails, when melting, waste,
 Or hasty Births decay,
9 Or as Thorns to a fiery Blast,
 To thy fierce Wrath give way.

10 The Righteous then shall droop no more,
 But God's just Vengeance view,
And wash their Feet in impious Gore,
 And joyful ways pursue.
11 Then all Mankind convinc'd shall see,
 The Just are well repaid.
A God to Rule the World must be,
 And his Commands obey'd.

Another Metre: *As the old* 125. *proper Tune.*

1 THE Place was dark,
 And far remov'd from searching Eyes,
No chearful Light
 Could break th' impenetrable gloom;
No starry Spark
 Could there the dark Cabal surprize,
But sullen Night
At once possess'd the dismal room.
There sate Saul's Council, there their Plots they laid,
Their Souls more black than Nights prevailing
 (shade.
 Vile Men, could you
There in a righteous Ballance weigh

The

PSAL. lviij.

    The Sufferer's Cause,
And neither Love, nor Pride, nor Hate,
    Nor Malice shew?
Did all impartial Justice sway
    Your equal Laws?
No Bribes an unknown Right create?
Did you in that obscure retreat conclude,
God's piercing Eye your Thoughts and Actions
                    (view'd.

    Alas! 'twas vain
To look for sacred Justice where
    Triumphant Sin,
With all its curs'd Attendance reign'd,
    Where Hopes of Gain
Could barbarous Violence endear,
    And all had been
By secret Wickedness maintain'd.
Yet such you all, great Counsellers, have been,
The Slaves of Tyrants, and the Tools of Sin.

    When born at first,
To entertain the World you ly'd.
    And Fraud and Lyes
Your Thoughts, and Words, and Actions fill'd,
    With Poisons nurst,
Your Looks the Basilisk out-vy'd,
    Your baleful Eyes
The Serpent at a distance kill'd.
Deaf Adders sooner hear the Charmer's Art,
Then you'd support the poor Afflicted Heart.

    How shall I pray?
What Judgments on the Miscreants call?
    Whose Lion rage
Would all the trembling World devour?
    Thy Wrath display,
Great God, and make their Furies fall,
    At once asswage

Their Spite and defolating Power.
Let all their Strength, like hafty Torrents, fly,
Which now o'reflow, now fink in Sands, and die.

7, 8   Snails melt away,
Confum'd in their own unctuous flime,
    When Mid-day's Sun
On them fhoots down his pointed Heat
    Thofe Births decay
Which Women loofe before their Time,
    Shapes juft begun
And not by Nature's Hand compleat.
9 So let them wafte, all ftrength their Members leave
Their broken Bows and Shafts their Hands deceive.

    Rife mighty God,
Let thy impetuous Fury break
    On their curs'd Heads
While yet they firmly ftand and thrive !
    O let thy Rod
Thy Wrath with dreadful Lafhes fpeak !
    As Ruines fpread
When fiery Tempefts fiercely drive,
And thorny Woods with crackling Flames embrac'd
Are laid at once, in one fhort Moment, wafte.

10   This Vengeance pafs'd,
The Sons of Heaven fhall droop no more,
    But every Mind
With Joys furprizing Raptures fwell,
    Their Feet be wafh'd
In flowing Streams of finful gore.
11   Till Men refign'd
To powerful Truth, with Praife fhall tell,
" God doubtlefs reigns, his care his Servants guard
" And all their Faith with endlefs Love rewards.

PSAL. lix.

1 FRom all my Foes, dear Lord, and those
    Who fierce against me stand;
2 From Men of Blood, who hate the Good,
    My Safety, Lord, command!
3 For those who hate my Soul lay wait,
    The mighty Men combine;
  And all agree to murder me
    For no Deserts of mine.

4 For no base Facts, no lawless Acts,
    Their Bands my Life pursue;
  For me thy Might then, Lord, excite,
    And all my Dangers view.
5 Thou God of Hosts, who guard'st their Coasts,
    For *Israel*'s Land declare;
  The Gentiles round in Wrath confound,
    No Sins of Malice spare!

6 Return'd at Night like Dogs they fight,
    And round the City go;
  And for the Prey they miss'd by Day
    Their snarling Temper show.
7 Their very Words are piercing Swords,
    For who can hear? *Th. y cry*,
8 Let Scorn on all those Heathens fall,
    With Smiles their Rage defy.

9 Since Force and Might against me fight,
    And God is kind and just,
  My Confidence in his Defence,
    Shall ever firmly trust.
10 To me afford thy Mercies, Lord,
    With them prevent my Woes,
  And ô let me thy Vengeance see,
    On my insulting Foes!

Part 2.

11 Lord, kill them not, left, soon forgot,
  My People sin the more;
But, ô, disperse, with Anger fierce,
  Their Substance, and their Store!
12 For all those Lyes their Hearts devise,
  And what their Tongues have told;
Let all their Pride be mortify'd,
  Their perjur'd Minds controll'd.

13 Those Brutes abhorr'd, in Anger, Lord,
  Consume, consume them so,
That they thy Grace to *Israel*'s Race,
  And all the World, may know.
14 Return'd at Night, like Dogs they'll fight,
  And round the City prowl:
15 And long to eat, and get no Meat;
  But murmur loud, and howl.

16 Thy Strength I'll sing, my God, my King;
  Thy Mercies early praise:
For in my Grief, their kind Relief
  My drooping Fancies raise.
17 I'll spread, dear God, thy Strength abroad,
  Thy Mercies store disc'ose;
Till all have known from whence alone
  My kind Assistance flows.

PSAL. lx.

1 O Why so distant, Lord! so far
  From *Israel*'s chosen Line
When in a sad destructive War
  So mighty Kings combine.
See how our trembling Armies move,
  When not reviv'd by Thee:

O let us now thy ancient Love,
    Thy former Mercies see!

2 The Land beneath thy Furies shook,
    Nor could its Fears conceal.
Oh, with thy kind restoring Look
    Its dismal Breaches heal!
3 Hard Things thy People, Lord, have try'd,
    To deadly Fears betray'd:
4 But now thy Banners, on their Side,
    Are for the Truth display'd.

5 That thy Belov'd at large may live,
    From Chains and Bondage free;
Let thy Right Hand Salvation give,
    And hear and answer me.
6 God spoke, and, in his Holiness,
    My Heart with Joys supply'd:
And now I'll Sichem's Lands possess,
    And Succoth's Plains divide.

7 *Gilead* is mine, *Manasseh*'s mine,
    My Head on *Ephraim* rests:
But *Judah*'s Tribe, by Right Divine,
    The Royal Crown invests.
8 *Moab* my meanest Slave shal be,
    And *Edom* kiss my Feet;
And *Palestine*, subdu'd, shal me
    With humblest Tributes meet.

9 Who'll me through Cities fortify'd,
    And *Edom*'s Barriers, lead?
10 Lord, sha' n't thy Help, so long deny'd,
    Our marching Armies head?
11 Man's Help in Trouble's vain; for me
    Then, Lord, thy Aids dispose.
12 Through God we'll bravely Act, for He
    Sha'l crush our angry Foes.

Another Metre. As Psal. 121. *proper Tune.*

1 WHY, Lord, are we rejected? why
   Thus off in Anger thrown,
   And wretched Dastards grown?
O turn, and with a gentler Eye
   All our late Disasters view,
   And thy ancient Loves renew!

2 Thy Anger shook the trembling Land,
   And made its Pillars bow:
   O heal its Breaches now!
3 On Thine, dear Lord, thy weighty Hand
   Has a Thousand Hardships brought,
   And impos'd a deadly Draught.

4 But on thy Servants side at last
   Thy sacred Banner stands;
   Thy Truth has arm'd their Bands,
And all their pressing Fears are past.
5   Free that thy Belov'd may be,
   O support and answer me!

6 God's Oracle of Holiness
   My Heart with Joy supply'd:
   I'll *Sichem* soon divide,
And *Succoth*'s fertile Plains possess.
7   *Gilead*'s mine, *Manasseh* too,
   And what *Ephraim*'s Strength can do.

Judah the Royal Crown must wear.
8   The meanest Slaves, to me,
   Shall *Moab*'s Off-spring be;
And *Edom*'s Youth my Shooes shall bear.
   Palestine, my conqu'ring Feet,
   With triumphant Garlands meet.

9 Who

9 Who, through strong Forts, to Lion's Head.
   Our trembling Bands will guide,
   Or in our Camps preside?
10 Thou, Lord of Hosts, our Armies lead;
   Though of old we oft were thrown,
   Now our Cause and Armies own!

11 In all our Streights, assist us, Lord;
   For Man's poor Helps are vain.
12 Through God we'll Honour gain.
   God's Strength to us shall Strength afford,
   And his unresisted Blows
   Batter down our angry Foes.

PSAL. lxj.

1 Lord, hear my Cries; my Pray'rs attend.
2 From Earth's last Quarters I
   On Thee, though languishing, depend;
   To Thee, for Comfort, fly.
3 O Thou, my Help of old, my Strength
   Against fierce Enemies!
   Fix me on that high Rock at length,
   Which all their Force defies!

4 Within thy holy House, my Rest
   Beneath thy Wings shall be:
5 For all my Vows, to Heav'n address'd,
   Were kindly heard by Thee.
   To those who fear thy Name, thy Grace
   Shall large Possessions give.
6 The King shall still, before thy Face,
   A Thousand Ages live.

7 Let Truth and Mercy guard his Head
   From ev'ry threat'ning Storm,
8 And I his Praise, in Songs, will spread;
   And daily Vows perform.

PSAL. lxij.

1 BUT still on God, my Saviour, I
   With humble Silence wait:
2 My Rock, my Health; who sets me high,
   And then confirms my State.
3 How long shall your base Plots assail
   My Life? Your selves shall fall;
   And like old tott'ring Fences fail,
   Or like some batter'd Wall.

4 They fain would thrust my Glories down,
   And old in Lyes they grow:
   Their Language Oily Blessings crown,
   Their Hearts with Curses flow.
5 But still on God, my Saviour, I
   With humblest Silence wait:
6 My Rock, my Health; who sets me high,
   And then secures my State.

7 God's my Salvation, Glory, All
   My Strength, my Hope, my Trust.
8 Pour out your Hearts with Faith; O call
   On Him, ye suff'ring Just!
   Our God's a Guard, who ne'er can fail:
9   But Men are Vanity.
   Nay, that against 'em turns the Scale,
   They're all an empty Lye.

   Those Men by Providence depress'd,
   And those exalted high;
   The Rich, the Poor; the Worst, the Best,
   Are all an empty Lye.
10 O ne'er in Wrong nor Force confide,
   Nor swelling Thoughts disclose;
   Nor on your Treasures multiply'd
   Your careless Hearts repose.

11 Once

11 Once God hath spoke, and twice have we
    His Declaration heard,
That Might belongs to God, and He
    Will for his Might be fear'd.
12 And Mercy, Lord, is only thine,
    And thy impartial Hand
Will, as Men's various Works incline,
    Their due Rewards command.

PSAL. lxiij. *as the 100th.*

1 BEfore the Morning-blushes rise,
    To Thee, dear God, I lift my Eyes;
For thou alone my God shalt be.
To Thee my thirsty Soul aspires;
Thy Smiles my longing Flesh desires,
    Where I no Springs of Comfort see.
2 As oft within thy holy Place,
I met of old thy quick'ning Grace,
    I'd now thy Strength and Glory view.
3 More swift than Life, thy Mercies flow;
And I with chearful Lips would show
    Thy Works, thy ancient Praise renew.

4 Thy Works, with Blessings I'll proc'aim
While Life shall last; and in thy Name
    My Hands and Heart devoutly raise.
5 Sweet Marrow's Juice the Taste invites,
But more in Thee my Soul delights;
    And Thee my joyful Lips shall praise.
6 In Bed I think on Thee, dear Lord;
Thy Loves I through the Night record,
    And on thy Goodness meditate.
7 From Thee my Health and Safety springs;
And, shadow'd by thy glorious Wings,
    I'll all thy Works with Joy relate.

8 To Thee my steady Soul adheres;
   Thy Hand my strong Support appears.
9   But those who would my Life betray
   Shall sink in Death's Eternal Shade:
10 Their Lives to cruel Swords be made,
   And Wolves, and savage Beasts, a Prey.
11 Then in his God the King shall be
   Exalted high; the World shall see
   His flowing Joys: and all who swear
   To him, shall in their Oaths be bless'd;
   And Lying Lips, with Shame suppress'd,
   No more to blast his Crown appear.

PSAL. lxiv.

1 Lord, hear my Voice in Pray'r; secure
      My Life from angry Foes!
2 From Sinners Plots ô hide me sure,
      And wicked Workers Blows!
3 Sharp though they whet their temper'd Swords,
      Their Tongues are sharper far;
   And out they shoot their bitter Words,
      Like Shafts prepar'd for War,

4 In dark Retreats the Plotter lies,
      To wound the perfect Heart;
   And, fearless, there, with bo'd Surprize,
      He throws his deadly Dart.
5 Mischief's their Life, to mischief they
      Encouragements apply;
   And talk of spreading Snares, and say
      Who can our Snares descry?

6 Deep are their Hearts, their Counsels deep,
      And a their Thoughts profound;
   And all a Search for Mischief keep,
      And practise Mischief found.

7 Bu

PSAL. lxv.

7 But God, with more surprizing Darts,
    Their wounded Hearts shall reach:
8 Their Tongues shall soon betray their Hearts;
    Themselves, themselves impeach.

9 Aloof the wond'ring World shall stand;
    And all around, with Fear,
Acknowledge God's revenging Hand,
    And all his Acts revere.
10 Then shall the Just in God rejoice,
    Their Faith more strongly raise;
And each good Man exalt his Voice,
    To sing his Maker's Praise.

PSAL. lxv. *as the* 100*th.*

PRaise, Lord, in *Sion* waits for Thee;
    To Thee our holy Vows we pay.
Thou hear'st us; whence, in Misery,
2   To Thee the suppliant World shall pray.

3 My Sins are, Lord, too strong for me:
    But Thou shalt all my Sins forgive.
4 O happy's he, whose Eyes may see
    Thy House, and in thy Presence live:

When him Devotion kindly warms,
    His inward purer Joys abound;
His Soul with bless'd Religion's Charms,
    Is in thy sacred Temple crown'd.

5 What though a Thousand Dangers rise
    To us? our sure Salvation springs
From Thee: thy Flock for Shelter flies
    To thy protecting Mercy's Wings

For us thy dreadful Judgments move,
    And scatter all our Fears and Woes.

Whence all in Thee their Trust improve,
     Where Earth extends, or Water flows.

6 Thy Might the lofty Mountains rais'd,
    And Pow'r thy wondrous Throne surrounds;
  And at thy Voice, the Seas, amaz'd,
    Laid down their Billows roaring Sounds.

7 Thy Terrours smooth the Wat'ry Plain,
    And all the murm'ring Nations quell;
  When ruffling Storms disturb the Main,
    And stubborn Hearts with Madness swell.

Part 2.

8 When earth is shock'd, and Comets blaze,
    And thy prodigious Signs appear,
  At them the trembling Nations gaze,
    And them at utmost distance fear.

  The blushing Dawn, the Morning-Skies,
    Through all the World thy Praise proclaim;
  And when Night's gloomy Shadows rise,
    They celebrate thy glorious Name.

9 Thy Eyes the lower World survey,
    Thy Hand their various Need supplies;
  Thy Dews and Rains prepare the Way
    For Grass, and Herbs, and Plants to rise.

  What mighty Treasures, Lord, hast Thou
    Within thy wat'ry Chambers laid?
  Whence all our vast Provisions now,
    Our Corn, and Wine, and Oil's convey'd.

10 The rising Grounds thy Fountains make;
    Their wealthy Crops and Fatness yield:
  The lower Lands thy Smiles partake;
    Thy Blessing warms the springing Field.

1 The joyful Year, with Goodness crown'd,
   Owes all its Plenty, Lord, to Thee:
Thy Clouds with fat'ning Drops abound,
   And we their large Production see.

2 The barren Wilds, the burning Sands,
   Those cooling Drops in Season bless:
The dancing Hillocks join their Hands,
   And Mirth and Gratitude express.

3 Huge Flocks the fruitful Pastures yield,
   Huge Crops the burthen'd Valleys bring;
Joys eccho through the chearful Field,
   And all their Maker's Praises sing.

Another Metre, to the old 104th proper Tune.

1 IN Sion's bless'd Gates,
      Lord, Praise waits for Thee:
   To Thee holy Vows
      Shall justly be paid.
2 Thy Goodness creates
      All our Confidence: we
   By't mov'd in thy House,
      Our Petitions have made.

3 Man's impious Art
      Against me prevails;
   O purge, O remove
      Our Follies away!
4 How happy's his Part,
      Whom thy Mercy ne'er fails!
   Thy Choice can approve,
      And thy Service can stay!

   That Man in thy Sight
      And Temple may dwell;

Thy

Thy Altars draw near,
   Thy Favours enjoy;
And in Thee delight,
   And be satisfy'd well
With Goodness: and there
   All his Service employ.

5 By terrible Things
   In Righteousness shown,
Thou'lt answer our Cares,
   Our Saviour to be.
Our Confidence springs
   From thy Goodness alone:
Whence Strangers make Pray'rs,
   And rough Sailers, to Thee.

6. The Mountains stand fast,
   Fix'd strongly by Thee;
Thy powerful Arm
   Has girt 'em secure.
7 Loud Storms are soon past,
   For thy Fury, we see,
Mad People can charm,
   And their Quiet procure.

8 Thy Wonders and Signs
   All Nations afright,
Where Comets e'er blaze,
   Or Earth-quakes can tear,
The Morning, which shines,
   And the dark gloomy Night,
Rejoice in thy Praise,
   And thy Glories declare.

9 Thou visit'st the Earth,
   Its Waters abound;
Vast Rivers, with Wealth,
   The Countries o'erflow:

Thence Corn has its Birth;
   And the Fie'ds, with it crown'd,
New Vigour and Health
   On the Nations bestow.

10 The highest ridg'd Field
   Thy Water partakes;
The Furrows, laid low,
   Are drench'd with the same:
The Clods quickly yield,
   Earth its Hardness forsakes;
The Crops, which they show,
   Then God's Blessing proclaim.

11 By Thee the rich Year
   With Goodness is crown'd;
And al thy bless'd Ways
   Pure Fatness distil:
12 Rich Pastures appear
   All the Desarts around;
All ecchoing Praise
   From each neighbouring Hill.

13 With Thousands of Sheep
   The Pastures are clad;
The Valleys with Corn
   Are cover'd quite o'r:
Hence Nature may keep
   Now its Revels; and glad,
With Praises adorn
   Both her Lord, and her Store.

PSAL. lxvj. *as the* 113*th.*

1 IN God, ô all ye Lands, rejoice;
2 Let ev'ry Man's triumphant Voice
   Advance his Name, his Glories sing.

3 How

3 How dreadful, Lord, thy Works appear!
  Thy Terrours make thy Foes, with Fear,
    To Thee their forc'd Submissions bring.
4 To Thee the Nations round shall bend;
  Thy Name shall in their Songs ascend
    Above the Clouds, above the Skies.
5 Come, see God's Operations here;
  How when his dreadful Works appear,
    Their Terrours Humane Hearts surprize.

6 When from *Egyptian* Bondage He
  His *Israel*'s happy Race set free,
    God through the Seas contriv'd a Road;
  Where, fenc'd by Watry Walls, they went
  Safe o'er a spacious Continent,
    And all their Hearts with Joys o'erflow'd.
7 God, by his Pow'r Eternal, reigns;
  His Look the Rebel-World restrains,
    And beats their swelling Humours down.
8 O all ye serious People, bless
  That God, whose Name our Tongues confess:
    His Name with lofty Praises crown.

9 The Lord our Souls in Safety keeps;
  He never slumbers, never sleeps;
    He ne'er permits our Feet to slide:
10 Yet, as the Silver's oft refin'd,
  When for the noblest Works design'd,
    Our Sou's as oft his Hands have try'd.
11 We fell in strong, perplexing Snares;
  Our Strength sunk down with weighty Cares;
    Our Heads we bow'd to conqu'ring Foes.
12 But through Affliction's scorching Heat,
  Through Floods of Tears, thy Mercies great
    Convey'd us to a sweet Repose.

Part

Part 2.

3 My Thanks his Temple now shall see.
4 I'll pay my Vows, dear Lord, to Thee;
  My Vows in Times of Danger sign'd.
5 My upright Mind, my Heart sincere,
  My guiltless Hands, shall Favour there,
    More than a Thousand Oxen, find.
6 Come, hear me, all that fear the Lord;
  O hear, while I, with Praise, record
    What for my Soul his Hands have wrought:
7 I cry'd, his Name I rais'd on high;
8 Yet, had my Heart been faulty, I
    His Smiles, alas! had vainly sought.

God reads the inward Parts, and views
What Ways the righteous Soul pursues,
  And hears his earnest Pray'rs and Cries:
But Hypocrites, whose various Arts,
Divide their glosing Tongues and Hearts,
  Are odious to his piercing Eyes.
9 But God has heard my Pray'rs, and He
  With Favour gently answer'd me;
    His Ears to my Petitions bow'd.
10 O bless'd be He, whose gracious Ear
  His suppliant Servant's Pray'rs would hear,
    And Mercy to his Pray'rs allow'd!

PSAL. lxvij.

TO us, with Mercy free,
    Lord, shew thy glorious Face:
O let thy happy Servants see
    Thy Blessing, and thy Grace!
That all the Earth may know
    Salvation's certain Way,
Thy Truth to all the Nations show,
    Thy saving Health display.

3 Let

3   Let all the Wor'd, ô God,
       Exalt thy glorious Name:
O let the Nations all abroad
    Thy wondrous Praife proclaim!
4   To Thee, with loud Applaufe,
       The govern'd World fhall fing,
When Thou fhalt all, by equal Laws,
    To righteous Judgment bring.

5   Let all the World, ô God,
       Exa t thy glorious Name:
O let the Nations a'l abroad
    Thy wondrous Praife proc'aim!
6   Then fhall the fruitful Land
       Its ancient Burthen fhow;
And on our felves, from God's free Hand,
    Shall endlefs Bleffings flow.

7   Then God fhall blefs us all;
       And at his awful Feet,
With Fear the fartheft Tribes fhall fall,
    And to his Laws fubmit.

PSAL. lxviij. *As the* 100*th.*

1 LET God arife, his angry Foes
    Will quickly turn themfelves to Flight:
Their Malice can't his Wrath oppofe,
    Nor bear the Terrours of his Sight.

2 But as Smoak flies before the Wind,
    As Wax diffolves before the Fire,
So Impious Men their Weaknefs find,
    And, by his Frowns confum'd, expire.

3 But holy Men, with joyful Hearts,
    Before their God fhall Praifes fing.

PSAL. lxviij.

Sing then, ye Saints; fing all your Parts;
 Exalt the great Celeftial King.

See where your God triumphant rides;
 His Name with boundlefs Glory fhines.
In Him each raptur'd Soul confides,
 And gladly in his Praife combines.

For Widows Tears, and Orphans Cries,
 God, like a Judge and Father, cares;
Starves Rebels, makes the Captives rife,
 And fills the lonefom Houfe with Heirs.

Lord, when thou led'ft thy People o'er
 The barren Wilds, and Defart-Lands,
Earth's Bofom ftrong Convulfions tore,
 And Heav'n, diffolv'd at thy Commands,

A Thoufand Dewy Sweats diftill'd.
 Nay, *Sinai* too, fupreamly blefs'd,
Great *Ifra*.*i*'s God with Terrours fill'd,
 With Light's immoderate Beams oppreſs'd.

9 But cooling Dews, and fruitful Rains,
 On thy exhaufted *Canaan* flow'd;
10 Which now thy People entertains,
 Thy Goodnefs on thy Flock beftow'd.

Part 2.

1 God gave the Word, and out in hafte
 All Nature's ready Armies flew,
 And fpoke God's Will; and as they pafs'd,
 Did all oppofing Force fubdue.

2 God's Houfhold then, with Spoils, grew fair,
 Of routed Hofts, and flying Kings;
As Doves, which feem to cut the Air
 With Silver Plumes, and Golden Wings.

13 On that great Day, though b'ack before,
  Among the Brick-Kilns newly laid;
14 They more than *Sal'mon*'s Whiteness bore,
  When in his Snowy Robes array'd.

15 God's *Sion*, *Bashan*'s Pride out-vies;
  And God in *Sion*'s Hill delights.
16 Why then should other Hills despise
  What God's own Residence invites?

17 A Thousand Thousand Chariots, steer'd
  By fiery Angels, round Him wait;
  As once in *Sinai*'s Mount appear'd,
  When there, enthron'd, his Glory sate.

18 Lord, when thou took'st thy Seat on high,
  Both Death and Hell were Captives led:
  Thy Gifts made stubborn Hearts comply,
  And Rebels own their sacred Head.

19 O bless'd be God, from Day to Day,
  Who us with bounteous Goodness loads:
20 Our Saving Health, our Lord, our Stay,
  Our Guide from Death's obscure Abodes!

21 But sinful Fools, his thoughtless Foes,
  God in their Heads, their Vitals, wounds.
22 I too, says God, will rescue those
  Whom *Bashan*, or the Sea, surrounds.

  My Friends shall live at large, and free;
  Ill us'd, restrain'd, oppress'd no more.
23 Their Steps o'er bleeding Foes shall be,
  Where Dogs shall lick the streaming Gore.

Part

Part 3.

24 My God, my King; thy glorious Ways
  Are oft with awful Wonder view'd,
When in thy House, on Holy Days,
  Thou meet'st the suppliant Multitude.

25 First all the charming Voices move,
  Then those who touch the tuneful Strings;
The Damsels next their Fingers prove,
  And loud the merry Timbrel rings.

26 Praise God in all Assemblies; praise
  Your God, ô all of *Israel*'s Race!
27 Let *Benjamin* his Anthems raise,
  Whom first the Regal Ensigns grace.

28 With Him let *Judah*'s Head combine,
  And all the Tribes their Leaders bring,
Till Mid-land Tribes and Coasters join
  And All their Maker's Glories sing.

29 Strength, Lord, on us thy Hand bestows;
  O let our Graces stronger be!
30 While Strength from *Salem*'s Temple flows,
  Great Kings shall offer Gifts to Thee.

31 Rebuke th' *Egyptians* Force! confound
  The Brutes, in Idol-worship strong:
Those who in Pride and Wealth abound,
  And who for Wars and Tumults long.

To God then mighty Kings shall fly,
  From *Egypt*, and *Arabian* Lands;
And cast their Crowns and Sceptres by,
  And raise to him their suppliant Hands.

32 Sing

32 Sing, sing to God, his Praise unfold,
    His Name yee Earthly Kings adore.
33 He rides above the Skies of old,
    And speaks in Thunders dreadful roar.

34 Ascribe to God all Strength and Might,
    VVho o're his Israel's Lot presides,
VVhose Power, and whose Majestic light,
    Above the highest Orb resides.

35 VVhat Terrours in that sacred Place,
    Israel's Eternal God surround!
The Saints his Might and Courage grace,
    His Name be still with Praises crown'd.

PSAL. lxix.

1 O Save me, Lord! Thy Floods prevail,
    The Floods my Strength controul.
2 The Mud, the rugged VVaves assail,
    And sink my fainting Soul.
3 To Thee till weary'd quite I cry,
    My Throat grows hoarse and dry,
My very Ey-strings crack, while I
    On Thee for Help rely.

4 More than my Hairs my Foes increase,
    And they whose causeless Hate,
Pursue my Soul, and break my Peace,
    Are strong, and Fortunate.
To lay their Spite, I paid with Care,
    VVhat ne'er was due from me.
5 Thou, Lord, my Follies know'st, nor are
    My Faults conceal'd from Thee.

6 Thro me let none endure Disgrace,
    VVho on thy Love depend,

PSALM lxix.

None blush thro' me who seek thy Face,
   Or for thy Grace attend:
7 For thy Name's sake I suffer scorn,
   To all Reproach confin'd,
8 My Mother's Sons, my Brethren born,
   To me are grown unkind.

Part 2.

9 Lord, for thy House with zealous Flame.
   My Soul consumes, and dies,
And those who dare affront thy Name,
   My Heart with grief surprize.
10 I fast, my fasting Tears succeed,
   But I'me reproach'd for all.
11 I Sack-cloth wear, my Sack-cloth weeds,
   Among their Proverbs fall.

12 Where all the senseless Rabble sit,
   I'me made their constant Theme;
Each Drunkard tries his brutish Wit,
   My Glories to blaspheme:
13 In thy accepted Time, dear Lord,
   Receive my Soul's address,
With Mercy by thy faithful Word,
   My cruel Foes repress.

14 From miry Deeps, Lord, raise my Head,
   From mighty Waters save,
15 And from the stormy Tempests dread,
   And from the gaping Grave.
Let not the Floods devour me quite,
   Nor Whirlpools swallow me.
16 But in thy Mercies, Lord, delight.
   And hear my Prayers to Thee!

Part 3.

With Pitty view my mournful Case,
　　And ease my dismal Woes.
17 From me ô never hide thy Face,
　　When Sorrows round me close.
18 Draw near, redeem my Soul from those,
　　Who, in my Fall delight.
19 My shame, reproach, and all my Foes,
　　Are ever in thy sight.

20 Shame breaks my Heart, my panting Soul,
　　For Comfort looks in vain,
No Friends my mournful State condole,
　　Nor feel my dreadful Pain,
21 They gave me bitter Gall to eat,
　　Sharp Vinegar to drink,
22 But let thy Wrath their Joys defeat,
　　Their spiteful Pleasures sink.

O let thy Curse a deadly snare,
　　Of all their Plenty make,
And when their Souls for Mirth prepare,
　　All Mirth their Souls forsake,
23 O let their Eyes be dark, their Loins
　　With strange Diseases shake.
24 Till Wrath with utmost Fury joins,
　　And they of both partake.

Part 4.

25 Let all their lofty Palaces,
　　Their Tents deserted ly,
26 For they on thy Afflicted press,
　　And Wounds to Wounds apply.
27 Punish their Sins with Sins; nor let
　　Them Righteousness behold!

28 Their

PSAL. lxx.

28 Their Names i'th' Book of Life unset,
    Nor with the Just enroll'd.

29 But me, oppress'd with mighty Woes,
    Thy Health, dear God, shall raise.
30 And Songs I'll to thy Name compose,
    And ever sing thy Praise.
31 And these shall Thee, my God, much more
    Than Firstling Bullocks, please.
32 The Humble, who thy Face implore,
    Shall see't, and live at Ease.

Joys shall their happy Hearts possess
    At this triumphant Sight:
Their Souls shall wondrous Mirth express;
    Their Lives, supream Delight.
33 God hears the Poor and Bond-men call,
    And sends Deliverance:
34 Then let Heav'n, Earth and Seas, and all
    Their Hosts, his Praise advance.

God saves his own, and they, in Peace
    Within their Countries rest:
6 And there their happy Heirs increase,
    Who love their Maker best.

PSAL. lxx.

HAste, Lord; ô haste to aid,
    And set thy Servant free!
Asham'd let all those Fools be made,
    Who seek to ruin me!
With Shame confound them al',
    Who would my Life destroy;
And when they think I'm like to fall,
    Express unmanly Joy.

H   4 But

4   But where Men seek thy Face,
      Let constant Joys reside :
Let those who love thy saving Grace,
      Say, *God be magnify'd.*
5   But I am weak and poor ;
      O haste to help me, Lord ;
And, as thou oft hast done before,
      Thy speedy Aids afford !

PSAL. lxxj.

1 IN Thee, dear Lord, I only trust :
    From Shame ô keep me free !
2 And, as thy Promises are just,
    Hear, help and rescue me !
3 Be thou my mighty Fortress, where
    I, when oppress'd, may fly.
Thou art my Rock, my Fort ; in Fear
    I on thy Word rely.

4 Save me, my God, from impious Hands
    From Fraud and Violence.
5 In Thee my Hope, my Safety stands ;
    My Lord, my Youth's Defence !
6 I from my Mother's Womb, at first,
    By Thee was brought to light ;
And by thy Providence was nurs'd,
    And in thy Praise delight.

7 Though I a Monster seem to most,
    In Thee my Hopes are strong.
8 O let thy Honour be my Boast ;
    Thy Praise, my daily Song !
9 Cast me not off when elder Days,
    When Age comes creeping on :
O leave me not when Strength decays,
    And youthful Years are gone !

10 My Foes, who watch my Soul, declare,
   Where they in private meet,
11 See now how God withdraws his Care,
   And leaves his Favourite!
   Up! let us seize him now; pursue
   Where-e'er the Dastard flies:
   He has, alas! no Help in view;
   None to his Aid will rise.

Part 2.

12 Haste then, my God; to help me, fly;
   No more thy Helps delay!
13 But let my Foes confounded lie;
   Their Spite, with Shame repay.
14 On Thee I'll still with Patience wait,
   And praise Thee more and more;
15 And all thy righteous Acts relate,
   And thy Salvation's Store.

   These all Accounts so far transcend,
   That none their Numbers know.
16 But, Lord, I'll on thy Strength depend,
   Thy Justice only show.
17 As taught by Thee from Childhood, I
   Thy wond'rous Works have shown
18 O let me not deserted lie,
   When weak and ancient grown!

   Lord, leave me not when hoary Hairs
   Invest my aged Head:
   Till to this Age, and future Heirs,
   I've all thy Wonders read.
19 On high thy righteous Actions shine,
   And great thy Judgments are.
   What Being, Lord, though call'd Divine,
   Can e'er with Thee compare?

H 2   20 Thou

20 Thou show'st me mighty Griefs and Woes,
    Yet shall thy Smiles revive;
And from Earth's hollow Deeps below,
    Present my Soul alive.
21 My Head thy Loves shall greatly raise,
    Thy Comforts guard my round:
22 And I thy Truth with Songs shall raise,
    And Harp's melodious Sound.

23 O *Israel's* holy God, to Thee
    My Lips will gladly sing;
My Soul, redeem'd from Misery,
    Its Tribute-Praises bring.
24 Thy Righteousness my Tongue shall trace,
    And daily talk of thee,
Since they are crush'd with dark Disgrace,
    Who sought to ruin me.

Psal. 72. *As the* 100*th. or Mr.* Sandys's 14*th*

1 LOrd, to the King thy Judgments give,
    Thy Justice on his Son bestow,
2 Then shall the World his Judgments know;
    The Humble, by his Justice live.

3 Then those advanc'd to noblest State
    Shall all for publick Peace declare:
The meanest Officers, with Care,
    Their Princes Goodness imitate.

4 He'll judge the Poor, their Off-spring save,
    And break the bold Oppressor's Force.
5 While Sun and Moon maintain their Course,
    His Fear shall ev'ry Heart enslave.

6 His Goodness, like soft Rains and Dews
    Which on the new-mown Grass descend,

7 Shall

7   Shall to the Moon's laſt Age extend,
    And Peace, abundant Peace, diffuſe.

8 The Righteous, in his happy Reign,
    Shall thrive; his mighty Empire ſtretch
    As far as Lands or Waters reach,
  Or fartheſt Springs their Streams maintain.

9 To Him th' *Arabian* Troops ſhall bow;
    His Enemies the Duſt embrace.
10   And *Saba*'s Kings, to court his Grace,
    Their nobleſt Gifts and Off'rings vow.

    The Iſles, the Continent, ſhall ſend
      Their Kings, to kiſs his ſacred Feet.
11   All Kings ſhall in his Worſhip meet,
    And Nations to his Service bend.

12 For He'll the praying Poor diſcharge;
    Th' Oppreſs'd, who no Aſſiſtance find.
13   He'll to the needy Soul be kind;
    And He'll the humble Heart enlarge.

14 From Violence He'll ſet them free;
    From ſhameleſs Fraud, and baſe Deceit.
    And in his Sight in Value great
    The Blood of all his Saints ſhall be.

15 Long ſhall He live; pure Gold as long
    To Him th' *Arabian* Bands ſhall pay:
    To Him th' obedient World ſhall pray,
    And Him with daily Bleſſings throng.

16 And though his Truth at firſt may ſeem
    Of meaneſt Worth, and ſmalleſt Force,
    'Twill ſoon, with a reſiſtleſs Courſe,
    Command the wiſer World's Eſteem.

Its Fruit to nobler Heighths shall grow
　　Than *Lebanon*'s immortal Heads:
　　More thick than Grass the Valleys spreads,
Vast Crouds shall to his Doctrine flow.

17 His Name Eternity possess'd,
　　God's Son, before reflecting Streams,
　　Threw back the Sun's first Infant-Beams;
And in Him ev'ry Nation's bless'd.

18 All Lands shall bless his sacred Name.
　　O bless'd be God, the mighty Lord,
　　Whose Name old *Jacob*'s Tribes record,
Whose Name his wondrous Works proclaim!

19 With Blessings let his Name be crown'd,
　　Till Time's run out; and ev'ry Day
　　His Glories through the World display;
And loud Amens, Amens resound!

Another Metre, as Mr. Sandys's 5th.

1 Lord, let the King thy Judgments find!
　　Enrich the Prince's Royal Mind,
For Crowns and Governments design'd.

2 Then sha'l He Sentence wisely give;
　　And safe in his Prerogative
Shall all the Poor, Afflicted, live.

3 Then Righteousness and Peace shall reign,
　　The mighty Men sha'l Peace maintain,
And Justice all the Vulgar gain.

4 He'll vindicate and save the Poor,
　　And all their Race from Harms secure:
But Tyrants must his Wrath endure.

5 Him

5 Him all, from Age to Age shall fear,
As long as Mid-day's Suns appear,
Or Moons the gloomy Mid-night chear.

6 Sweet be his Rule, and soft his Reign,
As gentle Dews which cool the Plain,
Or Show'rs which Grass and Herbs maintain:

7 The Just shall flourish in his Days;
Abundant Peace her Head shall raise,
While Moons shall shine, or Stars shall blaze.

8 His Empire shall be vast, and wide;
As far as Seas can feel the Tide,
Or Rivers flow, or Winds can ride.

9 In him th' *Arabians* wild shall trust:
His Foes, beneath his Foot-stool thrust
Shall fall, and humbly lick the Dust.

10 Him shall the Island-Kings obey;
To Him Black *Æthiopians* pray,
And Off'rings on his Altars lay.

11 Their Kings, by Truth convinc'd, shall be
His Servants, and his Slaves; and He
All Nations at his Feet shall see.

12 For He the poor Man's Cries shall hear;
The Suff'rers and Afflicted chear,
When neither Help nor Friends appear.

13 He'll to the Weak in Want be kind:
The humble and submissive Mind
Shall always his Assistance find.

14 Where Fraud and Wrong triumphant seem;
He'l all their fainting Souls redeem,
And dear their precious Lives esteem.

15 Long may He live; and long may they
To Him their Golden Tributes pay,
And daily praise, and daily pray!

16 Where little Hope or Seed was found,
May mighty Crops adorn the Ground;
Like *Libanus*, with Cedars crown'd.

Their Towns, before with Widows fill'd,
A new and num'rous Off-spring yield,
Thick as the Grass which shades the Field.

17 To Him may all the Nations haste;
His Name, with endless Blessings grac'd,
Beyond the Sun, Eternal last.

18 Bless'd be the Lord, our God! May He,
Whose wond'rous Works we daily see,
Prais'd by his grateful Churches be!

19 Bless'd, ever bless'd his glorious Name!
May all the World advance his Fame!
While we Amen, Amen proclaim!

PSAL. lxxiij.

1 IT's true, God to his *Israel*'s kind,
  To those whose Hearts are pure:
2 Yet all my Confidence declin'd,
  My Faith was scarce secure.
3 Envy, uneasie Envy gain'd
  An Empire in my Breast,
  To see how impious Mad-men reign'd,
  With Peace and Plenty bless'd.

4 No racking Pains their Deaths fore-show'd,
 Their Strength no Sickness broke:
5 They never bore Grief's common Load,
 Nor felt God's angry Stroke.
6 Hence are they crown'd with haughty Pride,
 And rob'd with Violence:
7 Their Looks are high; their Lusts supply'd,
 Beyond their utmost Sense.

8 They in excessive Leudness walk,
 And in Oppressions boast;
And with their thund'ring lofty Talk
 O'er-awe the neighb'ring Coast.
9 Nay, Heav'n it self their Words defy,
 And trembling Earth subdue:
10 And, while they make their Treasures fly,
 Allure the hungry Crew.

11 And yet they cry, " Can God above
 " Our secret Practice know?
" Can God our gallant Acts reprove,
 " Or greater Wisdom show?
12 Such are the wicked Workers, who
 Can, with a prosp'rous Gale,
And still increasing Riches, through
 The World's rough Ocean sail,

Part 2.

13 This I observing, fondly cry'd,
 " I've cleans'd my Hands in vain;
" In vain my Heart I purify'd,
 " And Innocence maintain.
14 " In vain, alas! my strugling Lust
 " I've daily mortify'd;
" And grovel'd in Affliction's Dust,
 " By sharp Temptations try'd.

15 But soon I this Reflection made,
    "Should I such Thoughts embrace,
"I must God's Providence upbraid,
    "And damn his chosen Race.
16 In vain I trod, without a Guide,
    The dark, perplexing Maze:
In vain by Reason's Methods try'd
    Thy Wisdom's secret Ways;

17 Till I could to thy Holy Place,
    With humble Thoughts, ascend;
And there their wretched Fortunes trace,
    And read their dismal End.
18 Oh, on what slip'ry Ground they stand!
    How quickly ruin'd all!
19 And, crush'd by thy destroying Hand,
    With Terrours wasted, fall!

23 As Dreams fly off from drowzy Eyes
    When Sleep the Man forsakes,
So Thou their Image shalt despise
    When once thy Fury wakes.
21 Thus now my Thoughts are satisfy'd,
    Though long perplex'd before;
Though Grief did then my Heart divide,
    And Pains my Bosom tore.

Part 3.

22 Such Ignorance and Folly then
    My untaught Soul betray'd:
And I, beneath the Rank of Men,
    With senseless Beasts was laid.
23 I see I'm always now with Thee;
    Thy Hand my Life supports:
24 Thy Counsels, Lord, my Guide shall be,
    To thy All-glorious Courts.

25 On whom but Thee, dear Lord, above,
    Can my Affections be?
And none on Earth my Soul can love;
    O none, compar'd with Thee!
26 Though here my Flesh my Heart decline,
    Thy Strength my Heart supplies.
Thou art my God, my Part Divine,
    When Time, expiring dies.

27 Loe, those whose vain Affections rove
    From Thee, shall sink, and die:
Those Fools who doat, with wanton Love,
    On curs'd Idolatry.
28 But when I draw to God, how nigh
    His flowing Mercies are!
On Him I've fix'd my Trust, that I
    Might all his Works declare.

PSAL. lxxiv.

1 O Why thus absent, Lord! Shall we
    No more thy Smiles obtain?
Shall thy poor Flock eternally
    Thy Fury's Weight sustain?
2 O think on those redeem'd of old;
    Those Lands, by Thee possess'd:
With Pity *Sion*'s Mount behold,
    Which once thy Presence bless'd?

3 O Thou Eternal God, to ease
    Our Desolations, haste;
For cruel Foes thy Temple seize,
    Thy sacred Dwellings waste.
4 Hark! how their Bands, insulting, roar,
    Where thy Assemblies met!
And their triumphant Banners o'er
    Thy mournful Altars set!

5 When safe thy glorious Temple stood,
   The curious Carver rais'd
Rare Figures on the yielding Wood,
   For Art and Softness prais'd.
6 But now those noble Works are all
   By barb'rous Axes spoil'd :
7 In Flames those sacred Buildings fall,
   With ruin'd Heaps defil'd.

8 Nay, in their cruel Hearts they say,
   Let's all at once destroy !
And on each Place of Worship they
   Devouring Flames emp'oy.
9 We see our Mystick Signs no more ;
   No Prophets speak thy Will :
And none our Term of Woes explore,
   By Wisdom's sacred Skill.

Part 2.

10 How long, Lord, shall Reproaches rise
   From thy insulting Foes?
How long shall horrid Blasphemies
   Thy glorious Name expose?
11 Rouse, Lord, thy Might ! make bare thy Arm !
   Stretch out thy dreadful Hand !
Their bloody Insolence alarm !
   And their Designs withstand !

12 For Thou'rt our King of old ; from Thee
   The World's Salvation flows :
To Thee its ancient Liberty
   Poor Jacob's Portion owes.
13 From Thee, of old, the parting Seas
   With sudden Haste recoil'd
And Israel, marching through, with Ease
   The ransack'd Ocean spoil'd.

14 'Twa

14 'Twas there the furious Monarch's Heat,
    In mighty Waters, dy'd:
Nor wou'd the rolling Waves retreat
    From *Pharaoh*'s haughty Pride.
The King, his Lords, his Troops were thrown
    Around the Purple Shore;
A Prey to Wolves and Vultures grown,
    But to be fear'd no more.

15 Thy Word unseal'd the Springs, and made
    The Rocks their Waters yield:
And through old *Jordan*'s Bosom laid
    A spacious, Sandy Field.
16 Thou bid'st the smiling Morning rise,
    And draw'st the gloomy Night;
And mak'st the Sun adorn the Skies,
    The Moon advance her Light.

17 Thy Hand has fix'd Earth's utmost Bounds,
    With winding Seas embrac'd:
And Heat, and Cold, in Yearly Rounds,
    Thy wondrous Wisdom plac'd.
18 Such were thy wondrous Acts of old:
    O now revive the same!
Since Foes in Scorn thy Wisdom hold,
    And Fools blaspheme thy Name.

Part 3.

19 Thy mournful Turtle, Lord, no more
    To cruel Hands resign;
Nor pass the poor Afflicted o'er,
    As if they ne'er were thine.
20 Thy ancient Covenant re-call,
    With our bless'd Fathers made;
For Rapine now our Quarters all,
    And barb'rous Force invade.

21 To Thee alone thy Suff'rers cry;
   Dear Lord, remove their Shame;
And, though in Woes and Poverty,
   They'll still exalt thy Name.
22 Rise, Lord! thine own great Cause maintain!
   Think how the scoffing Crew,
How Fools each Day, with deep Disdain,
   Thy glorious Name pursue.

23 Oh, ne'er forget th' insulting Voice
   Of thy triumphant Foes!
Who Thee, with fierce advancing Noise,
   And growing Spite, oppose.

To Father, Holy Ghost, and Son,
   One God, in Persons Three,
Be Glory paid, and Homage done,
   Through all Eternity.

PSAL. lxxv.

1   TO Thee, great God, to Thee,
       We offer Thanks and Praise;
   Thy Goodness we so near us see,
       In all thy wond'rous Ways.
2   When I, at thy Command,
       The Royal Crown shall wear,
   Through all the Land my righteous Hand
       With Justice shall appear.

3   See what Convulsions shake
       The Tribes, and all the Lands!
   And when they shake, I only make
       Its Pillars firmly stand.
4   I said to Fools, of old,
       O cast your Follies by!
   I Sinners told, O be n't so bold,
       Nor let your Horns on high!

5   Ne'er set your Horns so high,
       With such a lofty State;
Nor stubbornly your God defy;
       Nor so perversely prate:
6   For Pow'r and great Renown,
       Not Chance, but God bestows:
7 He gives the Crown, and he casts down
       Who Justice only knows.

8   Ne'er strive, with God to fight;
       He holds the deadly Bow!!
The dreadful Sight may well affright
       The wretched guilty Soul.
What horrid Drugs compound
       The Crimson baleful Draught!
The Nations round, as guilty found,
       To th' very Dregs are brought.

9   But still I'll praise the Lord;
       To *Jacob*'s God I'll sing:
And my sharp Sword, o'er those abhorr'd
       For wicked Actions, bring.
10   I'll make their Stiffness bend,
       While all the Just around,
Through God, their Friend, shall high ascend,
       With Mirth and Glory crown'd.

*Psal.*lxxvj. *as the* 148*th. or as Mr.* Sandys's 47*t*.

1 GOD's Name in *Judah*'s known,
    It's great in *Israel*:
2 His House in *Salem*'s shown;
    His Smiles on *Sion* dwell;
3   For there his Stroke,
Swords, Bows and Shields,
For Martial Fields,
   And Arrows broke.

4 Thy

4 Thy glorious Name's more bright
   Than theirs, whose num'rous Bands
In Violence delight,
   And spoil their Neighbours Lands;
      Who proudly boast,
      No Force can stay
      Their conqu'ring Way,
      Or guard our Coast.

5 But Desolation now
   Their daring Hearts attends;
And on each drowsie Brow
   An heavy Sleep descends.
      The Men of Might
      Grope, but in vain,
      Their Swords to gain,
      In that dark Night.

6 At thy Rebuke they fall;
   And Horse and Charriot lie,
Profoundly bury'd all,
   In one deep Lethargy.
7   Thou, on'y Thou,
      Deserv'st our Fear:
      For, who can bear
      Thy angry Brow?

8 When we thy Judgments heard,
   With Terrours from the Sky,
The World, to what it fear'd,
   Submitted si'ently.
9   Then God arose,
      To save and seek
      The patient Meek,
      And crush their Foes.

10 Man's hottest Wrath thy Name,
    Great God of Hosts, shall praise:
And though the raging Flame,
    With spreading Fury, blaze;
      Yet suddenly
    Their Rage, restrain'd
    By thy just Hand,
      Shall sink, and die.

11 Ye who the Lord adore,
    Your Vows before him lay;
And what was vow'd before,
    With grateful Gladness pay.
      To that great King,
    Whose angry Brow
    Aws all be'ow,
      Your Off'ring bring.

12 For his victorious Arm,
    With unresisted Force,
Fierce Monarchs shall disarm,
    And stop their head-strong Course.
      His Awful Frown
    Strange Terrour brings
    On Earthly Kings,
      And casts them down.

Another Metre, applied to our own Cases in this Nation.

GOD's Name i'th' *British* Isles is known,
    And is in *England* great:
Bless'd *England* is his happy Throne,
    His highly favour'd Seat.
Here, with his pow'rful Arm, He broke
    The Bow, the Sword, the Shield:
His Word alone, without a Stroke,
    Secur'd the Martial-Field.

4 Though mighty Tyrants mighty Fame
 With Scandal mix'd, may gain,
Yet, Lord, thy more illuſtrious Name
 No baſe Reproach can ſtain.
5 But ſudden Deſolations now
 Thoſe daring Hearts purſue;
And Sleep on ev'ry drowſie Brow
 Diſtils its weighty Dew.

In vain, alas! the Man of Might
 Dreams o'er his former Broi's:
In vain i' th' Dark he ſtrives to fight,
 And for a Conqueſt toils.
6 At thy Rebuke, great God, they fall;
 And Horſe and Chariots lie
Confounded quite, and bury'd All
 In one deep Lethargy.

7 Thou, only Thou, art juſtly fear'd:
 Thy Fury, who can ſtand?
8 VVhen we thy Heav'nly Judgment heard,
 It huſh'd the trembling Land.
9 VVhen God, the patient Meek to ſave,
 VVith Riſing Judgment reign'd,
10 To Him Man's Rage new Glories gave,
 And He their VVrath reſtrain'd.

11 O ye, who *Britain*'s Lord adore,
 Your Vows before him lay!
And what your juſt Engagements bore,
 VVith grateful Gladneſs pay.
12 Your Off'rings make to Him, whoſe Frown
 Reſiſtleſs Terrour brings;
Bold Princes daunts, and batters down
 The proudeſt Earthly Kings.

PSA.

PSAL. lxxvij.

TO God I cry'd, I strongly cry'd;
    And He receiv'd my Pray'r.
The Lord, when by Afflictions try'd,
    I sought with earnest Care.
All Night my wretched Soul was pain'd,
    With mighty Woes oppress'd;
And Sorrows, unresisted, reign'd
    In my afflicted Breast.

On God I fix'd my thoughtful Mind,
    But was perplex'd the more:
My Soul, to sad Complaints resign'd,
    Its Burthen hardly bore.
Thy Terrours hold my wakeful Eyes,
    And banish needful Sleeps.
My wretched Soul Grief's strange Surprize
    In heavy silence keeps.

I all my former Years survey'd,
    Those happy Days of old:
Those Songs, in better Seasons made,
    Which God's great Name extoll'd.
Distractions still, by Nights, by Days,
    Confus'd my weary'd Mind:
I mus'd, and sought the secret Ways
    Of Providence to find.

But still unsatisfy'd, I cry'd,
    " Is God for ever gone?
8 Will God his Presence always hide,
    " His former Loves disown?
9 What! Are his Days of Mercy past?
    " His sacred Promise void?
" His Smiles with angry Clouds o'er-cast?
    " His Goodness all destroy'd?

10 At last, I said, "My Follies all,
 "These faithless Thoughts create,
 "But God can yet my Hopes recall,
 "And change my mournful State.

Part 2.

11 I'le now thy ancient Actions, Lord,
    Thy Miracles of old.
12 And all thy wondrous Works record,
    Thy wise Designs unfold.
13 Thy Ways, tho' dark to Humane Eyes,
    Are holy, Lord, and pure.
What God with Thee in Greatness vyes,
    Or can thy Frowns endure.

14 Thy Works so many Wonders are,
    Thy Might the Nations know.
15 Thy Arms blest Freedoms welcome Air,
    On *Jacob*'s Race bestow.
16 The Waters, Lord, the Waters saw
    Thy Face, and parting fled.
The Deeps with one prodigious flaw
    Display'd their sandy Bed.

17 The Land unceasing Rains o're-flow'd,
    At thy commanding Voice,
The pointed Lightnings went abroad,
    With Thunders roaring noise.
18 Thy ratling Thunders roar'd around,
    And streaks of dismal Light
Shot thro' the Air; the trembling ground
    Quak'd with the dreadful fright.

19 Thy Road was thro' the Seas; thy way
    Thro' mighty Waters made,
Thy secret Paths could none survey;
    Or where thy steps were laid.

PSAL. lxxviij.

Moses and Aaron thro' the Deep,
   And trackles Deserts lead.
Thy Tribes, and them, like tender sheep,
   Securely kept and fed.

PSAL. lxxviij.

MY People mark my Precepts well,
   Your Ears to my Discourses bow,
My mouth shall weighty Matters tell,
   And Truths obscure and ancient show.

Which we their happy Sons have known,
   From what our hoary Fathers told.
That we with Praise to all our own,
   Might God's miraculous Acts unfold.

God gave his Laws to *Jacob*'s race,
   And bade our Fathers teach their Seed,
That each descending Age might trace
   His Will, and his Injunctions heed.

That so his sacred Worship might,
   Unmix'd from Age to Age descend.
All trust in God, and with delight,
   His Works declare, his Laws attend.

That they their Father's Guilt might fly,
   Whose Hearts perversly false rebell'd,
Let God's prodigious Wonders dy,
   And neither Faith nor Conscience held.

What broke arm'd *Ephraim*'s Archers? what
   So turn'd their coward Backs in figut?
God's Covenant they quite forgot,
   And from his Laws began their flight.

They

11 They soon forgot his tender Care,
    And all his mighty Wonders shown;
12 Which *Ægypt*'s Ruines still declare,
    And *Zoan*'s fields have dearly known.

Part 2.

13 He led them thro' the parted Seas,
    While all the crouding Waters gaz'd,
14 His Cloud by Day contriv'd their ease,
    By Night bright Flames before them blaz'd.

15 He burst the desert Rocks, and thence
    Sweet Waters as from Fountains drew,
16 Made Springs from stubborn Flints commence,
    Which soon to spacious Rivers grew.

17 Yet they, who saw it, trespass'd still
    And in a Desart hungry Land,
18 Ask'd Meat aloud to eat their fill.
    Yet question'd God's Almighty Hand.

19 To urge his Wrath, the faithless Crew,
    Thus, with a taunting boldness, said,
    " Can God his Wonders here renew?
    " Full Tables in a Desert spread?

20 " He smote the stony Rocks indeed,
    " And out the wholesom Waters broke:
    " But can his Magick Rod proceed,
    " Will Bread and Flesh attend the stroke?

21 With Anger God their murmurings heard,
    And at them soon his Fury smok'd,
22 When *Israel*'s seed so false appear'd,
    And faithless Fools their God provok'd.

Part 3.

13 To try them more, He bade the Skies,
  From their unbounded Treasures rain,
14 Streight heavenly Wheat before them lyes,
  And tastful Manna fills the Plain.

15 The Bread of Angels there they find;
  To glut their hungry Appetite.
16 Then God commands the Eastern Wind,
  And Southern fruitful Gales excites.

27 Less Dust in rapid Whirlwinds flies.
28   Then Flesh within their Trenches rain'd,
  Less Sand around the Ocean lies,
  Then Fowls about their Tents remain'd.

29 They fed, and fill'd themselves, and He,
  On them their utmost wish bestow'd:
30 But they no inward Guilt could see,
  Nor feel their Lusts confounding load.

31 Hence, e'er their Meat was down, their Pride
  God with a dismal blast surpriz'd,
  Their noblest Youth, and Princes dy'd,
  All to his Anger sacrific'd.

32 Yet unreclaim'd from sinful Ways,
  They'd still his wondrous Works oppose,
33 And He consum'd their Years and Days,
  In fading Joys, and lasting Woes.

34 If Death among their Armies flew,
  For God they'd seek, to God they'd fly,
35 Then God was all their Strength they knew,
  Their great Redeemer, God most high.

36 Their God with fawning Tongues they prov'
 With lying lips to Him they pray'd,
37 But still their Hearts perversly mov'd,
 Their Hearts their faithless Works betray'd.

38 Yet He forgave their Sins, and spar'd,
 Their Tribes, and laid his Anger by;
39 He knew they common Frailties shar'd,
 Would quickly change, and quickly dy.

Part 4.

40 How oft in desert Lands they mov'd,
 And urg'd, and vex'd his Heav'nly mind!
41 How oft, relaps'd, his Patience prov'd,
 And *Israel*'s Holy God confin'd!

42 They quite forgot that powerful Hand,
 Which them from slavish Bonds redeem'd,
43 When *Zoan*'s Field, and *Ægypt*'s Land,
 With dreadful Signs and Wonders teem'd.

44 How He their pleasant Waters chang'd,
 To nauseous Blood, and mystick Gore,
45 Mix'd Swarms in all their Quarters rang'd,
 And Frogs their Royal Chambers bore.

46 Their Fruit-trees blasting Whirlwinds peel'd,
 And Locusts all their Toils enjoy'd,
47 Their Vines, Figs, Cattel, and the Field,
48 Hot storms of fiery Hail destroy'd.

49 Since still the stubborn Land rebel'd,
 With fiercer flames his Fury glow'd;
 And as his burning Fury swell'd,
 The Coals malignant Angels blow'd.

Thick thro' the solid Dark they flew,
 With horrid shrieks, and dismal Cries,
And laid Hell's endless Pains in view,
 Before their Intellectual Eyes.

No Torch, no Star, no Middays Beams,
 No peaceful Thought, no comforts Light,
But Ghosts with frightful Howls and Screams,
 Could pierce th' unfathomable Night.

No sleep could seal their labouring Eyes,
 But dreadful Dreams of fo'lowing Woes,
And roaring Storms, and rattling Skies,
 And trembling Earths convulsive throws.

Part 5.

50 While thus with weighty Gloom o're thrown,
 Lost Ægypt lay; God's dreadful Hand,
Heavy with ripening Vengeance grown,
 Does newer Wounds and Plagues command.

Now a thick pestilential Air,
 Is rais'd from late corrupted Gore,
And sullen Stars malignant glare,
 And Locusts rotting round the shore.

From Fens and Bogs, and poisonous Lakes,
 And what rank venemous Weeds produce,
From Scorpions, Basilisks and Snakes,
 And Toads and Hemlocks baleful Juice.

All these in One, with deadly skill,
 Infernal Spirits temper sure;
That every Atomes force may kill,
 And neither Art, nor Nature, cure.

I

Out streight commanded *Michael* flies,
  A thousand Spirits round him wait,
  And on his Spear the mixture tries,
  And loads it with resistless Fate.

51 No wretched Shed, nor homely Stall,
  Where Men repos'd, or Beasts were laid,
  But Death at once attack'd 'em all,
  And one continued Slaughter made.

The first-born Prince, the first-born Slave,
  Of Flocks and Herds the Firstlings dy'd,
  Each Floor assign'd its Heir a Grave,
  Each Roof entomb'd its Owner's pride.

With dying Shrieks, and Groans, and Cries,
  The frighted Hills and Walls resound,
  All *Ægypt* now in mourning lies,
  In Sorrows boundless Ocean drown'd.

Part 6.

52 But while Heaven's warlike Prince at large,
  Thus ravag'd all the sinful Land,
  God of his *Israel* took the Charge,
  And led them with a gentler Hand.

53 He was their Shepherd, He their Guide,
  His Flock, his own Peculiars they,
  His Care their growing Wants supply'd,
  And led them safely all the Day.

Those Foes, who, with a furious Will
  Pursu'd, beneath the Seas He drown'd;
54 And brought them to his Holy Hill,
  With his protecting Presence crown'd.

55 He all the Nations round expel'd,
    And gave their Lands to *Jacob*'s Race;
    Who, then their Towns securely held,
    And in their Cities took their place.

56 Yet still they tempted God, and still
    To Anger mov'd their mighty Lord,
    Nor would their holy Vows fulfil,
    But his Commands, and Laws, abhorr'd.

57 They sinn'd, as all their Fathers us'd,
    And like an ill-set Bow they broke.
58 Their Lord with graven Gods abus'd,
    Which might his jealous Rage provoke.

    Each lofty Hill, each shady Grove,
    They with their gaudy Idols fill'd,
    Against their Maker boldly strove,
    And there their Sacrifices kil'd.

59 God heard of all; his Anger flam'd,
    And off th' ingrateful Nation threw.
60 And *Shilo*'s Holy Place disclaim'd,
    That Ark which once his Glories knew.

Part 7.

61 Now God, their Strength, and all their Pride,
    Resign'd to their insulting Foes.
62 Who with their Blood their Javelins dy'd,
    And fil'd his Heritage with Woes.

63 Hot feverish flames their Youth consum'd,
    Their mateless Virgins, Virgins dy'd.
64 Altars their mangled Priests entomb'd,
    Their own sad Widow's Tears deny'd.

65 Thus Justice rang'd the Field; at last,
    On Golden Wings bright Mercy rose;
And God, his hotter Fury past,
    Made Love her ancient Smiles disclose.

    Like some fierce Giant, rous'd from Sleep,
        Or high with sprightly Wines inflam'd;
66 God struck his Foes, their Wounds were deep,
    And their Eternal Shame proclaim'd.

67 Yet, for their Sins, He *Joseph*'s Fields,
    And *Ephraim*'s Tribe, though fruitful, scorns
68 His Rest more happy *Judah* yields;
    His House lov'd *Sion*'s Mount adorns.

69 There high his lofty Turrets rise,
    And all the Town beneath command:
And deep the vast Foundation lies;
    As Rocks, the solid Buildings stand.

70 Then from his Sheep, and meaner Cares,
71   Our God, his Servant *David* takes;
And him his *Israel*'s King declares,
    His holy Nation's Pastor makes.

72 That nobler Flock, with faithful Art,
    He watches, feeds, and safely folds;
And with an upright, prudent Heart,
    Our happy Church and State upholds.

PSAL. lxxix. *As the* 130*th.*

1 Lord, the Heathen-Troops have spoil'd
    Thy bless'd Inheritance;
And thy holy House defil'd,
    And still their Arms advance.

Sal'm's Walls on Heaps are laid :
    Thy murther'd Servants lie,
Preys to Wolves and Vultures made,
    Beneath the open Sky.

See a spacious Crimson Flood,
    By dying Martyrs shed :
Salem's Streets, with flowing Blood,
    And mangled Corpses spread.
Jacob's Tribes, alas ! are grown
    Their nearest Neighbour's Scorn ;
Out to vile Derision thrown,
    By cruel Scoffs o'er born.

Ah ; how long, dear Lord ! how long
    Shall thy fierce Fury burn !
O, on all the Godless Throng
    Thy weighty Vengeance turn !
Let the Gentile-Nations all,
    Who ne'er acknowledge Thee,
Underneath thy Judgments fal',
    And just Severitie.

They, with cruel Teeth, devour
    Poor *Jacob*'s wretched Race ;
And Destruction's Tempests pour
    On *Isra'l*'s Dwelling-place.
All our Sins, bless'd God, forgive,
    And speedy Mercy show ;
For by Thee alone we live,
    Though now reduc'd so low.

Part 2.

Lord, to our Assistance fly;
    From Thee our Safety springs :
Honour to thy Name, Most High,
    Such Saving Mercy brings.

10 Why, ô why should Heathens cry,
    "Now where's their mighty God?
Let them now the Lashes try
    Of thy revenging Rod!

Grant that, Lord, our longing Eyes
    Thy just Revenge may see!
While the Blood of Martyrs cries
    So loud, great God, to Thee!
11 Let the Pris'ners Sighs ascend
    Before thy Majesty;
And with mighty Pow'r defend
    The Souls, condemn'd to die.

12 To our Neighbours, Lord, repay
    Their base, reproachful Spite;
Such who in the Scorners Way,
    And Blasphemies, delight.
13 So shall we, thy Flock, thy Sheep,
    For ever praise thy Name;
And, through endless Ages keep
    Thy everlasting Fame.

Or thus,

1 DEar Lord, the Heathen Bands have spoil'd
    Thy bless'd Inheritance;
And have thy holy House defil'd,
    And still their Arms advance.
Poor *Salem's* Wal's in Heaps are laid:
    Thy murther'd Servants lie,
As Preys to Wolves and Vultures made,
    Beneath the open Sky.

3 See, Lord, a spacious Crimson Flood,
    By dying Martyrs shed;
And *Salem's* Streets, with flowing Blood,
    And mangled Corpses spread.

4 Sad

4 Sad Jacob's Tribes, alas! are grown
    Their barb'rous Neighbours Scorn;
And to Derision vilely thrown,
    By cruel Scoffs o'er-born.

5 But, ah! how long, dear Lord! how long
    Shall thy fierce Furies burn!
6 At last, on all the Godless Throng
    Thy weighty Vengeance turn!
O let the Gentile Nations all,
    Who ne'er acknowledge Thee,
Beneath thy heavy Judgments fall,
    And just Severity!

7 For they with cruel Teeth devour
    Poor *Jacob*'s wretched Race;
And total Desolation pour
    On *Israel*'s Dwelling-place.
8 O all our Sins, bless'd Lord, forgive,
    And speedy Mercy show;
For by thy Mercy, Lord, we live,
    Though now reduc'd so low.

Part 2.

9 Now, Lord, to our Assistance fly;
    From Thee our Safety springs:
For G'ory to thy Name, Most High,
    Such saving Mercy brings.
10 And why, ô why, should Heathens cry,
    "Now where's their boasted God?"
Let them too all the Scourges try
    Of thy revenging Rod!

Permit, bless'd Lord, our longing Eyes
    Thy just Revenge to see!
While yet the Blood of Martyrs cries
    So loud, great God, to Thee!

11 O let the Pris'ners Sighs ascend
    Before thy Majesty!
  And with Almighty Pow'r defend
    The Souls condemn'd to die.

12 And to our Neighbours, Lord, repay
    Their base reproachful Spite,
  To such as in the Scorners Way,
    And Blasphemies delight.
13 And so shall we, thy Flock, thy Sheep,
    For ever praise thy Name;
  And, through Eternal Ages keep
    Alive thy glorious Fame.

PSAL. lxxx.

1 HEar, gracious Shepherd! Thou, whose Love,
    Like Flocks, thy *Israel* guides!
  Shine forth, ô Thou, whose Strength above
    The Cherubs Wings resides!
2 Before our drooping Nation, rouze,
    Great God, thy wondrous Might;
  And with thy saving Strength espouse
    Thy ancient People's Right!

3 Change, Lord, ô change our mournful State,
    And let thy Beams Divine,
  Our Health and Safety to create,
    With doubled Lustre shine.
4 How long, great God of Hosts, shall we
    Thy Fury's Heat sustain?
  How long thy People, Lord, to Thee
    Address their Pray'rs in vain?

5 Tears are our Meat, our Drink is Tears;
6   When they our Spoils divide,
  Our Neighbours quarrel; and our Fears
    Malicious Foes deride.

7 Change, Lord, ô change our mournful State;
 And let thy Beams Divine,
Our Health and Safety to create,
 With doubled Lustre shine!

Part 2.

8 Of old, from *Egypt*'s fruitful Soil,
 Thy Hands a Vine remov'd;
And made the *Canaanites* recoil;
 And here the Plant improv'd.
9 Large was its Room, and large its Root,
 Through all the Country spread:
And with the weighty Purple Fruit,
 It bow'd its noble Head.

10 Its Shade the Mountains cover'd o'er;
 Its Arms, like Cedars stood:
11 Down to the Seas its Branches bore,
 And reach'd *Euphrates* Flood.
12 Oh, why are all her Fences gone?
 Her Fruits by all destroy'd?
13 Her Roots by Forest-Boars o'erthrown,
 And savage Beasts annoy'd?

14 Turn, Lord of Hosts! ô turn at last!
 And, from thy lofty Skies,
On thy poor Vineyard, void, and waste,
 O cast thy gentler Eyes!
15 The Vineyard which thy mighty Hand
 In *Canaan* planted first;
And made its Branches strongly stand,
 By Peace and Favour nurs'd.

16 But now the Boughs are scorch'd, the Trunk
 By cruel Hands cut down:
Thy People's Hopes and Vigour sunk
 Beneath thy angry Frown.

17 Smile,

17 Smile, Lord! ô turn thy gracious Eyes
    On him that's rais'd by Thee,
With Strength to ease our Miseries,
    And set the Bond-men free!

18 So we'll no more from Thee dec'ine,
    Nor thy Commands transgress:
Our Hopes, our Lives, shall all be thine;
    Thy Name we'll daily bless.
19 Change, Lord, ô change our mournful State,
    And let thy Beams Divine,
Our Health and Safety to create,
    With doubled Lustre shine.

Psal. lxxxj. *As the 100th. or Mr. Sandys's 8th.*

1 TO God, our Strength, your Voices raise!
    Aloud the God of *Jacob* praise!
2 A Psalm to th' merry Timbrel suit,
The pleasant Harp, or charming Lute.

3 The Moon her Infant-Horns displays:
Let's feast on these appointed Days;
And with the shriller Trumpet's Voice,
In God, our Strength, our King, rejoice.

4 For this, by his supream Commands,
A Statute firm in *Jacob* stands;
A Monument of Love; since He
From *Egypt*'s Bondage set them free.

There we, when God, our Help, appear'd,
An unknown, awful Language heard.
6 " Through Me, said God, thy Burthen ceas'd;
" And I thy Hands from Pots releas'd.

7 " Thou pray'dst in suff'ring Times to me;
  " And I, in Mercy, answer'd thee

" From

" From the dark Closets of the Sky,
" Where Thunder's secret Treasures lie.

" At *Meribah* thy native Pride
" I with prodigious Waters try'd.
8 " Hear then, my People; hear the Law,
" Which I, for thy Direction, draw.

Part 2.

9 " With thee no Foreign God shall be:
" To such thou ne'er shalt bend the Knee;
" To such no guilty Worship pay,
" Nor Off'rings on their Altars lay.

10 " For I'm the Lord, thy God; my Hand
" First led thee out from *Egypt*'s Land.
" Let me thy largest Wishes know,
" My Gifts shall still as largely flow.

11 " But they, my People, disobey'd;
" And *Israel* no Submissions paid:
" Their Hearts no kindest Acts could gain;
" No Love, their wandring Steps restrain'd.

12 " I then the wilful Fools resign'd,
" To Ways to which their Hearts inclin'd,
" Such Ways as they'd themselves invent;
" At once their Crime, and Punishment.

13 " Oh, had my People wisely weigh'd
" My Laws, and my Commands obey'd,
14 " My Hand had quickly humbl'd those
" Who durst their thriving State oppose.

15 " Those Men who durst effront their Lord,
" Had been, as Lyars, all abhorr'd;
" Consum'd, destroy'd, and bury'd quite
" In dark Oblivion's gloomy Night.

But

"But *Israel*, of my Love possess'd,
"Had been to endless Ages bless'd.
16 "Their Bellies purest Wheats had fill'd;
"And Honey from the Rocks distill'd.

  To Father, Spirit, Son, bless'd Three,
  One only God, one Trinity,
  As is, as was e'er Time begun,
  Be Praise, and endless Homage done. Amen.

Another Metre: Proper Tune.

1 Aloud to God, our Strength, aloud,
  With chearful Voices sing!
To *Jacob*'s God, through all the Croud,
  Let hearty Praises ring!
2 A Psalm to merry Notes compose,
  And let the Timbrels sound!
While pleasant Harps their Sweets disclose;
  And Lutes maintain the Round!

3 See where the Moon her Horns displays,
  With Infant-Beauty dress'd!
Your solemn Joys with Trumpets raise,
  At that appointed Feast.
4 For this your God ordain'd of old
  To *Isra'l*'s faithful Race:
And we must still the Laws, enroll'd
  By *Jacob*'s God, embrace.

5 This was to them, from Bondage clear'd,
  His Pledge of endless Love,
When they an unknown Language heard
  From rending Clouds above.
6 "Thy Shoulders I, *said God*, releas'd,
  "And made from Labours free:
"Through me thy weary'd Fingers ceas'd
  "From Bricks and Slavery.

7 " To Me thou pray'dſt, and I appear'd,
      " And ready Aids app'y'd:
   " And thee, through gloomy Thunders heard,
      " At Maſſah's Waters try'd.
8 " Hear me, my deareſt People! hear!
      " To thee I'll teſtifie:
   " If Iſrael's Race my Words can bear,
      " And with my Laws comply.

   " Thy Seed no other God ſhall own;
      " No Sacrifice allow
   " To Gods by other Nations known,
      " Nor to their Idols bow.
10 *I only live*; thy Lord, thy God,
      " Who thee from *Egypt* freed:
   " And I'll my largeſt Stores afford,
      " To ſerve thy utmoſt Need.

11 " But they, my People, careleſs, all
      " My juſt Commands refus'd:
   " My *Iſrael* from their Vows could fall,
      " And all my Loves abus'd.
12 " So I their Sight with Slight repay'd,
      " And let the Fools purſue
   " Their fooliſh Ways; and as they ſtray'd,
      " Return'd their Wages due.

13 " Oh, had my People's Thoughtleſs Seed
      " my kind Advice obey'd;
   " Nor, by their own falſe Hearts miſ-led,
      " From Ways of Wiſdom ſtray'd!
14 " I then had quickly cruſh'd their Foes,
      " And turn'd my dreadful Hand
   " Againſt the wretched Heads of thoſe
      " Who durſt againſt them ſtand!

15 " God's Haters ſoon had ſunk, betray'd
      " By Lyes themſelves had fram'd:

But

"But Mine had been a Nation made,
"Through endless Ages fam'd.
16 "I had their hungry Souls supply'd,
"With Wheat's pure Fatness fill'd;
"And them with Honey satisfy'd,
"From flowing Rocks distill'd.

PSAL. lxxxij.

1 GOD sits the Judge, where mighty Kings
    Their secret Counsels hold:
2 How dare ye then unrighteous Things,
    And wicked Laws uphold?
3 The Weak, the Orphans Cause decide;
    Th' afflicted Soul relieve:
4 The Poor, by long Oppressions try'd,
    From wicked Hands retrieve.

5 To Fools, alas! I vainly speak,
    Who on in Darkness reel;
Through whom Earth's strong Foundations break
    And strange Convulsions feel.
6 I've said, "You all are Gods, and all
    "The Sons of God, most High;
7 "But must like meaner Princes fall,
    "Like common Mortals die.

8 Arise! thy Justice, Lord, declare!
    And o'er the World advance!
For all the scatter'd Nations are,
    Thy just Inheritance.

PSAL. lxxxiij.

1 LOrd, unconcern'd no longer prove,
    Nor wrap'd in Silence lie:
2 Our Foes, who hate Thee, fiercely move,
    And bear their Heads on high

3 Against

PSAL. lxxxiij.

3 Against thy People all combin'd,
    Their secret Counsels take;
And those who thy Protection find,
    Their hated Objects make.

4 "Come on! *they cry*; let *Israel* bear
    "No more a Nation's Name!
"Let's from Time's largest Records tear
    "Their long-detested Claim!
5 In Mischief thus their Hearts agree,
    And horrid Plots design;
Leagu'd in a strong Conspiracy,
    Against thy self, and thine.

6 See, Lord, What Tents o'er-spread the Field,
    Where *Edom* takes his Place;
What Bands fierce *Moab*'s Countries yield,
    And *Agar*'s slavish Race!
7 *Gebal* and *Ammon*'s Companies
    Curs'd *Amalek* commands;
And *Palestine*'s Battalion lies,
    With *Tyre*'s assisting Bands.

8 With these, proud *Assur*'s Forces join,
    And *Ammon*'s Side embrace;
And Desolations all design
    On *Abraham*'s faithful Race.

Part 2.

9 Bless'd Lord, for us at last appear;
    And let thy daring Foes
The Lot of ruin'd Midian bear,
    Who durst the Saints oppose;
As *Sisera*'s and *Jabin*'s Hosts,
    Near *Kishon*'s Torrents dy'd,
10 In *Endor* slain; and all the Coasts
    With Blood, for Dung, supply'd.

11 Let

11 Let all their valiant Captains slain,
   With *Zeeb* and *Oreb*, dwell
Where *Zeba*'s and *Zalmunna*'s Train,
   With all their Princes, fell.
12 For thus the boasting Wretches said,
   "Come, let's at once go seize
" The Tents their God inhabited,
   " His sacred Palaces!

13 Lord, hurl them off, as Chaff before
   The rapid Whirlwind flies:
14 As Flames through ancient Forests roar,
   Or Mountain-Shrubs surprize;
15 So them with fiercest Storms pursue,
   With Tempests terrifie!
16 Till they with Shame their Errours view,
   And to thy Service fly!

17 Else let them all confounded lie,
   Crush'd with Eternal Shame;
And know God only rules on high,
   By Great *Jehovah*'s Name.

PSAL. lxxxiv.

1 AH, how my Soul thy Dwelling-place,
      Great Lord of Hosts admires!
Ah, how thy Courts, thy glorious Face,
      My longing Soul desires!
2 In Thee, the God of Life, alone,
      My Flesh, my Heart rejoice
To see thy sacred Earthly Throne,
   And hear thy Heav'nly Voice.

3 Around each House the Sparrows find,
      The Swallows build their Nests;
Where, with their yet unfeather'd Kind,
      The Dam in Safety rests.

But, ah, thine Altars! wretched I
    Near them no more can sing,
While, banish'd from thy House, I fly,
    Dear Lord, my God, my King!

Ah, happy Souls! who in thy House
    Can live, and praise thy Name!
Whose Arms thy Heav'nly Strength endows;
    Whose Hearts thy Ways can frame!
Though through the Vail of Tears they go,
    Their Eyes with Sorrows drown'd;
Yet Blessings on their Teachers flow,
    With Fruit their Pains are crown'd.

From Strength to Strength, from Grace to Grace,
    Th' improving Learners go;
Till them the God of Gods embrace,
    And Rest on them bestow.

Part 2.

8 My Pray'r, great God of Hosts, receive,
    And kind Assistance bring:
9 Consider, O our Shield; relieve
    Thy once anointed King!
10 For in thy Courts, one Day appears
    More bless'd, more sweet to me,
Than could a Thousand Thousand Years,
    At any Distance, be.

I'd rather keep thy Temple's Door,
    And find thy Presence there;
Than in a Palace reign secure,
    Where Sins uncheck'd appear.
11 For God, their Sun, their Shield, to those
    Will Grace and Glory give,
Who with his Laws sincerely close,
    And on Obedience live.

12 Happy

12 Happy, ô happy that good Man,
　　Great Lord of Hosts, must be,
Who, through all Worldly Changes, can
　　Unmov'dly trust in Thee!

To Father, Holy Ghost, and Son,
　　One God, in Persons Three,
Be Glory paid, and Homage done,
　　Through all Eternity.

PSAL. lxxxv.

1 THY Favours, Lord, have kind at last
　　To *Israel*'s Captives been;
2 And all thy People's Follies past,
　　And cover'd all their Sin.
3 Thy gentler Thoughts, with tender Love,
　　Thy Jealous Furies eas'd:
And He who pleads for us above,
　　Has all thy Wrath appeas'd.

4 To us, ô God, our Saviour, now
　　From Anger kindly turn!
Some Limits to thy Wrath allow,
　　Which, else, would always burn.
5 On us, dear God, new Life bestow,
　　To us new Vigour give;
6 That we our Joys in Thee may show,
　　And in thy Favour live.

7 To us thy Mercy, Lord, extend,
　　And thy Salvation show!
8 What God shall answer, I'll attend,
　　Who will his Peace bestow
On all his own: His Saints shall find
　　The Sweets of Heav'nly Peace,
When they, from Sin's foul Dross refin'd,
　　From careless Follies cease.

9 God's kind Salvation's always nigh
  The Wise, who fear his Name;
That Glory o'er our Land may fly,
  And raise our ancient Fame.
10 Kind Peace and Righteousness embrace,
  And Truth and Mercy close:
11 Truth springs from Earth; from Heav'n, her Face
  Impartial Justice shows.

12 All Good on us shall God bestow,
  Our Land shall fruitful prove:
And Justice, with a wondrous Flow,
  Before his Face shall move:
While we, who err'd so oft before,
  Bless'd with so sure a Guide,
From God shall never wander more,
  But in his Paths abide.

Another Metre: As the old 125th proper Tune.

BLess'd Lord, thy kinder Thoughts at last
 Did *Jacob's* Captive Tribes restore:
And, all the People's Follies past,
 Their Sins with Mercies cover'd o'er;
  Thy Jealous Furies eas'd,
  And all thy Wrath appeas'd.

To us, ô God, our Saviour, now,
 From thy tempestuous Anger, turn!
Shall thy fierce Wrath no Bounders know,
 But through Eternal Ages burn?
  Us, Lord, again revive,
  And in thy Joys we live!

To us thy Mercy, Lord, extend!
 To us thy bless'd Salvation show!
To God's kind Answer I'll attend;
 For Peace he'll on his Saints bestow. His

His Servants shall have Peace
When they from Follies cease.

9 To pious Men Salvation's near,
   That Glory may possess the Land.
10 Mercy and Truth conjoin'd appear;
    And Peace and Justice, Hand in Hand.
11   From Earth, Truth; from the Sky,
    Fair Justice casts her Eye.

12 Our God on us shall Good bestow.
    Our happy Land shall fruitful prove;
13 And Justice, with a wondrous Flow,
    Before his glorious Presence move.
    And we, with such a Guide,
    Shall in his Paths abide.

PSAL. lxxxvj.

1 Lord, to my Pray'r thine Ears incline,
    For I'm distress'd, and poor!
2 I'm wholly, Lord, and only thine:
    Bless'd God, my Soul secure!
3 My God, thy faithful Servant save,
    Who hopes thy Grace to see:
Mercy, thy Mercy, Lord, I crave;
    And daily cry to Thee.

4 To Thee alone my Heart I raise:
    O make my Soul rejoice!
6 Love, Pardon, Mercy are thy Ways;
    Thou hearst my humble Voice.
6 Lord, hear my Pray'rs, receive my Cry,
7   In Woes address'd to Thee!
8 Thy Might, thy wondrous Works out-vye
    The Gods of Vanity.

9 All Nations, whom thy Hands have made,
   Shall fall before thy Face;
And, with pure Worship, duly pay'd,
   Thy glorious Name embrace.
10 For Thou art God, thy Works are great;
   Thy self art God alone!
11 To me, bless'd God, thy Ways repeat,
   And make thy Doctrines known!

I'll walk in Truth; then, Lord, unite
   My Heart to fear thy Name!
12 My Heart shall then thy Praise recite,
   And all thy Praise proclaim.
13 Thy Mercy's great to me; from Hell
   Thou brought'st my sinking Soul;
14 Though Tyrants at me proudly swell,
   And would my Life control.

No Sence of Thee the Rebels show:
15   But Pity, Lord, we see,
Grace, Patience, Mercy, Truth, we know,
   In plenty dwells with Thee.
16 To me, dear God, with Mercy turn!
   Thy Strength on me bestow!
To him who's of thy Hand-maid born,
   Thy kind Salvation show.

17 With me some Mark of Favour leave,
   And shame my spiteful Foes,
When they thy Aid to me perceive,
   And all thy Love disclose.

PSAL. lxxxvij. *as the* 113*th.*

8 WHen God, in his All-searching Mind,
      To fix his Church on Earth design'd,
   Deep he her strong Foundations laid.

2 But *Sions* Mount, that sacred Place.
 (Tho' well He lov'd a'l *Jacob*'s Race)
   He his peculiar Darling made.
3 How vastly wide, how wondrous high,
 Shall thy Immortal Glories fly.
   Blest City of th' Eternal King!
4 When *Ægypt*, *Assur*, *Palestine*,
 And all th' *Arabia*'s shall be thine,
   And Vows to thy Protector bring!

 Envy in Them no more shall reign,
 But Saints to fill thy blissful Train,
   Shall come from each converted Land.
5 In *Sion* yet those Sons of Peace,
 Shall more than other Lands encrease,
   And in her God securely stand.
6 When God shall all his Saints enrol,
 The *Gentiles* Tribes shall fill the Scroul,
   From Thee, blest God! our Joy shall spring
7 And all the Sons of Harmony,
 Shall tune their chearful Strings to Thee,
   And thy Eternal Praises sing.

PSAL. lxxxviij.

1 Blest God of my Salvation! I
   Call Day and Night to Thee,
2 O hear my Prayer, accept my Cry,
   And kindly answer me!
3 My Soul alas! is fill'd with Woes,
   The Grave attends my Fate.
4 I'me left by Life and Sense, like those,
   Just in a dying state.

5 Among the slaughter'd dead I ly,
   Ith' Grave from Sorrows free,
 Where Men thrust out from Memory,
   Are cut from Earth by Thee.

PSAL. lxxxviij.

6 Down in the Pits unfathom'd Night,
    Thou throw'st my trembling Soul,
7 On me thy angry Judgments light,
    And all thy Tempests roul.

8 Thou mak'st my Friends aloof remain,
    And less than Strangers kind,
  Nor can I Liberty obtain.
    By Chains of Hate confind.
9 Whole Seas of Tears my mournful Eyes,
    Thro' deep afflictions shed.
  To thee I send my daily Cryes,
    My Hands submissely spread.

Part 2.

10 What? Shall thy mighty Works be shown,
    Where Death triumphant Reigns?
  The Dead to make thy Wonders known,
    Shake off their Icy Chains?
11 What? shall the Grave, the silent Tomb.
    Advance thy Mercies Fame?
  Or shall Destructions utmost Doom,
    Thy Faithfulness proclaim?

12 Or shall thy wondrous Works appear,
    Where all thick Darkness hides?
  Thy Righteousness be publish'd where
    Forgetfulness presides?
13 To Thee, dear Lord, I cry, to Thee
    My morning Prayers are made.
14 O why's my Soul cast off? to me
    Thy Beams no more displaid?

15 From my first Youth afflicted I
    With constant weakness prest,
  Have born thy Terrors constantly,
    In my Distracted Breast,

16 Like breaking Seas with mighty Force,
    Thy Terrours bear me down.
17 And with a vast united Course,
    My baffled Comforts drown.

18 Thou mak'st my Friends, who lov'd me too,
    To mighty Distance fly,
  And those I intimately knew,
    In unknown Darkness ly.

PSAL. lxxxix. *Metre first*; *as the* 113*th.*

1 I'Le ever sing thy Mercy Lord
  Thy Truth from Age to Age record,
    My Lips shall praise thy glorious Name,
2 Thy Mercies everlasting are,
  Thy Truths with Heaven it self compare,
    Thy Faithful Promise I'le proclaim.
3 "A Covenant long since I made,
  " And to my Servant *David* said,
    " (My chosen King,) and firmly swore.
4 " Thy seed Eternally shall stand,
  " Thy Royal Scepter'd Heirs command,
    " Till Sea and Earth and Times no more.

5 The Heaven's, thy Wonders Lord shall praise,
  Thy Holy Congregation raise,
    Thy Faithful Works above the Skys.
6 For who above's compar'd with Thee?
  What God-like Man thy Mate can be?
    What Lord to equal Glories rise?
7 Gods Presence strikes a reverend Fear,
  Where his Assembling Saints appear.
    And his attending Angels aws.
8 Great God of Hosts whose strenth like Thine,
  Whose Truth so breaks with Beams divine:
    Receiv'd by every Worlds applause.

9 Thy Hands the mighty Ocean sway,
  And make its angry Waves obey,
    Thy Word its stormy Tempest quells.
10 By that th' *Egyptians* wounded dy'd,
  Thy dreadful Arm the gathering Pride,
    Of all thy fiercest Foes dispells.
11 Thy Hands Heaven's vaulted Arches made.
  Thy Hands this Earth's Foundations laid,
    And all the World with Plenty stor'd:
12 The North and South thy Creatures are,
  Tabor and *Hermon* both declare,
    Thy Name, and Thee, their mighty Lord.

13 Thy Arm All-mighty strength endues,
  Thy Hand resistless vigor shews,
    Thy glorious Hand's exalted high.
14 Justice and Judgment make thy Throne,
  Thy truth, and ancient mercy known,
    Thy Steps to all the World descry.
15 Thrice happy they, whose Souls are warm'd,
  By holy Trumpets sounds alarm'd,
    And live enlightned, Lord, by Thee!
16 They'l always in thy Name rejoice,
  With solemn Musicks moving voice,
    Thy Righteousness their strength shall be.

17 Such happy Men securely stand,
  And with a settled strength Command,
    But God is still their Strength and Pride,
  Thy Goodness, and thy boundless Love,
  Has rais'd our happy Strength above,
    Since thou hast own'd our sinking side.
18 The Lord is our Defensive shield,
  That Holy One can shelter yield,
    Who's *Israel*'s God, and *Israel*'s King.

19 But, that thou might'st our Hearts uphold,
A smiling Vision, rais'd of old,
Did thus of thy Anointed sing.

Part 3.   Metre 2.   As the 100th.

20 " Help on a pow'rful Arm I've laid,
" A Man above the Vulgar plac'd;
" My King my Servant *David* made,
" His Head with holy Unction grac'd.

21 " Him shall my strength'ning Hand secure,
" My Arm his strong support shall be:
22 " No En'my shall his Hurt procure;
" No Sinner, his Destruction see.

23 " I'll dash his Foes before his Face,
" And batter those who hate him down:
24 " With him my Truth and Mercy place,
" And in my Name exalt his Crown.

25 " No River's Bank, no Ocean's Wall,
" Shall his unbounded Reign confine:
26 " He'll me his God, his Father call,
" His Saving Health, his Rock Divine.

27 " And him, my First-born Son, I'll make
" Above Earth's Kings, exalted high:
28 " With him my Mercy ne'er shall slake,
" Nor my immortal Cov'nant die.

29 " His Seed shall ever last; his Throne
" Out-shine, out-wear the Rolling Skies.
30 " But if his Sons my Laws disown,
" Or e'er against my Judgments rise;

31 " If they my stated Laws prophane,
" My Precepts or Injunctions slight,

32 " With Rods their Follies I'll reſtrain;
   " Their Sins, with Strokes deſerv'd, requite.

33 " Yet not my Mercies quite remove,
   " Nor break my faithful Word of old;
34 " Expoſe my Covenanted Love,
   " Nor change what Prophets once foretold.

35 " Once by my Holineſs I've ſworn,
   " And can't my *David*'s Hopes deceive;
36 " His Seed, to Crowns and Scepters born,
   " No Time ſhall of their Rights bereave.

37 " The Sun, the Moon, which guild the Skies,
   " Thoſe faithful Signs, to Mortals known,
   " May ceaſe to ſet, and ceaſe to riſe;
   " But nothing ſhock his glorious Throne.

Part 4. Metre 3.

38 Such was thy Promiſe, Lord, of old:
      But, at a diſtance, now
   Terrours thy dear Anointed hold
      From thy contracted Brow.
39 Thou'ſt thrown thy ſacred Cov'nant by,
      Defil'd his trampled Crown;
40 Let all his Walls in Ruins lie,
      And trod *his Fences* down.

41 Him, all who paſs, may ſpoil; and all
      His neighb'ring Foes deſpiſe:
42 On him their Troops, inſulting, fall,
      And high their Forces riſe.
43 No Wounds his Edgeleſs Sword beſtows,
      He flies the Martial Field:
44 His Throne's caſt down; nor can his Brows
      Their former Luſtre yield.

45 His youthful Bloom now fades with Woes,
    And he's o'erwhelm'd with Shame.
46 How long shall we thy Favour lose,
    And feel thy Fury's Flame?
47 Think, Lord, how vain is Man: How I
    Have but a While to live.
48 What Man now breaths, but once must die?
    What Art can Lives retrieve?

49 Where are thy Mercies, Lord, of old,
    By Oath to *David* due?
50 Think how our Lives to Shame are fo'd;
    What Scorns thy Friends pursue!
51 Think how thy Foes black Scandals raise
    On thy Anointed King;
52 While we, to thy immortal Praise,
    Amens devoutly sing.

PSAL. XC.

1 Thou, Lord, from Age to Age, hast been
    Our certain Resting-place,
2 Before the lofty Hills were seen
    On Earth's extended Face:
Before this Earth to Shape was grown,
    Before the World was fram'd,
Thee, Lord, the mighty God alone,
    Eternity proclaim'd.

3 When Man, fix'd in a glorious State,
    With thriving Beauty shines,
His proudest Shows thy Frowns abate,
    And he to Dust declines.
When grov'ling in the Dust he lies,
    Thy Smiles his Fortunes raise.
" Weak Man, *fay'st Thou*, return, and rise!
    Weak Man thy Word obeys.

A Thousand Years no longer last
    In thy unbounded Sight,
Than Yesterday, so lately past,
    Or its succeeding Night.
So Floods, with rapid Swiftness, slide;
    So Dreams, in Slumbers, fly;
So Meadow-Greens, with chearful Pride,
    Salute the Morning-Sky.

They flourish with the Morning's Tears,
    And shoot their Branches high;
But e'er the shady Night appears,
    Are mow'n, and scorch'd, and die.
When thy impetuous Anger burns,
    Our Lives are soon consum'd;
And by thy Wrath's severe Returns,
    To deep Afflictions doom'd.

Thou view'st our wretched Actions o'er;
    And thy All-searching Eyes
Examine all that secret Score
    Which now in Darkness lies:
Far off our flying Days are blown,
    Before thy Fury's Blast:
Our Years, like empty Tales, are gone
    Which scarce one Moment last.

Part 2.

Through Seventy Years our common Lives
    May hold their constant Course;
And if to Eighty one arrives,
    By Nature's rarer Force,
Yet his declining, batter'd Strength
    Meer Pains and Sorrow brings,
And fails, and swiftly flies at length
    On Time's impatient Wings.

11 But, ô, what wretched Man can know
    Thy Anger's utmost Might!
Which, as thy Fear, through all must go,
    With an unbounded Flight.
12 O teach us, Lord, to count our Days,
    And so our Hearts apply,
That we, through Wisdom's peaceful Ways,
    May reach Eternity.

13 Turn, Lord, at last, and grant some Rest
    To all thy Servants Woes!
14 Our Hearts, with early Mercies bless'd,
    To holy Joys dispose!
15 O let us now thy Favours share,
    Thy gentler Smiles obtain;
Proportion'd to our long Despair,
    And Years of constant Pain!

16 Lord, to thy happy Servants now,
    And all thy faithful Race,
Thy Works, thy wond'rous Glories show;
    And send thy quick'ning Grace!
17 O let our Maker's Beauty here,
    On all our Labours rest,
Till all our Handy-works appear
    By thy Protection bles'd!

PSAL. xcj.

1 HE's safe from Death, secur'd from Harms,
    Who to his Maker flies;
And on his kind, protecting Arms,
    For Help and Health relies.
2 "Thou, Lord, art all my Hope, my Trust!
    To God I'll freely say,
"My strong Defence; on Thee it's just
    "My Hope shou'd firmly stay.

3 Do Thou the same! He'll rescue thee
 From Death's surprizing Snare;
And keep thee from th' Infection free
 Of Pestilential Air.
4 He'll shade thee with his gracious Wings,
 His Feathers o'er thee spread,
While his unfailing Promise brings
 A Shield to guard thy Head.

5 What though strange Terrours fill the Night?
 Death's Shafts obscure the Day?
He'll guild them both with wholsom Light,
 To keep thy Fears away.
6 What tho' fierce Plagues, through horrid Gloom,
 With wild Destruction reign?
7 Though Thousands, nay, the gaping Tomb
 Ten Thousand Morsels gain?

Though Death the Day and Night command,
 And gasping Corpses lie,
Heaps upon Heaps, on either Hand,
 And almost Mountain-high?
8 Thine Eyes shall still securely see
 How God's revenging Stroke
Distinguishes, where carelesly
 Vile Men their God provoke.

Part 2.

9 Since now thy Heart my God alone
 Thy sacred Refuge made;
And has it self, for Shelter, thrown
 Beneath his saving Shade;
10 No Mischief shall attempt thee there,
 Nor Mischief-boding Chance;
No cruel Plague, to give thee Fear,
 Shall near thy Tents advance.

11 For if in those delightful Ways,
  Where God and Nature lead,
Thy Feet, through all thy mortal Days,
  With Care exactly tread.
He'll give his Angel-Armies Charge
  About thy Paths to wait;
To lay their watchful Guards at large,
  And to secure thy State.

12 Their Hands shall waft thee gently o'er
  The Rocks of Sin below,
Where strong Temptation's fatal Store
  And daily Scandals grow.
13 Let Hell's old Lion roar, enrag'd,
  With all th' Infernal Crew;
And Men, in Hell's vile Work engag'd,
  Their pois'nous Arts pursue.

His Feet shall quickly tread them down,
  Whose Heart my Loves inflame;
And Freedom shall with Honour crown
  The Man who knows my Name.
15 To Me shall he, in Dangers, cry:
  His Cries I'll kindly hear;
Be with him, and exalt him high,
  And rid his Life from Fear.

16 Long Life, with ever peaceful Days,
  I'll on my Friend bestow;
And to him, by a Thousand Ways,
  My kind Salvation show.

PSAL. cxij.

1 HOW bless'd are we, thy Praise to sing
    On all thy Holy Days,
  Great God, when all thy Churches ring
    With thy exalted Praise!

2 To shew thy Mercies e'er the Sun
    Unfolds the Morning-Light ;
Thy Truth, e'er Clouds have first begun
    To form the gloomy Night.

3 When, with the Harp and Lute, the Voice
    Its chearful Notes can raise ;
And Organs can with Shalms rejoice,
    To sound thy lofty Praise ;
4 Thy Works, thy wondrous Works inflame
    My Soul's triumphant Joys.
3 To show thy deeper Counsels, Fame
    Her shrillest Notes employs.

6 Poor Brutish Man can never know
    This wondrous Happiness ;
Nor can the B'essing's Balmy Flow
    The foolish Heart possess.
7 His Thoughts to meaner Subjects move ;
    And watch the Sinner's Race,
How they like Summer-Plants improve,
    Their Branches thrive apace :

Yet think not how, when pleasant Blooms
    Have spread the Wicked o'er,
They sink beneath their weighty Dooms,
    And live on Earth no more.
8, 9 Thy Foes, since, Lord, Thou reign'st above,
    Thy wretched Foes, shall die :
And those who wicked Actions love,
    Dispers'd, confounded, lie.

Part 2.

10 But, Lord, Thou'lt raise my humble Head,
    With Strength exalt it high ;
On me fresh Oil of Gladness shed,
    And fill my Heart with Joy.

11 My happy Eyes my Wish shall see
 On all my angry Foes:
My Ears shall hear their Doom, who me
 With envious Spite oppose.

12 The Righteous, with a thriving Pride,
 Like Palms, their Heads shall raise:
Their Seed, like Cedars, multiply'd,
 Which *Libanon* displays.
13 Those whom their Maker's skilful Hand
 His House has p'anted round,
Shall in his Courts securely stand,
 With constant Verdure crown'd.

14 Their Sappy Trunks, in Hoary Age,
 Shall spring with lively Shoots;
Their thrifty Leaves long Life presage
 To their extended Roots;
15 That they the Lord, my Rock, may show,
 His Righteous Works declare;
And make the wiser Nations know
 How just his Actions are.

PSAL. xciij.

1 THE Lord, the great *Jehovah*, reigns,
 With Majesty and Glory crown'd;
The Lord Almighty Strength retains
 With that, like Garments girt around.

His Hand the World's vast Frame secures;
 He stays it with his Awful Nod.
2 Thy Throne from Days of old endures;
 Thy Self an everlasting God!

3 The Floods, great God, the rolling Croud,
 At Thee, like mighty Waters, roar;
And dash, like breaking Waves, aloud,
 Which threaten all the neighb'ring Shoar.

4 And

4 And let tempestuous Passions raise
 Their Hearts, their swelling Furies high;
Their utmost maddest Rage obeys
 That God who rules above the Sky.

5 Thy Promises, dear Lord, are true,
 And all thy Testimonies sure:
Thy Flocks pure Holiness pursue,
 And ever, like thy Self, endure.

Another Metre: As the 111*th, proper Tune.*

1 THE Lord a King remains,
 The great *Jehovah* reigns,
  With Awful Glories crown'd:
As with a Robe of Light,
The Lord with wondrous Might
 And Strength is girt around.

By his Divine Commands
The World securely stands,
 From Alterations free.
2 Thy Throne was fix'd of old,
Thy Deity extoll'd
 From all Eternity.

3 Great God, th' uncertain Croud
Against thy Kingdom, loud,
 Like mighty Waters, roar;
And with a surly Spite,
As breaking Billows, fight,
 And shock the neighb'ring Shoar

4 But let tempestuous Rage
Their furious Hearts engage,
 And Heav'n it self defy;

His stern Command alone
Can beat their Madness down,
Who ever rules on high.

5 Thy Testimonies true
Thy Promises renew;
Both faithful, both secure.
Thy Saints, with Holiness,
Shall tow'rds thine A'tars press,
And ever bless'd endure.

PSAL. xciv.

1 GReat God, to whom Revenge belongs;
Great God of Vengeance, rise.
2 The Proud, thou mighty Judge of Wrongs,
With just Rewards surprize.
3 How long shall wicked Workers, Lord,
Uncheck'd, triumphant reign?
4 Their impious Words, and Pride, abhorr'd,
With haughty Boasts maintain?

5 Lord, shall they crush thy People still?
Afflict thine Heritage?
6 Their Widows and their Strangers kill?
Nor spare their Orphans Age?
7 Yet thus they do; and thus they cry,
" Can God our Actions see?
" We Jacob's unknown God defy:
" From his Observance free.

8 But think, ye stupid Fools, a while!
Think well, ye senseless Crew!
9 Can you his sacred Ears beguile,
Who Ears bestow'd on you?
What, can't he see, whose Hands the Eyes,
Those Orbs of Wonders, made?
10 He, whose Hand the World chastise,
From Your Correction stay'd?

Can't He who Senſe on Man beſtows,
    Their ſecret Thoughts deſcry?
Men's Hearts, alas! He throughly knows,
    And knows their Vanity.
Lord, happy's he, who, taught by Thee,
    Has all thy Laws obey'd!
He, in ill Times, at Reſt, ſhall ſee
    The Pit for Sinners made.

Part 2.

4 Our God his Servants can't deſert,
    Nor his Inheritance:
5 But Judgment will to Right convert,
    And upright Souls advance.
6 Who'll me from wicked Workers ſave,
    Or my Aſſiſtant be?
7 God only help'd me, or the Grave
    Had quickly ſilenc'd me.

8 My Foot, ô Lord, which ſeem'd to ſlide,
    Thy Mercy's He'p enſur'd:
9 In Cares and Fears thy Comforts try'd,
    My Soul's Delight procur'd.
10 Wilt thou ſupport the Tyrant-Crew,
    Who ſettle Sin by Law?
11 Whoſe Armies righteous Souls purſue;
    And Blood of Martyrs draw.

12 Though ſuch their cruel Practice be,
    My God will raiſe my State:
My ſolid Rock, my Refuge He;
    Whoſe Loves my Faith create.
13 Our God obſerves their Wickedneſs;
    Their Malice He'll repay:
With ſudden Strokes their Pride repreſs,
    And cut their Hopes away.

PSAL. xcv.

1 O Come your chearful Voices raise,
  To our Eternal King!
The Lord, our strong Salvation praise,
  His Goodness loudly sing!
2 With Thanks approach his awful sight,
  And pleasant Anthems sing.
3 The Lord's, a God of boundless Might,
  O're all the Gods, a King.

4 Earth's secret Deeps, and Mountains high,
  His powerful Hand commands.
5 The Seas were made by Him, and dry,
  He laid the rising Lands.
6 O come let us our Lord adore,
  And at his Foot-stool low,
Our humbly bending Knees before,
  Our great Creator show!

7 For he's our God; his People we,
  And in his Pastures feed,
Those wandring sheep which kindly He,
  From Death and Darkness freed.
To day, ô hear his Voice, to day!
8   For thus th' Almighty spoke.
No more your own false Thoughts obey,
  My Wrath no more provoke!

" No more with hardned Hearts refuse,
  " My necessary Grace;
" Nor, as in former times, abuse
  " My Word, or Holy Place!
9 " Such Arts your Fathers us'd of old,
  " Who all my Wonders saw,
" And many Years perversly bold,
  " Despis'd my righteous Law.

" At laſt thus, by my ſelf, I ſwore,
" With juſt Diſpleaſure mov'd,
" This wretched Nation ſin the more,
" The more by Goodneſs prov'd.
" They neither know my ſelf, nor know
" Thoſe Rules to them addreſt,
" Nor will I e're their Souls beſtow,
" In my Eternal Reſt.

Another Metre: As Mr. Sandys's 15*th.*

1 COme, ô come, and let us ſing,
 To our Lord, and to our King!
Let us make a joyful Noiſe,
To that God whoſe Love employs,
All his ſaving Health, and Grace,
To protect his faithful Race.
2 Let us all, with Thanks, and Praiſe,
Come before his Glorious Face,
And our Pſalms, and cheerful Airs,
Join with Vows and humble Prayers!
3 For the, Lord, our God, is great,
Lofty his Eternal Seat.
Every God to Him ſubmits,
He a King above them ſits.
4 All the Earths Foundations deep,
Solid Rocks and Mountains ſleep,
All their ſtrength's by Him poſſeſt,
And by his Protection bleſt.
5 Him, the rolling Seas regard,
By *his* mighty Hands prepar'd,
Earth to Him, ſubmiſsly bows,
And his forming Power avows.
6 Come, ô come, let's all adore,
And his Footſtool kneel before!
Let us kneel, and proſtrate all,
To our Lord, and Maker, fall!

7 He's

7 Hee's our God, our Lord, alone,
   We are all his People known;
   Us His Hands securely keep,
   Hee's the Sheepheard, we the Sheep,
   Hear, ô hear, his voice to Day,
   And that sacred Voice obey!
8 Humble let your Hearts appear.
   Let no Hardness center there,
   As of o'd your Father's pride,
   All my kindest Cares defy'd,
   When their wandring Armies past,
   Tho' the Deserts sandy waste.
9 Oft they tempted, oft they try'd me,
   Often to Believe deny'd me.
   Tho' my Wonders all they saw,
   Knew my Power, and heard my Law.
10 All their Follies large Arrears,
   Forty tedious rolling Years,
   I with wondrous patience bore,
   But at last in Fury swore.
" 11 These a wretched People are,
" All involv'd in Error's snare.
" Soon they have my Laws forgot,
" Seen my Works, but know them not;
" By my Self, my Self alone,
" (That's the greatest Oath that's known)
" These shall never, never blest,
" Enter my Eternal Rest.

PSAL. xcvj.

1 NEw Songs to great Jehovah sing!
      Sing all the Earths around!
   Your Blessings to his Altars bring,
      His saving Health resound!
2 Each Day your active Tongues employ,
      To spread his glorious Name!
3 Thro' all the Nations round with Joy,
      His wondrous Acts proclaim!

Our Lord is great, and greatly prais'd,
    More to be feard then those.
6 Who by Vain Men to Godhead rais'd,
    On Vainer Fools impose.
Our God stretch'd out the lofty Syes;
    How glorious Majesty,
How strength with lovely Beauty vyes,
    We in his Temple see.

O give to God, ye Nations all,
    Give strength and Glorys due!
On his great Name with Honour call;
    To him with Offerings sue!
Before his Seat of Holiness,
    Let all devoutly bow,
And Fear before his Face express;
    And to his service vow!

Among the Nations round proclaim,
    The great Jehovah reigns!
Through Him the World's establish'd frame,
    Unmov'd and Firm remains.
Hee'l Judge the People righteously;
    Then let the Skys rejoice;
Let Earth be glad, the Ocean high,
    Exalt its roaring Voice!

2 Let all the Flocks, and Fields their Joys,
    Express in various ways;
And Forrests with a murmuring Noise,
    Their great Creator praise!
3 He flys to judge the Earth! He flies
    To make the World confess,
All Justice in His Bosom lies,
    And Truth and Righteosness.

PSAL. xcvij. *As the* 100*th*.

1 THE Lord, the Great *Messiah*, reigns;
    No more to *Jewish* Bounds confin'd.
Since all the World the Blessing gains,
    Let all express a grateful Mind!

O let that spacious Continent
    Which *Adam*'s num'rous Heirs possess,
And all the Isles, with sweet Consent,
    Their Saviour's wond'rous Love confess!

2 Thick Clouds and gloomy Darkness hide
    The God from Faithless, curious Eyes.
On Judgment too, by Justice try'd,
    His Throne's Eternal Pillars rise.

3 Bright Flames before his Presence fly,
    And melt the Hearts of angry Foes.
4 His Beams the World with Light supply;
    And trembling Earth its Master knows.

5 Vain Men, blown up with lofty Pride,
    Like Wax, before his Flames appear:
And those whose Thoughts their God defy'd,
    The mighty God of Nature fear.

6 His Righteousness the bending Skies,
    Aloud, with wond'rous Signs declare:
His glorious Works before the Eyes
    Of all th' astonish'd Nations are.

7 Shame be their Lot who Images
    Adore, and in their Idols boast!
Our God with humblest Worship please;
    Bow to Him, all ye Heav'nly Host!

8. *Zion.*

8 *Zion*'s and *Judah*'s Daughters true
  With Joys thy Judgment, Lord, embrac'd :
9 The Earth her mighty Maker knew,
  With more than Angel-Glorys grac'd.

10 O ye who love our Saviour, hate
   All Sin for Him, in each Degree !
 He'll Safety for his Saints create ;
   And from the Wicked set them free.

11 Light's largely for the Righteous sown,
   And Joys for upright Hearts prepar'd.
 In Him ô let our Joys be shown ;
   His Holiness, with Thanks, declar'd !

Another Metre.

1 THE Lord, the great *Jehovah*, reigns ;
    Let all the Earth rejoice !
 Let all those Isles the Sea contains
    Exalt a chearful Voice !
2 Thick Clouds and heavy Darkness hide
    Our God from Humane Eyes :
 On Righteousness, by Justice try'd,
    His Throne's Supporters rise.

3 Fierce Flames before his dreadful Face
    Consume his angry Foes.
4 His Lightnings fright the World : His Place
    The Earth, with trembling, shows.
5 The Hills, before Earth's mighty Lord,
    Like Wax, dissolving, flow :
6 The Heav'ns declare his righteous Word ;
    And All, his Glory know.

7 Shame be their Lot who Gods can make,
    And in their Idols boast.

But

> But for your God our Saviour take,
>   Ye bright, Angelick Host!
> 8 *Zion*'s and *Judah*'s Daughters heard
>   Thy Judgments, Lord, with Joy:
> 9 For Thou, above the Gods, art fear'd;
>   O'er Earth, exalted high.
>
> 10 O ye who love the Lord, with Hate
>   All wicked Works pursue!
> For He'll secure his Servants State
>   From all the sinful Crew.
> 11 For upright Hearts, true Joys and Light
>   Are sown: Ye Righteous, all
> Rejoice; and God's All-sacred Might,
>   With grateful Thoughts, re-call.

Another Metre, to the Notes of the 114*th,*
as translated by Mr. Cowley.

> 1 THE Lord, a King triumphant reigns!
>   Let all the Earth around,
>   The Isles with Joys resound!
> God alone a King remains!
> 2 Thick Clouds, and heavy Darkness, round him fly;
> Justice severe, and Judgment, waiting by.
>   His glorious Throne prepare.
> 3   Bright Flames before his Face,
> With dreadful Flashes, rake the Air;
>   And all his Foes malignant Race,   (embrace.
> With all their impious Works, one burning Pile
>
> 4   See how the pointed Lightnings roll;
>   With what a dismal Glare
>   They fill the glowing Air,
>   Soaring tow'rd the frighted Pole!
> Shock'd with the Vision, trembling Nature quakes;
> The shatter'd Earth a strong Convulsion shakes.

5 The lofty Mountains melt,
  Like Wax before the Fires:
 Whate'er his scorching Fury felt,
 Before the World's great Lord retires;
And by his awful Frown dissolv'd, at once expires.

6 The Heav'ns his Righteousness declare;
  And all the People see
  His glorious Majesty,
 How it fills the Purpled Air.
7 May Shame deserv'd, and dark Confusion seize
 Those Fools, whose Thoughts their empty Ido's
  Fools, who absurdly boast (please!
  In Gods themselves can frame!
 But, ô ye bright, Angelick Hosts,
 Adore our Great *Jehovah*'s Name; (claim!
And on your bended Knees, the God of Gods pro-

8 His Condescensions *Sion* heard,
  And *Judah*'s Daughters too;
  And at the wondrous Shew,
 Extasy'd with Joys, appear'd:
 Thy Goodness then before the Nations shone;
 Thy sacred Judgments through the World were
9 But, though so lowly now, (known.
  Thy glorious Godhead still
 Makes all the World submissly bow;
 Bless'd Angels thy Commands fulfil:
And All Subjection yield to thy Immortal Will.

10 Ye who the Great *Jehovah* love,
  With God-like Hatred due,
  All wicked Works pursue:
 Fix your happy Souls above!
 He, like a Father, guards his faithful Souls;
 And all their Foes, and all their Force, controls.
11 But Mirth and Light to all
  The Just and Good shall shine:

PSAL. xcviij.

12 O, then your ancient Joys re-call!
    In your *Jehovah*'s Praise combine;
And all his holy Acts record in Songs Divine!

PSAL. xcviij.

1 THE Lord, who wondrous Works hath wrough
    With Anthems new proclaim!
His Hand, his holy Arm, hath brought
    Himself the Conqu'ror's Name.
2 He makes his great Salvation known,
    To give the Nations Light:
His Righteousness the Lord hath shown,
    In all the People's Sight.

3 His Mercies he hath call'd to mind,
    His Truth to *Israel*'s Race:
And all those Bounds which Earth confin'd,
    His Saving Health embrace.
4 Sing to the Lord, ô Earth! aloud!
    Sing chearful Notes around!
The Lord, among the grateful Croud,
    The Lord's just Praise resound.

5,6 To God, with Harps, your Voices raise,
    And Trumpets Martial Sound:
With ecchoing Cornets let the Praise
    Of God, the King, be crown'd!
7 Let Seas, with all their Fulness, roar!
    The World, and all its Host!
8 In Him each River's sounding Shoar,
    And lofty Mountain boast!

9 For now the Lord to Judgment's near,
    And Earth its Doom shall know:
His Righteousness the World sha'l hear,
    His Truth and Justice show.

Anoth

Another Metre, as Mr. Sandys's 13th.

1. O Sing to God, the Lord:
His wond'rous Works record!
Sing, sing an Anthem new.
Return his Praises due,
Whose Hand, whose ho'y Arm
Dissolv'd Hell's fatal Charm:
Whom we triumphant see,
And crown'd with Victorie!

2. The Lord's Salvation
Is now more clearly known:
His Truth and Justice He
Makes all the Nations see.

3. But with his *Isra.l*
His Mercies ever dwell:
And though a while a Cloud
His Truth and Mercy shroud
From their expecting Eyes,
Off soon the Shadow flies,
And both, with Beams Divine
More bright and strongly shine.
So all the Nations round
Have our Salvation found;
How God about us waits,
And all our Health creates.

4. Let all the Nations round
Their Maker's Praises sound:
O let the Earth rejoice,
And raise its chearful Voice;
And all the World combine
In Thanks, and Songs Divine.

5. Sing to the Lord! ô sing
To our Eternal King!
To well-tun'd Harps ô raise
Your Notes of Heav'nly Praise!

6 O let the Trumpets sound,
Let Cornets Notes rebound,
And with them loudly sing
To our Eternal King!
7 Let the loud Ocean roar
Its Joys from Shoar to Shoar:
Let Angels, bless'd on high,
With Earth in Praises vye!
8 O let the Waters sound,
The ecchoing Hills rebound;
And with a chearful Noise,
Express their boundless Joys!
9 Let All their Joyfulness
Before the Lord express!
For, loe! He comes with Haste,
And Awful Glories grac'd:
His dreadful Summons all
To his Tribunal call:
His Judgment then sha'l bless
The World with Righteousness:
Truth from his Lips shall flow;
And all the World shall know
Their glorious Judge, and see
His Love and Equity.

PSAL. XCIX.

1 CHrist reigns! Let all the People round
Beneath his Empire quake!
He sits above the Cherubs, crown'd:
Let Earth's Foundations shake!
2 The Lord in *Sion*'s great, and high;
Above the People rais'd.
3 O may his dreadful Majesty,
His holy Name, be prais'd!

4 Judgment our mighty Monarch loves,
And Equity prepares:

And Judgment with his Juftice moves
　　In *Jacob*'s blefs'd Affairs.
O then exalt the Lord our God,
　　Before his Foot-ftool bow;
And fpread his wond'rous Works abroad,
　　His holy Nature fhow!

So *Mofes* once, and *Aaron* fo
　　Among his Priefts appear'd;
And *Samuel* with his Prophets, who
　　The God of *Jacob* fear'd.
Thefe at his Footftool bow'd, and there
　　To him devoutly pray'd;
And always found his Anfwers near,
　　And all their Faith repaid.

They kept his Teftimonies fure,
　　His Statute-Laws obey'd;
And He to Them from Clouds obfcure
　　His gentle Anfwers made.
Sometimes indeed his Wrath fevere
　　Their Follies would purfue,
Yet oft their Cries He'd kindly hear,
　　His Mercies oft renew.

O praife our God's exalted Name,
　　Before his Altars bow!
Our God, our holy Lord proclaim,
　　With Praife his Glory fhow!

PSAL. C.

YE who enjoy Salvation's Light,
　　To God your Voices raife;
Appear with Gladnefs in His Sight,
　　And Sing your Saviour's Praife!
Our Lord is God indeed; it's He,
Not We our felves have made;

L　　　　　　　　　　Our

Our Shepherd, He; his People, we;
  And in his Pastures laid.

4 O then approach his Courts, his Gates,
    With Thanks, and hearty Praise:
  For Praise on his Assembly waits
    On all his holy Days.
5 O b'ess his Name, for God is good,
    And all his Mercies sure:
  His Truth from Age to Age has stood,
    And shall unchang'd endure.

Another Metre. As the old 100th.

1,2 O Ye enlighten'd Souls, with Praise,
    Before our mighty Lord appear!
  To Him your chearful Voices raise;
    Adore his Name with humblest Fear.

3 He's our Almighty God; not we,
    But He, to us our Substance gave:
  He's ours, we His, those Sheep which He
    Di'd, by his own pure Blood to save.

4 O then approach his Gates with praise,
    And in his Courts his Glories sing;
  On all his own appointed Days,
    Your Sacrifice of Praises sing.

5 He's always kind, and always good,
    His Favour great, his Mercy sure;
  His Truth has ever firmly stood,
    And shall from Age to Age endure.

PSAL. cj.

1 MErcy I'll sing, and Judgment praise,
    And sing my God to Thee.

PSAL. cij.

And wisely walk in perfect Ways:
    O come, dear Lord, to me!
Then with an undissembling Heart,
    I'l ever justly move;
And in my Court, in every part
    Thy sacred Rules improve.

No wicked Actions shall mine Eyes
    With Satisfaction see.
And those who things perverse devise,
    Shall ne're be great with Me.
From Me all froward Fools shall part;
    I'll none that's wicked own:
But cut off those whose sland'rous Art
    Against their Neighbour's shown.

The Heart that's proud, the Look that's high,
    I'll ne're at Court endure,
But through the Land my searching Eye
    Shall faithful Friends procure.
That Man who treads a perfect Path
    My Favourite shall be;
But Cheats, and those who break their Faith
    Shall never dwell with Me.

I'll bear no Liar in my sight,
    The wicked I'll destroy,
Till *Salem* freed from Sinners quite,
    Shall perfect Peace enjoy.

PSAL. cij.

A Soul with mighty Woes opprest,
    May thus complaining pray:
And in deep Sorrows Language drest,
    His weighty Griefs display.

1 Hear Lord, O hear my Prayers and Cries!
    To Me thy Face disclose!
2 My Soul, lost in Affliction, dies.
    O hear! O ease my Woes!
3 Grief wasts my Days like Smoke, and dries
    My Bones, like Hearths, with heat.
4 My Heart, like Grass quite wither'd, lies,
    And I forget my Meat.

5 My Bones break through my shriveling Skin:
    Through my unceasing Groans:
6 I'm like those doleful Birds, which in
    Wild Deserts vent their moans.
7 Like little Birds, which spent with Grief
    About their Nestlings mourn;
8 While taunting Foes against my Life,
    With bloody Oaths are sworn.

9 Ashes my Bread, my Drink was Tears,
    While I endur'd thy frown.
10 Thy Love once rais'd me up from Fears;
    Thy Wrath now hurls me down.
11 The Shaddow falls, my Lifes weak Flame
    So sinks; like Grass it wains;
12 But still *thou art*, thy glorious Name,
    From Age to Age remains.

13 Rise Lord! for *Sions* help return;
    In time her Woes relieve!
14 Thy Servants o're her Ruins mourn,
    And for her Ashes grieve.
15 All Nations then thy Name shall fear;
    All Kings thy Glory see:
16 When *Sions* Walls new built appear,
    And Glory springs from thee.

Part 2.

God hears the silent Mourner's Prayer:
    O write his Goodness down!
So shall Posterity declare
    Their mighty God's renown.
God from his Holy Throne, his Eye
    Turn'd down on Earth below.
To save the Men condemn'd to die,
    And let the Prisoners go.

That they in *Sion's* Walls might show
    His Praise, his Name record,
When thither Kings and Kingdoms flow,
    To serve their Mighty Lord.
My Strength, my shortned Days he broke,
    Then, " spare me Lord! I pray'd.
" Suspend, dear Lord, thy deadly stroke!
    " Thy Years can never fade.

Thy Hands this Earth's Foundations cast,
    And stretch'd the lofty Skies.
They perish, but thy Nature lasts,
    And Time it self defies.
They like a worn-out Garment fail,
    And shall be chang'd for new.
Thou'rt still the same, Age can't prevail,
    Nor time thy Steps pursue.

Our Lands sha'l quickly be suppli'd
    With thy obedient Race,
And their well-settled Heirs abide.
    Secure before thy Face.

PSAL. ciij. As the 100th.

1. O Praise the Lord with grateful Joy!
My Tongue my Soul his Praises sing!
2. O let his Praise thy Powers employ!
His Loves to kind Remembrance bring!

3. 'Tis He forgives thy Sins, 'tis He
Thy Weakness heals, thy Plagues removes,
4. Redeems thy Life from Misery,
And crowns thee with his tenderest Loves.

5. With good He fills the Youth and Age;
Thy Age with vigorous Youth renews.
6. His Arms for Saints opprest engage;
His just Revenge their Foes pursues.

7. He to his *Israels* Race of old,
By *Moses* made his Precepts known:
He, by *our Jesus*, still unfolds
His Will and Goodness towards his own.

8. Our Lord is kind, his Mercies great;
His Vengance, not his Mercy flow.
9. He'll not too oft his Strokes repeat.
Nor let his Anger alway glow.

10. So with our selves He dealt; our Crimes,
Though foul, with Rods he gently lasht.
His pittying Eyes a thousand times,
Our still repeated Follies past.

11. His Goodness so surrounds his own,
As Skies enclose our humbler Earth.
12. From us our Sins are farther thrown,
Then Sun-set's from the Mornings Birth.

Part

Part 2.

13 More love to pious Souls he shows,
   Then Fathers to their Darling Heirs.
14 Our frailer Constitution knows,
   Our mouldring Dust as gently spares.

15 Weak Man, like early Birds may rise,
   Or Grass which shades the cheerful Plains:
16 But struck with blasting Winds he dies,
   And neither House nor Name remains.

17 But Gods unfailing Grace pursues
   The Just, and all their faithful Seed:
18 Who on his Sacred Covenant muse,
   And all his righteous Precepts heed.

19 On high our God has fixt his Throne,
   And thence his boundless Empire guides;
   And o're the Subject World, alone,
   His Arbitrary Will presides.

20 Praise Him, ye Angel-flames, whose Might
   Does in compleat Obedience shine!
21 O praise Him all ye Sons of Light:
   Bless'd Ministers of Love Divine!

22 O all his Works your Maker praise!
   Praise through his spacious Empire sing!
   While I with grateful Anthems raise
   New Honours to my Glorious King.

PSAL. civ. *As the* 100*th*.

1 O Praise the Lord, my tuneful Soul!
   How great, blest God, how wondrous great.
   What Majesty, what Glories roll
   About thy Everlasting Seat!

2 Light robes Thee with her Radiant Streams;
   Thy Curtains are th' expanded Skies.
3 Floods bear thy Chambers weighty Beams:
   On humble Clouds thy Chariot flies.

   God walks on groaning Winds in State,
4   Attended with his Angel-Bands;
   And Servant-Flames around him wait,
   And fly to bear his great Commands.

5 He Earth's Foundations strongly laid;
   A well-pois'd never moving Load.
6 A wavy Deep its Covering made,
   Which o're the highest Mountains flow'd.

7 But off the head-long Waters flew,
   When his commanding Thunders roar'd.
8 They took their place, and strait in view,
   Sweet Plains appear'd, and Mountains soar'd.

9 The Floods their Bounds appointed know;
   Earth fears no more th' encroaching Deep:
10 Through Valleys Crystal Fountains flow,
   And round the Mountains softly creep.

11 To Them the Savage Creatures fly,
   And kindly cool their thirsty Flame.
12 The Birds above them sing on high,
   And there their curious Buildings frame.

Part 2.

13 His Rains refresh the parching Hills,
   And make our Earth with Fruits abound.
14 Thence Grass the hungry Cattel fills,
   And Herbs for Men are useful found.

'hrough Him rich Corn o're-spreads the Fields,
  And Wine to chear our drooping Hearts.
'at shining Juice his Olive yields;
  His Bread a vital Strength imparts.

Sap feeds the lofty Cedar-Groves,
  Where Birds of Prey their Eieries raise.
The Goat on Rocky Mountains roves;
  Through Rocks the Coney breaks her Ways.

The Moon, the Sun, their Seasons know,
  And when to rise, and when to fall;
Nights gloomy Clouds our World o'reflow',
  And out the Forrest-Rangers crawl.

The Wolves, the Tygers, howl for Prey,
  And loud the hungry Lions roar.
God for their Diet finds a way,
  And feeds them with his secret Store.

But when the Sun appears, they fly,
  And to their unknown Dens repare;
And Men their business safely ply,
  Till Night again o're-clouds the Air.

How various, Lord, how wisely fram'd;
  Great God, thy Works of Wonder are!
Thy Riches are through Earth proc'aim'd;
  Thy Wealth th' unfathom'd Seas declare.

Part 3.

There Fishes, great and small, in strange
  Unnumber'd Numbers cut their Way.
There Navies float, and Monsters range,
  And Whales in boundless Oceans play.

25 Those

27 These All, blest God, depend on Thee;
   Of Thee they beg their timely Food:
28 Thy Gifts they catch, thy Hands are free,
   And All are fill'd with needful Good.

29 Thou hid'st thy Face, affrighted, They
   Sink down to Dust, and Dust remain:
30 Thy Spirit commands, the Dead obey,
   And rise and fill the World again.

31 God's Glory lasts; He, pleas'd, reviews
   His Works; his Looks, his dreadful Stroke
32 Convulsions through the World diffuse,
   And make the trembling Mountains smoak.

33 To God, my mighty Lord, I'll sing,
   While Health, or Life, or Breath remains:
34 My Heart in Him with Joys shall spring;
   I'll praise his Name in lofty Strains.

35 He'll soon confound the Sinner's Race,
   And impious plotting Fools control,
   And all their Stock on Earth deface.
   O bless, ô praise the Lord, my Soul!

PSAL. cv. *as the* 100th. *or Mr.* Sandys's 8th.

1 O Praise the Lord! invoke his Name!
   His Acts through ev'ry Tribe proclaim!
2 Sing, sing aloud; your Anthems raise:
   Through all the World his Wonders praise!

3 Him, and his holy Name adore;
   His Smiles, with chearful Hearts, implore:
4 And seek the Lord, his Strength embrace;
   And ever seek his glorious Face.

5 O ye of *Abr'ham*'s faithful Seed,
  O ye of *Jacob*'s chosen Breed,
6 His strange, his dreadful Acts relate,
  And on his Judgments meditate!

7 He's our great God, our Lord alone;
  His Judgments through the World are known:
8 His Covenant, his Word of old,
  Shall through a Thousand Ages hold.

9 What He to *Abraham* spoke before,
  What He to *Isaac* firmly swore,
10 And as a Law on *Israel* laid,
  And thus his lasting Cov'nant made.

11 " To you rich *Canaan*'s Land I'll give,
   " Where you, its lawful Heirs, shall live.
12 Though then their Seed were weak and small,
   And despicable Strangers all.

13 When they a Thousand Movements made,
   And round the neighb'ring Countries stray'd,
14 He them, against the World, maintain'd;
   And Ill-designing Kings restrain'd.

15 " From Wrongs be my Anointed free:
   " Let no malicious Injurie
   " My Prophets or my Friends approach,
   " Or on my chosen Sons encroach!

Part 2.

16 Sharp Famine *Canaan*'s Land annoy'd,
   And God the Staff of Bread destroy'd;
   And *Jacob*'s House, among the rest,
   The long-continu'd Want oppress'd.

17 Yet

17 Yet *Joseph*, sold a Slave, he sent
Before, who might their Fates prevent.
18 Chains were the wretched Captive's Dole,
The pinching Fetters reach'd his Soul.

19 Till Time might for his Help provide,
God's Word his faithful Wisdom try'd:
20 Then sent the King, and eas'd him; He
Who rul'd the People, set him free.

21 Him o'er his Royal House preferr'd,
To him his weighty Cares referr'd;
22 That Lords and Senators might know
His God-like Sense, and wiser grow.

23 Then down to *Egypt Israel* went,
And there his Hoary Age was spent.
24 There God his fruitful Seed increas'd,
With Strength, above their En'mies bless'd.

25 But then their ancient Hate reviv'd,
And they his People's Fate contriv'd.
26 But, to divert their spiteful Blows,
God *Moses* sent, and *Aaron* chose.

27 They God's fear'd Will, at ev'ry Stroke,
In Signs and dreadful Wonders spoke:
28 And Hellish Gloom, at his Command,
Imprison'd all the groaning Land.

29 Their Streams were turn'd to pois'nous Gore;
The poison'd Fish o'er-spread the Shoar.
33 Their Roads Frogs freckled Armies choak'd,
And round their Royal Chambers croak'd.

Part

Part 3.

31 He spoke, his Word the Dust alarm'd,
  And Lice in all their quarters swarm'd.
32 He hurl'd down Monstrous Hails for Rains:
  And burning flashes rak'd the Plains.

33 Their Vines, their Figs, their Trees, the stroke
  Of his prodigious Thunders broke,
34 He spoke, the Locusts marching round,
  And unknown Insects swept the Ground.

35 Their Herbs and Grass, no more appear'd,
  The Land of all its Fruits was clear'd.
36 Their First-born fell, Gods fatal stroke,
  Their early strength and Glory broke.

37 Then out their Vig'rous Tribes he led,
  With Jewels, Gold and Silver sped,
38 Tho' pillag'd Egypt joy'd to see,
  Themselves from Plagues and Terrours free.

39 He cool'd them with a Cloud by Day;
  By Night Flames pointed out their Way.
40 They ask't, He gave them Quails for meat;
  And let them Bread of Angels eat.

41 He struck the Rock, the Waters flow'd;
  And streams on parching Lands bestow'd,
42 For now his sacred Oath re-curr'd,
  To *Abraham* his unchanging Word.

43 He therefore bade his People be
  From Bonds, with joys triumphant, free.
44 And then consign'd to *Isaac*'s Hands,
  The Neighbouring Towns, and Heathen Lands.

45 He

45 He freely all on them bestow'd,
   That, sensible of what they ow'd,
   Their Seed, his Statutes might record,
   And keep his Laws: O praise the Lord!

Psal. cvj. *As the* 100*th: or Mr.* Sandys*'s* 1*st b.*

1 O Praise the Lord! his Goodness praise!
     For sure his Boundless Mercy stands,
2   The strength of his Almighty Hands,
   His Honour, who can justly blaze?

3 Thrice happy they, who Judgment keep,
     And always righteous Laws pursue:
4 Lord, let me, as thy People do,
     By thy Salvation guarded, sleep!

5 To me thy Favour then shall show,
     That good thy chosen Friends partake,
     That Mirth thy happy People make,
   Those Joys thy dear Possessions know.

6 We, Lord, have, with our Fathers, sinn'd;
     Their Crimes, their impious Crimes renew'd,
7   Who thy *Ægyptian* Wonders view'd,
   But to Forgetfulness resign'd;

   Forgot his Mercies stores, and near
     The Sea, so lately pass'd, rebel'd:
8   Yet still He all their Fears dispel'd,
   To make his Name and Power appear.

9 He cut the Seas, and dry'd the Sands,
     While they through Deeps as Desarts, pass'd;
10   And brought them safe to shoar at last,
   Redeem'd from Persecuting Hands.

11 Their

PSAL. cvj.

   Their Foes the loofned Waves o'erflow'd,
     Not one his wretched Life retriev'd;
   Then, they his Word a while be'leved,
  And Gratitude with Praifes fhow'd.

13 But foon they all his Works forgot,
     Nor his Divine Advice improv'd;
14   Their raging Lufts his Anger mov'd,
  And made it in the Defert Hot.

15 And tho' he gave their Proud requeft,
     Their Stomachs eafelefs Hunger tore;
16 On *Mofes* then their Envy bore,
  And *Aaron*, God's Anoynted Prieft.

16 Then *Dathan*'s and *Abiram*'s Crew,
     Earths hollow gaping Womb devour'd:
18   Fierce Lightnings on th' Affembly pour'd;
  And Flames the Godlefs Rebels flew.

Part. 2.

19 Next, They the Calf in *Horeb* fram'd.
     And to the fenfelefs Idol bow'd;
20   A grazing Brutes dead fhape, aloud,
  They both their God and Guide proclaim'd.

21 They ne'er on God, their Saviour, more,
     Nor *Egypt*'s Slavifh fuffrings, thought;
22   What Wonders there his Hand had wrought,
  And on the Ocean's Purple fhore.

23 He then their Ruin had decree'd,
     But in his chofen *Mofes* came,
   He ftay'd th' approaching dreadful Flame,
  And facred Wrath, impetuous fpeed.

                    24 Yea,

24 Yea, they the promis'd Land disdain'd,
  His Word with them no Credence found;
25   Base Murmurs fill'd their Tents around,
  And off they threw their Lords command.

26 Then God against them rais'd his Hands,
  That they in Desart-Wilds might die;
27   Their scatter'd Race confounded lie,
  And perish all in barb'rous Lands.

28 Yet, unreclaim'd, the senseless Crew,
  Their Souls to *P....*'s God betraid.
  And eating Sacrifices made,
  To him; an Idol's Servants grew.

29   Thus they, with studied Art, rebell'd,
  And out the Plague among them broke;
30   Till *Phineas*, with a righteous stroke,
  The Plagues infectious Rage repell'd.

31 That gallant Action rais'd his Fame,
  When God's just Wrath his Zeal atton'd;
  His God the Righteous Action own'd,
  And blest him with a Deathless Name.

32 Nay, more they durst their God provoke;
  At *Meff..*'s springs they mischief made:
33 *Moses*, that meekest Soul betrays,
  Till Passion in him rashly spoke.

Part 3.

34 The Nations, to Destruction doom'd,
  By God's Command, they fondly spar'd;
35   And for their Pity's just Reward,
  Their Sins, and all their Plagues, assum'd.

36 Among

6 Among a Thousand snares they fell,
   While to their graven Gods they bow'd:
7   Their wretched Sons, and Daughters, vow'd
To Devils, they sacrific'd to Hell.

8 The Blood of Sons and Daughters round,
   Poor Innocents, to Idols flow'd:
   Canaan a dismal shambles show'd,
And Infant Gore the Country drown'd.

9 Their Works, and vile Inventions, both,
   Them to polluting Whoredoms drew,
10   Till God incens'd against them grew,
And could his own Possessions loath.

11 But God, with just Revenge, resign'd
   Them to their domineering Foes;
12   Where, vex't with long oppressing Woes,
Their Pride and lofty Thoughts declin'd.

13 Oft sav'd they sinn'd as oft, and made
   His Vengeance prosecute their Crimes:
14   Yet in their darkest suffring Times,
He saw and heard them while they pray'd.

15 He call'd his Covenant to Mind,
   And Sympathiz'd with all their Woes;
16   And soon their stubborn-hearted Foes,
Grew gentle, pittiful, and kind.

17 O save us, Lord! our Captiv'd Race
   From Heathen Chains and Lands recall,
   That we may sing thy Praise, and fall
With Thanks before thy Glorious Face,

18 The God of *Israel*'s Name record,
   His Praise from Age to Age resound;
   And let the joyful Tribes around
Sing out Amen: O praise Lord!

PSAL. cvij. Part 1. Metre 1.

1 O Praise the Lord! Exa't his Name;
  His Goodness celebrate!
Let Age to Age resound his Fame,
  His bounteous Acts relate!
2 Sing to His Name, ye whom from Chains
  His peaceful Arm redeem'd:
O be his Praise in grateful Streins,
  His glorious Works esteem'd.

3 He from Earth's utmost Quarters drew
  His *Israel's* scatter'd Race;
4 And the wild Desarts wandring thro',
  They found no Resting-place,
5 Tho' pinch'd with Hunger, scorch'd with Thirst,
  Their wasting Spirits fail'd;
Yet with their pittying God at first
  Their humble Cries prevail'd.

6 Thro' all their Streights his careful Hand
  Was their unfailing Guide,
7 And smooth'd their Ways, and made their Bands
  In well-built Towns reside.
8 O praise his Goodness! Praise his Name!
  His wond'rous Mercies praise!
Thro' all the World his Acts proclaim!
  His boundless Glories raise!

Part 2. Metre 2.

9 Praise God! His Springs we see
  Relieve the thirsty Soul;
The hungry Wretch revives, when He
  Bestows his plenteous Dole!
10 But when they, foolish all,
  His gracious Laws abus'd,

Despis'd

Despis'd their Maker's gentlest Call,
   And Love's soft Voice refus'd.

11 Then he the stubborn Crew
   In weighty Fetters chain'd;
Death's Chains around the Rebels flew,
   And Woes their Souls restrain'd.
12 Yet, when oppress'd, they bow'd
   Beneath the dismal Weight;
And when, in vain, they begg'd aloud
   For Men to ease their State.

13 When to their God they cry'd,
   And at his Footstool laid
Their pressing Griefs, and mortify'd,
   The softning Rebels pray'd.
14 He clear'd the Skies above,
   And every Slave unchain'd,
And with warm Beams of gentlest Love
   The Sufferers entertain'd.

15 O praise, O praise his Name,
   His bounteous Acts declare!
Let all Mankind with Thanks proclaim
   How great his Mercies are!

Part 3. Metre 3. As the 100th.

16 Praise God! At his Command the Gates
   Of massive Brass their Leaves unfold;
No Bars of Steel, nor sturdy Grates
   Against his powerful Words can hold.

17 When Fools, for Sins afflicted, griev'd,
   And with their Sins their Judge provok'd,
18 No Meats their Appetites reliev'd,
   Nor eas'd their Hunger's sickly Stroke.

Their

Their Stomachs loath'd bless'd Angels Food;
  Sweet Manna dropping from the Skies;
And Quails disturb'd their curdling Blood,
  Till Nature sunk without Supplies.

19 Yet when the fainting Sinners pray'd,
  He heard, and heard them when they cry'd;
God's Word their dying Swoons allay'd,
  And Appetites and Food supply'd.

20 New Life, new Spirits he bestow'd
  Where fading Nature's Force declin'd;
To them his healthful Favours show'd,
  And their distemper'd Blood refin'd.

21 O praise our God! Exalt his Name!
  Above the Skies exalt his Name!
22 Your Thanks with Sacrifice proclaim,
  And Trophies to his Goodness raise!

Part 4. *Metre* 4. *as the* 148*th*.

23 Such whose bold Courage o're
      The restless Ocean flies,
    And sail from Shore to Shore,
      For wealthy Merchandise
24   Such Men may see
        How wondrous there
        God's Works appear,
        How powerful He.

25   For if in Storms he speak,
        The swelling Tempest roars;
      And foaming Billows break,
        And lash the bounding Shores.
          While Wind and Tide
          On rolling Seas,
          Where-e'er they please,
          Triumphant ride.   26 Now

Now high the towring Fleet
   On Watry Mountains rife,
As if the Clouds they'd meet,
   Or brave the threatning Skies.
     Now down they come,
     Steep tumbling all,
     With dreadful Fall,
       To meet their Doom.

Strait every fhatter'd Sail
   Reels here, and ftaggers there,
While horrid Storms prevail,
   And Courage yields to fear.
     All Hopes are loft,
     And in Black Night,
     Ships guidelefs quite,
       At random tofs'd.

But when on God they call,
   He hears their mournful Cries,
Loud Storms in Silence fall,
   And Light remounts the Skies:
     Rough Billows flake,
     And gentle Gales
     Swell all their Sails
       Their Port to make.

There with Delights unfeign'd
   The wearied Sailers reft:
New Life and Safety gain'd
   Warms every fainting Breaft.
     Joys fweeter taft,
     And the dear Shore.
     Is va'u'd more
       For Dangers paft.

31   O praise, O praise the Lord,
       His Bounteous Actions praise!
     Let all the World record
       His Mercy's wond'rous Ways.
32   In thickest Throngs
       Where Princes are,
       His Loves declare
         With grateful Songs.

Part 4. *Metre* 4. *As the* 113*th*.

33 O praise the Lord; At his Commands
   Fair Streams desert the thirsty Lands,
     And Springs no more their Waters yield.
34 His Curse for Humane Crimes destroys
   Their blooming Hopes and ripening Joys,
     And sows with barren Salt the Field.
35 Yet for his own dear Servant's sakes
   He turns vast Lands to standing Lakes,
     And makes the Sands with Waters flow.
36 And then their hungry Troops he guides,
   And thro' the new-rais'd Fields divides,
     And makes new Towns and Cities grow.

37 With noblest Grains they sow their Fields,
   Rich Wines the grateful Vineyard yields;
     Their Crops are full, profound their Peace;
38 God's Blessing on their Labours waits,
   Their crowding Offspring throng their Gates,
     And all their pregnant Flocks encrease.
39 But when his ancient Love's abus'd,
   His Counsels, his Commands refus'd,
     A suddain Change o'returns their State.
   Down falls their haughty Pride, their Race
   Incessant Wars and Plagues deface,
     Expos'd to every Neighbour's Hate.

                                  40 Their

10 Their Princes with Contempt he treats,
    Confounds them in their proud Conceits,
    And lets their Hopes bewildred fall.
11 Then to the Poor despis'd before,
    Transfers his favouring Mercies store,
    And feeds, and multiplies them all.
12 Admire ye living Saints with Joy,
    (While silent impious Atheists ly)
    Admire his Providential Ways!
13 Let wise Men all their Thoughts confine,
    To meditate on Works Divine,
    And sing their great Protector's praise!

PSAL. CViij. *As the 110th.*

1 MY Heart is fix'd, ô God, my Heart
    Is fix'd, thy lofty Praise to sing,
    I'me ready with my noblest part,
    To praise my everlasting King.

2 Awake my Harp, awake my Lute,
    While I prevent the Morning's light.
3 And thy dear Praises prosecute,
    In all the wondring Nations sight.

4 Swift are the Clouds, and high the Skies,
    Above our Thoughts and Measures far:
    But higher, Lord, thy Mercies rise,
    More swift thy Truths vast Conquests are.

5 Lord, o're the Skies thy Brightness show,
    Let all the Earth thy Glories see.
6 O hear, ô save thy Servant! so
    I'le rescue those belov'd by Thee.

7 God swore once by his Holiness,
    And by his Oath my Joy maintains,

I'le

    I'le quick *Shechem*'s Fields possess,
       And measure *Succoth*'s fruitful Plains.

8 Fair *Gileads* mine, *Manasses* too,
       My Head on *Ephraim*'s strength relies,
    The Scepter's Royal *Judah*'s due,
       My Kingdom He with Laws supplies.

9 *Moab*, my meanest Slave shall be,
       And *Edom* prostrate at my Feet,
    And conquer'd *Palestina* me
       With humble Tribute gladly meet.

10 Who e'l me thro' Cities fortify'd,
      Or *Edom*'s rocky Frontiers lead?
11 Lord, let thy Help so long deny'd,
      At last our fainting Armies head.

12 Up Lord! in times of Danger aid!
      For Humane Helps are only shows,
13 And valiant thro' thy Influence made,
      Wee'l trample o're our vanquish'd Foes.

PSAL. cix.

1 O Thou, dear God, of all my Praise,
     No longer silent go!
2 For sinful Men, in sinful Ways,
     And Traitors bolder grow.
  Against me they their Rage excite,
     Their Tongues with Falshood whet.
3 And me with Words of deadly spite,
     And causeless Hate beset.

4 They, for my kindness, prove my Foes,
     But I in silence pray.
5 Malice to Goodness they oppose,
     And Love with Hate repay.

                        6 Make

PSAL. cix.

   Make Him some wicked Tyrant's slave,
     Let Satan bind his hands!
   And Sins severest Sentence have,
     When He in judgment stands!

   Nay, let his very Prayers be Sin!
     His Days be dark, and few!
   That Office fix another in,
     Which to himself was due!
   No Father let his Children see,
     His widow'd Wife go mourn!
10 His Off-spring common Vagrants be,
     Expos'd to Want and Scorn!

   Their Bread from cruel Hands intreat,
11   The Griping-Usurers trade,
   Seize all his Wea'th, and every Cheat,
     His Pains and Gains invade!
12 No Mercy let his Cries engage,
     Nor all his Orphan race,
13 But sink 'um all! in one short Age,
     Their very Names deface!

Part 2.

14 In God's revenging Presence let,
     Their Father's Crimes remain!
   No length of Time, or Years, forget
     Their Mother's viler stain!
15 Let them God's sleeping Vengeance move,
     Their Memory to destroy.
16 Since Grace could ne'er his Soul improve,
     Nor Love his Thoughts employ.

   But the dear Man, to Sorrows born,
     With humblest Thoughts indu'd;
   The broken Heart with Anguish torn,
     His bloody Hate pursu'd

17 Curfing, and hellish Words he lov'd,
　　His Lot may Curses be!
　His Heart no Blessings e'er approv'd,
　　Let him no Blessing see!

18 He Curses for a Garment us'd,
　　And with their poisonous draught
　His Bowels washt, like Oil diffus'd,
　　Quite thro' his Bones they wrought.
19 May He no other Garments wear
　　But Curses closely bound;
　And Curses for a Girdle bear
　　To gird him duely round!

20 Be this the Just reward of those,
　　From God's revenging Hand;
　Whose spiteful Words my Life oppose,
　　And who against me stand.
21 But Lord for thy Names sake appear!
　　My Party kindly own!
　Thy Mercy's Good; ô let it here
　　To rescue Me be shown!

Part 3.

22 For wretched and afflicted I
　　With inward Wounds decay,
23 And like an Evening Shadow fly,
　　Or Locusts hurld away.
24 My Knees with tedious Fastings fail,
　　And all my Leanness see,
25 My Foes with brutish scorn assail,
　　And shake their Heads at me.

26 Help ô My God! ô save Me! show
　　Thy former Mercies now!
27 That all thy Love to me may know
　　Thy Helps dear Lord allow!

28 T

PSAL. CX.

28 Then let them Curſe me ſtill! on me
    Thy Bleſſings Lord beſtow!
  Let Them, their own Confuſion ſee,
    But me thy gladneſs know!

29 When great they ſeem, like ſome large Cloke
    Let Shame be round them roul'd!
30 And I'le thy Name in Crouds invoke,
    Thy Praiſe at large unfold:
31 For God ſtill by the Poor Mans ſide,
    With ſure aſſiſtance ſtands:
  His Soul with ſaving Wings to hide,
    From partial Judges Hands.

PSAL. CX.

1 "SIT here on my Right Hand! the Lord
    Thus to my Lord, has ſaid
  Till thou ſhalt ſee thy Foes abhor'd,
    Beneath thy Footſtool lay'd;
2 From *Sions* Hill thy regal claime,
    Thy Scepter firſt ſhall riſe,
  Thence Reign and with thy awful Name,
    Command thy Enemies.

3 When thy Prodigious Might appears,
    Thy ready Armies move;
  And Preach thoſe happy gladſome years,
    The Reign of boundleſs Love:
  Tho' at a mighty diſtance now,
    The careleſs People ſtand,
  To Thee they'l then as ſwiftly flow,
    And own thy ruling Hand.

  Waſh'd from their Crimes and ſnowy white.
    Their Tempers undefil'd,
  And cloth'd with Innocence and Light,
    And like their Maſter mild.

These Conquests first belong'd to Thee,
E're dewy Mornings rose,
Or Time could thro' Eternity,
Thy sacred Birth disclose.

4 Then by himself thy Father swore,
And shook his awful Throne,
And when swift Time shall be no more,
He'el that Engagement own.
" Thou'rt an Eternal Priest, to Thee
" There's no succeeding Heir.
" And like *Melchisedec* shalt be,
" And Crown, and Miter wear.

5 The Lord shall in his angry Day,
Rebellious Kings destroy.
6 Among the Gentiles fierce'y sway,
And fill his own with Joy.
But where bold Opposition reigns,
The slaughter'd Corpses round,
And *dying* Kings shall spread the Plains,
And stain the purple Ground.

7 But he before the Conquest gain'd,
The Rage of Thirst shall know,
With Sorrow's streams be entertain'd,
And drink of deadly Woe;
Till, all those Difficulties past,
His Glory's largely spread,
And all shall see the Crown at last,
On his victorious Head.

PSAL. cxj.

O Praise the Lord! my Heart, prepare
To praise the mighty Lord!
Where-e'er his bless'd Assemblies are
Will I his Name record.

a Great

PSAL. cxij.

2 Great are his Works, and earnestly
    By Men of Wisdom sought:
3 His Works are all with Majesty,
    And comely Beauty wrought.

  His Righteousness eternally
4   Shall, with his Works, endure
In grateful Minds; his Clemency,
    And his Compassions sure.
5 For those who fear his sacred Name,
    The Lord at large provides:
His ancient Covenant the same
    Still in his Thoughts abides.

6 The Might wherewith his Works are wrought
    He to his People shows;
And Portions, from the Gentiles brought,
    On them at large bestows.
7 His Works in Truth and Judgment done,
    His Precepts just and sure;
8 As first in Righteousness begun,
    Through ev'ry Age endure.

9 The Lord his People once redeem'd,
    And gave them lasting Laws;
And still his holy Name, esteem'd,
    Our Veneration draws.
10 True Wisdom springs from Godly Fear:
    An Understanding pure
Will in Obedience best appear,
    And its just Praise endure.

PSAL. cxij.

1 O Praise the Lord! All Blessings wait
    On him who fears his Name;
In whom his just Commands create
    Pure Love's immortal Flame.

2 Mighty on Earth his Seed shall be,
    His Generation bless'd :
3 His Righteousness shall last, and he
    In Wealth and Plenty rest.

4 To Men of upright Hearts the Light,
    Through gloomy Darkness, shines.
 Mercy's the righteous Man's Delight :
    To Love his Soul inclines.
5 He's pitiful to Men distress'd,
    And lends to those in Need :
 In Judgment, from his milder Breast
    No cruel Words proceed.

6 He ne'er shall move; his Memory
    Shall ever sweetly last :
7 From Fear, through heavy Tidings, free;
    His Heart in God be fast.
8 His Heart, from cold Despair secur'd;
    Can on his God repose,
 Till of the Down-fall he's assur'd
    Of all his angry Foes.

9 With plenteous Doles his lib'ral Hand
    The needy Poor supp'ies :
 His Righteousness shall ever stand ;
    His Strength, with Honour rise.
10 Ill Men, enrag'd, his Happiness
    With envious Eyes shall view ;
 And gnash, and pine; and deep Distress
    Their blasted Hopes pursue.

PSAL. cxiij. *Proper Tune.*

1 O Praise the Lord ! his Praises sing,
    Ye Servants of th' Eternal King !
2 Bless, ever bless his sacred Name !

PSAL. cxiij.

1 From the firſt Buſhes of the Day,
  Till Night her ſable Wings diſp'ay,
    His Name's immortal Praiſe proclaim!
4 The Lord o'er all the Nations reigns:
  The Lord's iluſtrious Glory ſtains
    The brighteſt Star, the cleareſt Sky.
5 What Man, what God, would we compare
  With Him, whoſe lofty Dwellings are,
    Above all Heav'ns, exalted high?

6 Yet thence his Providential Eyes
  Survey the never-reſting Skies,
    And all our humble World below.
7 He helps the Wretched from the Floor;
  And from the Dung-hill lifts the Poor;
    His Goodneſs, and his Strength to ſhow.
8 Thence, He exalts their meaner Fate
  To Majeſty, and Princely State;
    And bids 'em Crowns and Sceptres claim.
9 He makes the barren Womb conceive,
  O'er-joy'd a youthful Race to leave.
  O praiſe! ô ever praiſe his Name.

Another Metre.

1   PRaiſe God! ô praiſe the Lord,
    Ye Saints, with one Accord!
  His holy Name, with Praiſe, proclaim;
    His holy Acts record!
2   His Name with Praiſe attend,
    Till Time it ſelf ſhall end!
3 His Fame diſp'ay, from dawning Day,
    Till Night's dark Shades deſcend.

4   God's o'er the Nations, high:
    His Glories paſs the Sky.
5 What God's ador'd as our great Lord;
    Or with his Height can vye?

6 Yet, condescending, He
  Through Heav'n and Earth can see,
7 The Poor to raise, who spend their Days
  In Want and Miserie.

8 His Smiles with Honour grace
  Those who the Dust embrace;
With Kings to vye in Majesty,
  And rule his chosen Race.
9 At his All-quick'ning Word
  The barren Womb's restor'd,
With Joy t' embrace a lively Race.
  Praise then, ô praise the Lord!

PSAL. CXIV.

1 WHen *Israel*'s Tribes, when *Jacob*'s Race
  From barb'rous *Egypt* went,
2 Then *Judah* was his holy Place,
  Israel his Government.
3 The Seas and *Jordan* saw their God,
  Advancing in their Head:
The Seas, amaz'dly parting, stood,
  And *Jordan* backward fled.

4 The Mountains, at the dreadful Sight,
  Leap'd up like frighted Rams:
The Hills, with the surprizing Fright,
  Skip'd like the trembling Lambs.
5 What terrify'd the parting Seas,
  That they divided stood?
What Fears could *Jordan*'s Currents seize,
  Or turn his hasty Flood?

6 What made the lofty Mountains leap,
  So like the frighted Rams?
The little Hills on crouded Heaps
  To run, like trembling Lambs?

7 Ne'er

PSAL. cxiv.

Ne'er ask the Cause! When *Jacob*'s God
    Appears, with Glories crown'd,
His dreadful Looks, his awful Nod,
    The trembling World confound.

3 And when his thirsty Nation prays,
    He turns the Rocks to Springs:
And from dry Flints, by wond'rous Ways,
    Unceasing Fountains brings.

Another Metre: As the 113*th.*

1,2 ISrael, of old; their Maker chose,
    His Empire, and his Name's Repose;
  And, more than all the Nations lov'd:
And with his own Almighty Hand,
From cruel *Egypt*'s barb'rous Land,
  Their happy Tribes in Peace remov'd.
3 The Sea his marching Armies view'd;
The Sea a while, as doubtful, stood;
  But soon, with wild Amazement, fled.
Old *Jordan*'s Streams, with headlong Haste,
Astonish'd *Merom*'s Waves re-pass'd,
  And backward flew, to find their Head.

4 The Mountains vast, which proudly bore
Their Heads above the Clouds before,
  Like Rams, from their Foundations leap'd:
The lesser Hills, as frighted Lambs
Run trembling to their he'pless Dams,
  Beneath their Parent-Mountains crept:
5 What made the Seas, divided, fly?
What made old *Jordan*'s Waters try,
  With backward Streams, to find their Spring?
6 What made the Mountains leap, like Rams?
The lesser Hills, like trembling Lambs,
  Close to their Parent-Mountains cling?

7 Slightly, alas! they mov'd or fear'd!
 At him the World amaz'd appear'd;
  The World before its Maker quakes:
 His look who now in *Jacob* reigns,
 And there his holy House maintains;
  The settled frame of Nature shakes.
8 Let then the Seas desert the Shore,
 Let *Jordan*'s Banks be fill'd no more,
  Let barren Sands around us ly,
 Our God can change with wondrous ease
 The Flints to Springs, the Rocks to Seas,
  And all his Peoples Wants supply.

PSAL. CXV.

1 TO us, dear Lord, to us no Praise,
   But to thy Name is due;
 For Mercy lays thy gracious Ways,
   And all thy Words are true.
2 Why should the foolish Gentiles cry,
   Where's He whom God they call?
3 Our God's on High above the Sky,
   And acts his Pleasure all.

4 Their Gods of other Tempers are,
   Fine Silver, weighty Gold:
 And Men with care such Gods prepare,
   And then their Gods uphold.
5 They ne're could speak, and ne're could see,
   Tho' made with Mouths and Eyes.
6 And louder he than Storms must be,
   Who can their Ears surprise.

6 The strongest Stench, the noblest Sweet
   Their Nostrils can't invade;
7 Their Hands can't meet, nor feel; their Feet
   Were ne're for walking made.

With

PSAL. CXV.

With all abusive Scorns appear
  Before their Deities,
Yet shan't you there one Murmur hear,
  So still their Anger lies.

8 Wise as their senseless Gods are those
  Who first advanc'd the Trade,
And such are those whose Souls repose
  On what their Hands have made.

Part 2.

9 O ye of *Jacob*'s wiser Seed,
  On God securely trust!
He'll help with speed in times of need,
  And ever shield the just.
10 O ye of *Aaron*'s sacred Breed,
  On God securely trust!
He'll help with speed in times of need,
  And ever shield the Just.

11 Ye who with Fear your Maker heed,
  In him securely trust;
He'll help with speed in times of need,
  And still defend the Just.
12 The Lord has kept us still in mind,
  His Priests shall all be bless.
Our Tribes shall find his Blessings kind
  On all their Dwellings rest.

13 The Lord will all his Servants bless,
  The Rich, Poor, Young and old;
14 And Happiness with vast access
  Shall you and yours uphold.
15 You're by that great Creator blest,
  Who bade the World to rise,
16 And who possest of sacred Rest,
  Lives high above the Skies.

17 O're Earth, and all that Earth contains,
    For mortal Men design'd,
 Man freely reigns, and God maintains
    The Gift to them resign'd.
18 The Dead, nor those can blaze thy Fame,
    Who sink to silence down;
19 But we thy Name with Praise proclaim,
    And endless Blessings crown.

PSAL. CXVI.

1 THe Lord who heard my Voice and Prayer,
    My Lord my Love shall be;
2 On him I'll call with constant Care,
    Who bow'd his Ear to me.
3 The Chains of Death engag'd me round,
    Me hellish Pains surpriz'd,
 And Troubles oft, and Anguish found,
    And Sorrows exercis'd.

4 Then in the Lord's prevailing Name
    To God I humbly pray'd,
 Thy Help, thy Favour, Lord, I claim,
    My Soul, dear Saviour, aid!
5 The Lord is kind, and righteous too,
    And Mercy freely shows,
6 He helps the weak, and swiftly flew
    To save my Soul from Woes.

7 Turn then my Soul, return to Rest!
    The Lord was kind to thee,
8 Thro' him I 'scap'd Death's cold Arrest,
    My Eyes from Tears are free.
 He keeps my Feet from Falls, and I
    My Woes, by him, survive,
9 And in return I'll gratefully,
    As in his Presence, live.

Part

Part 2.

10 So I believ'd, and so I spoke,
    But sore afflicted I
11 Thus out in hasty Passion broke;
    Men sure are sold to lye.
12 But what Returns, Lord, shall I make
    For all thy Loves to me?
13 Thy Blessed Cup with Praise I'le take,
    And duly call on Thee.

14 My Vows to God I''e offer here,
    Abroad in open Light;
15 The Death of all his Saints is dear
    In their Redeemer's Sight.
16 Lord, I'm thy Servant, humbly I
    My self thy Servant own,
  Thy Handmaid's Son, from Slavery
    By Thee discharg'd alone.

17 To Thee the Sacrifice of Praise
    My Sacrifice shall be;
  And in the Lords great Name I'le raise
    My suppliant Hands to Thee.
18 Here, Lord, to Thee I'le pay my Vows
    In all the Peoples Sight,
19 In *Salem*, in thy holy House;
    O praise the Lord of Might!

PSAL. cxvij.

1 O Praise th' Eternal Lord,
    Ye Nations all around!
  His Goodness thro' the World record;
    His glorious Acts resound!
2 On us, and all our Race,
    His Mercy largely flows,

PSAL. CXVIIJ.

His Truth no Time can e're deface,
Nor Force his Power oppose.

Or thus.

1. PRaise God ! & praise our mighty Lord,
Ye Nations all around !
His Goodness thro' the Wor'd record,
His wondrous Acts resound !
1 For on our selves, and all our Race
His Mercy largely flows,
His Truth no Time can e're deface,
Nor Force his Arm oppose.

PSAL. CXVIIJ.

1 THe Lord, the great *Jehovah* praise,
He's good in all his Ways :
His Mercies sure unchang'd endure,
His Goodness ne're decays,
2 Let *Jacob*'s long protected Race
Adore his wondrous Grace,
His Mercies sure unchang'd endure,
When Time resigns his Place.

3 Let *Aaron*'s sacred Heirs proclaim
The Lords exalted Name :
His Mercies sure unchang'd endure,
His Goodness still the same.
4 O ye who God's Commands obey,
With grateful Praises say,
His Mercies sure unchang'd endure,
His Mercies ne're decay.

5 In Streights I call'd on Him, and He
From Streights soon set me free.
6 To God I'm Dear, and ne're can fear
What Man can do to me.

7 The

7 The Lord, among my kindest Friends,
   His own Assistance sends.
My longing Eye shall soon descry
   My Foes expected Ends.

8 In God the Lord it's better far
      To trust our Hopes and Care,
   Then to repose our Hopes in those,
      Who wretched Mortals are.
9 In God the Lord it's better far
      To fix our Hopes and Care,
   Then to repose our Trust in those
      Who mighty Princes are.

Part 2.

10 I, When the Nations round me ply'd,
      In God their Strength defy'd;
11 They compassed me, but easily
      I so their Force out-vy'd.
12 Tho' me, like Bees, they closely ply'd,
      Like blazing Thorns they dy'd:
   In Gods great Name I quench'd their Flame,
      And all their Strength defy'd.

13 Oft hast thou push'd, unmanly Foe,
      To work my overthrow;
   But thro' Gods Aid, tho' oft afraid,
      I still in Safety go.
14 God by his Might has made me strong,
      My God's my daily Song;
   Salvation He ordain'd for me,
      Who to himself belong.

15 Sweet Tunes of Joy and Health abide
      Where righteous Men reside;
   Gods Hand is grown renown'd alone,
      For Deeds of Valour try'd.

17 His Hand's alone deserv'dly nam'd;
    His Hand on high proclaim'd,
His Hand is grown renown'd alone,
    For valiant Actions fam'd.

17 I still shall live, and still declare,
    How great his Actions are.
18 I felt his Rod, but still my God
    My Life wou'd kindly spare.
19 Let the wide Gates of Righteousness
    Now grant me free access;
I'le gladly there with Thanks appear,
    And God my Saviour bless.

Part 3.

20 Gods House his holy Gates are near;
    The Righteous enter there:
21 I'le praise the Lord, his Help record,
    Who would his Suppliant hear.
22 That Solid Rock, that Noble Stone
    Off by the Builders thrown;
Now all the Coines securely joyns,
    And makes the Building One.

23 The Lords great Work it was, and we
    Amaz'd the Wonder see.
24 God made this Day, now Joys shall sway,
    And Mirth triumphant be.
25 Hear, Lord, ô save at last, and make
    Our favour'd Actions take,
Our Business bless with kind Success,
    Lord, for thy Mercy's sake!

26 O blest be He who kindly came
    In Gods Almighty Name!
You who before his House adore,
    To you we wish the same.

7 Us God the Lord with Light supplies,
    O bind the Sacrifice!
With Cords it nigh his A'tars tie,
    Till there it bleeds and dies.

8 Thou, Lord, art God alone to me,
    I'le Praises sing to Thee.
By me thy Name, thy g'orious Fame
    Shall still exalted be.
9 The Lord our great *Jehovah* praise!
    He's good in all his Ways;
His Mercies sure unchang'd endure,
    His Mercy ne're decays.

PSAL. cxix. *Aleph*, 1. *Beth*, 2.

1 BLest are the Men whose perfect Ways
    Gods purer Laws confine,
2 Who keep his Word, and all their Days
    To Him in Heart incline.
3 No Sins to such can p'easing be
    As by his Orders move.
4 And thou commandedst, Lord, that we
    Thy Rules should keep and love.

5 Oh that my Footsteps guided sure,
    Could by thy Statutes tread!
6 Then should I live from Shame secure,
    When thy Commands I read.
7 I'le praise thee with an upright Heart,
    When I thy Judgments know.
8 I'le keep thy Laws; o ne're depart!
    To me no Stranger grow!

9 How may a Youth his Ways improve?
    If he thy Word obey.
10 To Thee with all my Soul I move,
    O never let me stray!

11 I in my Bosom hide thy Word,
　　From Sin to guard my Heart.
12 To me, b'est God, thy Grace afford,
　　And all thy Laws impart!

13 Thy Judgments, Lord, my Soul esteems,
　　My ready Lips declare;
14 To me thy Word more pleasing seems,
　　Then noblest Treasures are.
15 I on thy Precepts meditate,
　　Thy Laws before me set;
16 Thy Statutes all my Joys create,
　　Thy Words I ne're forget.

Gimel, 3. Daleth, 4.

17 Oh let me live! my God be kind,
　　So I thy Words shall keep.
18 Unclose my Eyes, by Nature blind,
　　To view thy Wonders deep!
19 O don't from me a Stranger, Lord,
　　Thy Testimonies hide!
20 For constant Cares to get thy Word,
　　My longing Soul divide.

21 Thy Judgments break the cursed Proud,
　　Who from thy Precepts stray.
22 Me, Lord, from flouting Scorners shroud,
　　For I thy Words obey!
23 Great Kings in Council curst my Name,
　　But I thy Statutes chose.
24 Thy Statutes all my Joys enflame,
　　My Counsels all compose.

25 My Soul, Lord, for thy Promise spare,
　　In Dust which prostrate lies.
26 Thou hear'st how I thy Ways declare,
　　O teach, and make me wise.

O Make me know thy Precepts, so
   I'le spread thy Works the more.
My Heart, with melting Cares brought low,
   Lord, by thy Word restore!

From me all lying Ways remove,
   To me thy Laws impart
For all the Paths of Truth I love,
   Thy Judgments fill my Heart.
I to thy Laws adhere, dear God,
   From Shame my Life discharge!
I'le run the Ways thy Saints have trod,
   If thou my Heart enlarge.

He, 5. Vau, 6.

Lord, teach me thy commanded way,
   And I'le observe it still.
My Heart let Understanding sway,
   Thy Laws my Heart shall fill.
By thy Commands, ô make me tread,
   For them I dearly love.
Let no false Lusts my Heart mislead,
   While by thy Rules I move!

From Vanity, ô-turn my Eyes,
   And make me live to Thee!
Thy Word on which my Soul relies,
   And fears, make good to me!
Reproach from me and Scandal take,
   But, Lord, thy Judgments give!
I for thy Precepts long, ô make
   Me by thy Justice live!

Thy Mercy, thy Salvation too,
   As promis'd, Lord, bestow!
So shall I hush the scornful Crew,
   And yet more faithful grow.

43 Never, ô never, Lord, withdraw
    Thy Word and Truth from me!
44 So thy just Judgments and thy Law
    My constant Guides shall be.

45 My happy Course at last I'le steer,
    In thy Commands secure.
46 Thy Testimonies Kings sha'l hear,
    Yet I no shame endure
47 I'le in thy lov'd Commands delight,
    For them my Hands I'le raise.
48 Thy Statutes study Day and Night,
    And thy Commandments praise.

Zain, 7. *Cheth*, 8.

49 Thy Word once pass'd, remember, Lord,
    In which thou mad'st me trust.
50 Thy Word my drooping Soul restor'd,
    Reviv'd my sinking Dust.
51 The scoffing Proud my Soul deride,
    Yet I thy Laws pursue.
52 With me thy Judgments pass'd abide,
    And all my Joys renew.

53 I trembled at their dreadful Fate,
    Who from thy Precepts stray'd;
54 But them I in my banish'd State,
    My daily Musick made.
55 Lord, on thy Name I muse by Night,
    And keep thy Righteous Laws:
56 Such Blessings from thy favouring Sight,
    A just Obedience draws.

57 Thou'rt all my Portion, Lord, I said
    I'de keep thy sacred Word:
58 And for thy Grace devoutly pray'd,
    Thy Grace, Dear Lord, afford!

9 I weigh'd my Works, and so thy Ways
   My careful Footsteps trac'd:
10 And that I might thy Laws obey,
   I flew with winged haste.

11 Tho' impious Bands my Wealth surprize,
   I can't forget thy Ways
12 But I, when I at Midnight rise,
   Thy righteous Judgments praise.
13 I love their Company, who fear
   Thy Name, and keep thy Word.
14 Thy Mercies round the World appear,
   Thy Statutes teach me, Lord!

Teth, 9. Jod, 10.

65 Lord, from thy Hands I Good receive,
   For all thy Words are true.
66 Teach me, since I thy Laws believe,
   Good Sense and Knowledge too!
67 I sinn'd, till by Affliction taught
   Thy sacred Words to know.
68 For me all Good thy Hands have wrought,
   To me thy Statutes show!

69 The Proud assau't my Soul with lies,
   But I sincerely move.
70 And while their Hearts with Fatness rise,
   Thy Laws entirely love.
71 Lash'd by thy Rod, my Heart enclines
   To keep thy Laws with Care.
72 Those Laws which richer far than Mines
   Of Gold and Silver are.

73 Thy Hands have made and fashion'd me,
   Thy Judgments make me know!
74 So thy pleas'd Saints my Care shall see,
   While in thy Paths I go.

75 I

75 I know thy Judgments Lord are just,
    Thy Love afflicted me.
76 Make good thy Word! my Comfort must
    Alone descend from Thee.

77 Lord send thy Mercys! quickned so
    I'le in the Laws delight.
78 Let shame thy treacherous Proud o're-throw
    But I'le thy Laws recite.
79 O let thy Saints, who know thy Will,
    With me as Friends appear!
80 When my sound Heart thy Statutes fill,
    I no Disgrace can fear.

Caph, 11. *Lamed*, 12.

81 Thy Health my longing Soul desires,
    And on thy Promise waits.
82 And while thy Comforts it requires,
    My Sight with Woes abates.
83 Dry'd up with Grief my strength appears,
    Yet I thy Laws retain.
84 How many are thy Servant's days?
    O now my Foes restrain!

85 The Proud for me their Pitts have made,
    Against thy righeous Law.
86 Me from their Wrongs by thy kind Aid,
    And Faithful Precepts draw!
87 Lord They'd consum'd me quite, but I
    Ne're from thy Precepts went.
88 In Goodness raise my Soul! I'le try
    To keep thy Testament.

89 Firm Lord as Heaven thy Promise stands.
90   Thy Truth from Age to Age,
    The Earth, form'd by thy mighty Hands,
    Stands by thy Patronage.

91 All by thine Ordinance ensur'd,
    To Thee their Service pay:
92 But Woes my Ruine had procur'd,
    But that I kept thy Way.

93 I'le ne're forget thy Precepts kind,
    Since oft by them reviv'd.
94 I'm thine, ô save me! for my Mind
    Has on thy Precepts liv'd.
95 The Wicked watch'd to ruine me,
    But I thy Statutes read;
96 And th' end of all Perfection see,
    But those all Bounds exceed.

Mem, 13, *Nun*, 14.

97 Lord, how I love thy Laws! by those
    My serious Studies move;
98 By them I far above my Foes,
    In Wisdom's Rules improve.
99 Thy Testimonies teach me more
    Than all my Teachers know.
100 I by thy Statutes wise before
    My reverend Elders grow.

101 My Feet all wicked Ways declin'd,
    To keep thy sacred Word.
102 Thy Judgments duly us'd my Mind
    With Heavenly Wisdom stor'd.
103 Honey to those pure Sweets must yield,
    With which thy Words are blest:
104 So I with thy wise Precepts fill'd,
    All lying Ways detest.

105 Thy glorious Words my Footsteps guide,
    And fill my Paths with Light:
106 I've sworn, and as by Oath I'm tied,
    I'le keep thy Judgments right.

107 I'me much distrest: ô by thy Word,
    My fainting Soul revive!
108 Accept my willing Praises Lord,
    To me thy Judgments give!

109 Tho' in my Hands my Life I bear,
    I can't forget thy Law.
110 Nor can the Sinners crafty Snare,
    From that my Soul withdraw.
111 Thy Will's th' Inheritance design'd,
    For my rejoicing Heart,
112 Which to thy Statutes all inclin'd,
    From Them can ne're depart.

Samech, 15. *Gnain*, 16.

113 I love thy Laws; but those that own,
    All vain Opinions hate.
114 Thou art my Covering Shield alone,
    And on thy Word I wait.
115 Begone ye sinful Crew! for I
    At pure Obedience aim.
116 With promis'd Help my Life supply,
    And guard my Hope from shame!

117 Uphold me, then I'me safe, and I
    Shall all thy Laws respect.
118 Trod down by thee those Straglers dy
    Who Cheats and Lies project.
119 Thy dear lov'd Word, like Dross, the Bands
    Of Sinners purg'd away.
120 And I the Judgments of thy Hands,
    With awful Fear survey.

121 I've done what's Just and Right; ô save
    Me from Oppressions Force!
122 Thy kind Assurance Lord I crave,
    To stop the Tyrants Course:

PSAL. cxix.

123 My Eyes for thy Salvation fail,
    And promis'd Righteousness,
124 With me, Dear Lord, in Mercy deal,
    And with Me Statutes bless!

125 Make Me thy Servant Wise; I'll then
    Thy Testimonies know!
126 He'p Lord, its time! lest impious Men,
    Thy Law should overthrow.
127 For this I love thy Precepts more,
    Then heaps of purest Gold;
128 I know their Justice, but abhor,
    The Paths which Lies uphold.

Pe, 17. *Tsadi*, 18.

129 Thy Testimonies wondrous are!
    My Soul to keep them tries,
130 Thy Words explain'd, the Truth declare,
    And make the Simplest wise.
131 Thy Words more sweet than cooling Winds,
    To fainting Spirits are.
132 That Pitty those who love Thee find,
    O let thy Servant share!

133 If by thy Rule thou fix my Ways,
    No Sinn shall conquer me.
134 And me from Mans Oppression raise,
    Then mine thy Laws shall be.
135 Smile Lord on me, and let thy Laws
    Thy Servants Soul convert!
136 Tears drown my flowing Eys, because
    Vain Men thy Laws desert,

137 Essential Justice Reigns in Thee,
    Thy Judgments all are right.
138 Thy Testimonies faithfully,
    To Righteousness evence.

PSAL. CXIX.

139 Zeal burns me up because my Foes,
　　Thy sacred Word forget.
140 That Word which as it purely flows,
　　On it my Heart is set.

141 I'm Lord despis'd and mean; but still
　　My Soul thy Law retains.
142 Thy Laws, the Truth, thy Righteous Will,
　　From Age to Age remains.
143 Delight to me, tho' compast round,
　　With Woes, thy Statutes give.
144 Their Justice every Age has found;
　　O make me Wise to Live!

Koph, 19. *Resch*, 20.

145 I cry aloud; Lord, hear my cry;
　　I'll keep thy Statutes sure.
146 I Pray, ô save me, and I'll try
　　Thy Testimonies pure.
147 My Crys Days early dawn prevent,
　　While for thy Word I Wait.
148 All Night my wakeful Heart's intent,
　　On them to meditate,

149 O Hear me, and my Spirits by,
　　Thy Judgments Lord renew!
150 For they approach who virtue Fly,
　　And Mischiefs ways pursue.
158 Thou Lord art ever near to Thine,
　　And thy Commands are True.
152 I knew long since thy Laws Divine,
　　Were strong and lasting too.

153 Weigh Lord, my sufferings! set Me free,
　　Who don't forget thy Laws!
154 And for thy promise quicken me,
　　O save and plead my Cause!

155 Salvations far from Sinners who,
　　Thy Statutes ne're pursue.
156 But as thy Mercys kindly flow,
　　My strength, just God, renew!

157 Tho cruel Foes unnumber'd are,
　　I don't thy Laws decline.
158 But see with Grief how Sinners dare;
　　Against thy Word combine.
159 See how I in thy Laws delight,
　　In Love revive my Soul!
160 Truth founds thy Word, thy Judgments right;
　　Shall Times last Force controul.

Schin, 21. *Than,* 22.

161 Pursued by Kings, with Causeless Hate;
　　Yet more thy Words I fear'd.
162 In me more Joys thy Words create,
　　Then Spoils in Battel clear'd.
163 Lies I with Hate and scorn disclaim,
　　But Love thy Laws to trust.
164 Seven times a day I praise thy Name,
　　For all thy Judgments Just.

165 They live in Peace, who love thy Word,
　　No Cares disturb their Rest.
166 I wait for thy Salvation, Lord,
　　With thy Commandments blest.
167 My Soul thy Testimonies takes,
　　And loves exceedingly.
168 Thy Laws its whole Employment makes;
　　My ways before Thee lie.

169 Lord, let my Crys approach thy Place,
　　Thy Statutes make me Wise!
170 My Prayers ascend, and from thy Face
　　My Promis'd Rescue rise!

N 2　　　　　　　171 My

171 My Lips shall utter Praises well,
    When all thy Statutes taught.
172 And on thy Word, my Tongue shall dwell,
    And Orders justly wrought.

173 Lord help me with thy gracious Hand,
    For I thy Precepts chose.
174 I long for thy Salvation, and
    My Joy thy Laws compose.
175 O let me live and praise thy Name,
    Thy Judgments help my Cause!
176 And me, poor wandring Sheep, reclaim
    Who n'er forget thy Laws!

PSAL. CXX.

1 TO God in deep Distress, I cry
    Who bows his Ear to me.
2 My Soul, Dear Lord, from Lips which lie,
    And Tongues deceitful free!
3 What shall be pay'd, what done to Thee;
    Thou false deceitful Tongue?
4 Thy Portion burning Coals shall be,
    And Arrows from the strong.

5 Wo's me that I constrain'd so long,
    In Forreign Tents abide!
  Wo's me who banish'd thus among:
    Men us'd to Blood reside!
6 My Soul hath sojourn'd long with those,
    Who hate the Thoughts of Peace,
7 If I the Name of Peace propose,
    Their Quarrels most encrease.

Another Metre, proper Tune.

1 TO God in Troubles I
    And deep Distresses cry,
  And He receives my Prayer.

2 Lord

PSAL. cxx.

2 Lord, save my Soul from those,
   Whose Lips with Falshood close;
      Whose Tongues deceitful are.

3 What shall be paid to Thee,
   Or what thy Portion be
      Thou while deceitful Tongue?
4 Hot Coals of Juniper,
   Shalt thou from Justice bear,
      And Arrows of the strong.

5 Woe's me alas! that I
   Must thro' necessity,
      In dismal Tents abide!
   Woe's me! who must so long
   In Banishment, among
      Blood-thirsty Brutes reside!

6 My Soul has sojourn'd long
   With those who live by wrong,
      But hate the Thoughts of Peace.
7 When I for Peace would move
   That Peace I dearly love.
      Their Feuds and Jarrs encrease.

PSAL. cxxj.

1 UP to the Hills I lift my Eyes,
      From whence my Aids descend?
2 The Lord who made the Earth and Skyes,
      Will sure assistance send.
3 Hee'l fix thy Foot secure: No sleeps
      Thy Watchman can surprize.
4 That God who *Israel* safely keeps,
      Ne're shuts his wakeful Eyes.

5 The Lord is thy Protector sure,
      And he defends thy Head.

Thy Maker will his shade secure
   O're all thy Dwellings spread.
6 So all the Sun's fierce Summer Beams
   Shall never make thee ill.
On thee the Moons unwholesome Gleams
   No hurtful Dews distil.

7 The Lord from Ills shall keep thee free,
   Thy Soul from Harms secure:
8 Go out, come in, he'll follow thee,
   His Loves unchang'd endure.

Another Metre: Proper Tune.

1 ABove the Hills I raise my Eyes,
      And thence assur'd expect,
      That God should me protect.
2 From God my certain Aid shall rise
      From that God whose Word gave Birth
      To the Skies, and humbler Earth.

3 No stumbling shall thy Feet surprize,
      Thy Guardian never sleeps,
4   That God who Israel keeps,
   Can never shut his wakeful Eyes;
5   But with his Protection blest,
      Thou beneath his Shade shalt rest.

6 The scorching Sun's directest Beams
      Unhurt thy Head shalt bear,
      And no Distemper fear:
   Nor shall the Moon's malignant Gleams,
      Poisonous Vapours, us'd to kill
      With her Midnight Dews distil.

7 The Lord from Harms shall keep thee free,
      And all those Ills controul,
      Which might affect thy Soul.

8 Go

PSAL. cxxij.

8 Go out, come in, he follows thee,
    And with Goodness thee secures,
    Which from Age to Age endures.

PSAL. cxxij.

1 WIth Joy I heard the Captives cry,
    Gods House is all our Quest.
2 Our wearied Steps shall chearfully
    In Salem's Entrance rest.
3 As where sweet Peace and Beauty join,
    So Salem's Buildingss grow;
4 And there God's holy Tribes combine,
    And to his Presence flow.

There Israels Testimony stands,
    And Gods great Name they praise.
5 The Throne of Justice there commands,
    And *David's* Offspring sways.
6 O pray for *Salem's* Peace! may those
    Who love thee prosper still!!
7 May Peace thy Battlements compose,
    Thy Houses Plenty fill!

8 For my dear faithful Brethrens sakes,
    O may thy Joys encrease!
And where my God his Dwelling makes,
    I'll seek thy Wealth and Peace.

Another Metre. Proper Tune.

1 I Heard with inward Joys
    The Captives cheerful Cries,
Gods holy House is a'l our Quest.
    Our often wand'ring Feet
    In one Design shall meet,
And in the Gates of *Salem* rest.

3   As where the Sweets of Peace
       With curious Arts increase;
So *Salem*'s happy Buildings rise,
4   For there the Tribes ascend,
       And *Israel*'s God attend,
And Thanks and Praises sacrifice.

5   There stands the Judgment-seat,
       There *David* once was great,
And still its to his Offspring due.
6   O pray for *Salem*'s Peace!
       O may thy Friends encrease!
And good Success their Loves pursue!
7   May Peace and Wealth abound
       Thy Walls and Houses round,
And for my faithful Brethrens sakes,
       Thy Cause I'le countenance,
       Thy Good and Peace advance
Where God his glorious Dwelling makes.

PSAL. cxxiij.

1 UP toward thy Dwelling-place the Skies,
       Almighty Lord to Thee
We raise our sad despairing Eyes,
       Consum'd with Misery.
2 As some poor beaten Slave would watch
       His Master's angry Hands,
Or some corrected Maid dispatch
       Her Mistresses Commands.

Yet view each Look, each turning Glance,
       To find if Pitty there
Would in their smoother Brows advance,
       Or in their Eyes appear.
So justly we, chastis'd for Sins,
       In patient Silence wait,
Till God, once more appeas'd, begins
       To raise our mournful State.

3 Pity, ô pity, Lord, our Woes!
    O hear our earnest Cries!
  And let thy Vengeance silence those
    Who our sad State despise.
4 Enough, dear Lord, enough we've born
    The scoffing World's Abuse,
  And all that Insolence and Scorn,
    Which Pride and Wealth produce.

PSAL. CXXIV.

1 Had not the Lord our Cause maintain'd,
    Sing now, and show a grateful Mind.
2 Had not the Lord our Right sustain'd,
    When Men of Blood our Fall design'd.

3 Our Land had been at once devour'd,
    All swallow'd by the barbarous Foe;
4 As Brooks by mighty Rains o're-pour'd,
    At once the Neighbouring Meads o'reflow.

5 Thus had our happy Days been past,
    Our Hopes, our Joys, our Souls Destroy'd.
  Our Foes yet scarce appeas'd at last,
    Or their inhuman Entrails cloy'd.

6 But blest, ô ever blest be He
    Whose careful Love our Souls redeem'd!
  And us from cruel Hands set free,
    His Name be prais'd, his Works esteem'd.

7 We 'scap'd as little Birds escape,
    When just beneath the Fowler's Hand;
  Our God disclos'd the Fatal Trap,
    And we, through Him, in Safety stand.

8 Let then the cruel World combine,
   And Malice private Plots devise,
  Our Help's at hand, our Hope divine
   On God, who made the World, relies.

Another Metre. Proper Tune.

1 THis grateful Song may shew a grateful Mind,
   Had not the mighty God our Cause maintain'd,
2 Had not our gracious Lord our Right sustain'd,
  When cruel Men, with barbarous Oaths combin'd,
  And to destroy our hated Land design'd.

3 Their Rage which for a proper Morsel sought,
  Their bloody Throats wide as Hell's dreadful Gate,
  Had gorg'd our Church, & swallow'd down the State.
4, 5 The Deeps the swelling Waves which proudly
    wrought
  A Flood quite o're our Souls at once had brought.

6 O blest be God who say'd the trembling Prey:
7 Our Souls as Birds from crafty Fowlers freed,
  And broke the Snares, and our Escape decreed!
8 Our Souls for Help on Him alone shall stay,
  Who made the worlds, and whom the worlds obey.

PSAL. CXXV.

1 THey fix'd, as *Sion's* Mount, endure,
   Who in their Maker trust:
2 As Mountains *Salem's* Walls secure,
   So God secures the Just.
3 Ill Men shan't o're the Good prevail,
   Or in their Quarters rest,
  Lest they beneath Temptations fail,
   Above their Strength opprest.

4 Be good and kind, dear Lord, to those,
   Who Peace and Goodness love!

PSAL. cxxvj.

To such thy gentle Smiles disclose,
  Whose Hearts are fix'd above!
5 But those who tread in Ways perverse,
  Gods just Revenge shall find:
Who'll Peace among his own disperse,
  And to his Saints be kind.

Another Metre. Proper Tune.

1 Those who on God have fix'd their Trust,
  Unmov'd, like *Sion*'s Mount, endure:
2 As Mountains *Salem*'s Walls secure,
So God Himself secures the Just,
  His Mercies endless store
  Shall last when Time's no more.

3 He checks the Wickeds angry Course,
  When they his holy Saints assail,
  They may, but never long, prevail:
Lest Faith crush'd by unequal Force,
  Should faintly quit the Field,
  And to the Tempter yield.

4 To those, dear God, who Goodness love,
  To Men of upright Hearts be kind!
  While those the Sinners Portion find,
Who stubborn and perversely move;
  But on God's Israel
  Shall Peace eternal dwell.

PSAL. cxxvj.

1 When Home the Lord his Captives lead,
    At first it seem'd a Dream;
2 But Joy was quickly round us spread,
    And Praise our glorious Theam.
  The very Gentile Nations round
    Cry'd out at once, amaz'd:

See how God's Favours there abound,
  How soon his Friends are rais'd!

3 God's Loves to Us indeed abound,
    Our Joys are truely great;
4 That Work which, Lord, thy Hands have found,
    O let thy Hands compleat!
  So *Judah*'s long deserted Lands
    Shall more Refreshments know,
  Then where soft Streams thro' Southern Sands,
    With constant Coolness flow.

5 Thus Men may sow in Tears, but hope
    To reap their Fields in Joy.
  Their precious Seed may give them Scope
    For Faith's Divine Employ.
6 Long may they wait, and long may fear
    Their Seed was vainly sown;
  Yet home their Sheaves triumphant bring,
    At last a Burden grown.

Another Metre. Proper Tune.

1 WHen God at last
      Return'd his happy Captives home,
  We all appear'd
      Like those who in their Slumbers dream.
2 Mirth from our Lips,
      Praise from our chearful Tongues would come.
  Mirth daily was
      Our Food, and Praise our daily Theam.
  The very Heathens round us wondring, cry'd,
  See how God's Love to them is magnifi'd!

3 God's Love to us
      Indeed is highly magnify'd.
  Our present Joys
      Are more than former Sorrows great.

4 Thou

4 Thou, Lord, who doſt
    Full Streams for Southern Lands provide.
O let our Re-
    ſtitution be at laſt compleat!
5 So *Judah*'s Lands ſhall more Refreſhment know,
Than Sands thro' which thy cooling Rivers flow.

    Thus, tho' ſwell'd Grief
        Rouls in with an impetuous Tide,
    Yet ſliding off,
        It ſoon its Place to Joy reſigns.
6 And he who pre-
        tious Seed on barren Mountains try'd,
    And thro' a fond
        Miſtake to cold Deſpair inclines:
Comes home at laſt with Joys triumphant Sound,
With weighty Sheves his fruitful Harveſt crown'd.

PSAL. cxxvij.

1 IF God to build the Houſe denies,
    The Workmen build in vain;
And Towns, without Gods wakeful Eyes,
    A needleſs Watch maintain.
2 Before the Mornings Buſhes riſe,
    Your daily Works renew,
And till the Stars remount the Skies,
    Your daily Works purſue.

Fare ne're ſo hard, it's all in vain,
    If yet by God unbleſt;
Do all, and but his Smiles obtain,
    You'll ſafely, ſweetly reſt.
3 Lo, Children from the pregnant Womb,
    By Gods beſt Influence grow,
4 Like Arrows, in their youthful Bloom,
    Shot from ſome Gyant's Bow.

5 O happy's he, whose Quiver's fill'd
   With such bright Shafts resound!
   He'll ne're to Force, nor Malice yield,
   While these his Foes confound.

Another Metre. Proper Tune.

1 IF God to build the House denies,
   The Workmen build, but build in vain,
   And Cities useless Guards maintain,
   If God withdraws his watchful Eyes.
      Gods Help out-does the Builders Art,
      And He performs the Watchman's Part.

2 Before the Morning-Blushes rise,
   Your daily painful Works renew,
   Your daily painful Works pursue,
   Till Night again obscures the Skies,
      Support your selves with meanest Fare,
      The Drink of Tears, the Bread of Care.

   In vain you toil, and build in vain,
   If God still at a Distance stands,
   And neither bless your Heads nor Hands.
   But if his Love you once obtain,
      Then rise, or watch, or fast, or weep,
      You'll safely live, and sweetly sleep.

3 Lo! Children from the pregnant Womb,
   By God's immediate Blessing grow,
4   Like Shafts sent from some Giants Bow
   They seem in all their youthful Bloom;
      They too can hurl their deadly Darts
      With steady Hands, and daring Hearts.

5 O happy's he, whose Quiver sounds
   With such important Shafts as these!
   The Man his Foes undaunted sees.

No Fear his Head or Heart confounds,
 Nor will he quit the Martial Field,
While these Support and Comfort yield.

PSAL. cxxviij.

HAppy, thrice happy Thou,
 Who in his own best way,
Dost to thy Great Creator bow,
 And his Commands obey!
His Blessings round thee wait,
 And on thy Labours rest,
Thy meaner, but contented State,
 With Peace and Safety blest.

Like some fair spreading Vine
 With purple Grapes o're-born;
So thy kind Mates chast Beauties shine,
 Her Fruits thy Walls adorn.
The lovely Mother she
 With hopeful Issue crown'd,
Her Sons, like Olive Plants, shall be
 Thy Tables planted round.

Thus sha'l the Lord his Grace
 On thee his Friend bestow,
To thee, from *Sion*'s sacred Place,
 A thousand Favours show.
Blest with a firm old Age,
 Thy happy Eyes shall see
Thy lively fruitful Heirs presage
 A long Posterity.

Thy happy Eyes shall see
 The Churches blest encrease,
Secur'd by long Felicity,
 And universal Peace.

PSAL. CXXIX.

1 ME from my Youth may *Ifrael* say,
    My Foes have oft oppreſt.
2 In vain, from Youthful Years have they
    Diſtur'd my Peaceful Reſt.
3 Deep o're my Back the Wicked plow'd,
    And long their furrows drew,
    And would of ſhort ſucceſſes proud,
    Their ſpiteful ways purſue.

4 But God, the Righteous Judge, with eaſe
    Their Cords in Pieces tore.
5 May Shame and Fear, theſe Wretches ſeize,
    Who hate to *Sion* bore!
6 Let them, like Corn on Houſes, dy
    Which Springs but quickly dyes,
7 Which Mowers paſs regardleſs by
    And Reapers, all deſpiſe.

8 No Paſſengers would kindly call,
    To ſuch as labour'd there,
Gods Bleſſing on Your Labours fall,
    His Name your Harveſt cheer!

PSAL. CXXX.

1 FRom gloomy Deeps, Dear Lord, to Thee
    From gloomy Deeps I cry'd.
2 O hear me! let thy Mercy be
    No more to me deny'd!
3 Shouldſt thou our Sinns ſeverely weigh,
    Who Lord thy Wrath could bear?
4 But Pardon is thy gentler Way,
    The Spring of Godly Fear.

5 My Soul, Lord, waits, it waits for Thee,
    And on thy Word depends.

PSAL. CXXX.

E're I the dawning Morning see,
   My Soul the Lord attends.
To him ô raise your Humble Eies,
   Poor *Israels* scatter'd Race!
With him kind Mercy treasur'd lies
   And never failing Grace.

From Him Redemption freely flows,
   And Hee'l redeem Thee too.
From all thy Sinns and all those Woes,
   Which justly Sinn pursue.

PSAL. CXXXj.

NO Prides aspiring Rage,
   No swelling Thoughts engage.
Dear God my Heart to bear a part
   With this corrupted Age.
I ne'r at Empire aim'd,
   Nor Crowns, nor Scepters claim'd,
Nor soar'd above with wanton Love,
   Of Mysteries enflam'd.

But as some Babe at Rest,
   Wean'd from its Mothers Breast;
Close Silence keeps with gentle sleeps,
   Or Smiling Slumbers blest,
So Lord my Soul set free
   From careful Vanity.
From Earths delights and unknown Flights,
   In Silence waits on Thee.

O Ye of *Israels* race,
   O seek his glorious Face!
On Him besure your Faith secure,
   And his Commands embrace!

PSAL. cxij.

1 Remember *Davids* Troubles Lord,
  How in Affliction He,
2 With faithful Vows engag'd his Word,
  O *Jacobs* God to Thee!
3 High tho my lofty Palace rise,
  With Cedar nobly ciel'd.
  And Beds with Golden Canopyes,
  Would downy Slumbers yield.

4 I'll ne'r my Rooms of State approach,
  Nor stretch my self at ease:
  No sleep shall on my Brows encroach
  My Lids no Slumbers please.
5 Till I that happy Place have found,
  By Heavenly Favour blest;
  Where *Jacobs* God on Holy ground,
  Will fix his glorious Rest.

It's done! and as our Meaner Race
  Of old their Maker chose.
So rough and mean's that wondrous Place
  Where hee'l at last repose,
6 *Ephrata's* Fields and *Shilohs* Plains,
  Are all alas! destroy'd!
And *Sions* Mount unsmooth'd remains,
  And rough, obscure, and void;

Yet there his Arke is fix'd, and there
  His sacred Altars stand;
Till there his Temples roofs appear,
  And all the Mount command.
7 Come let's approach the place! before
  His holy Altars bow,
And at his glorious Feet adore,
  And due Submission show!

Part

Part 2.

8 Rise Lord, thy Arke of Glory raise,
　　Assume thy chosen Seat!
　And on thy flock which humbly prays,
　　Thy Blessings Lord repeat!
9 Thy Priests with Righteousness invest,
　　Thy Saints for Joy shall sing,
10 For *Davids* sake his Offspring blest,
　　To Crowns and Scepters bring!

11 The Lord to *David* sware of old,
　　His Oath in Truth was made,
　Thy Seed shall still the Kingdom hold,
　　From Heirs to Heirs convey'd.
12 And if thy Sons with prudent Care
　　My Covenant observe.
　And from those Rules my Laws declare,
　　Shall never vainly swerve.

　I too will them as Kings support,
　　And thy continued Line:
　On *Salems* Throne in *Juda's* Court
　　From Age to Age shall shine.
13 *Sion* is Gods Election, where
　　Hee'l hold his Residence.
14 " Here will I always dwell, and here
　　" My long'd for Rest Commence.

15 " I'le their Provisions largely bless,
　　" Their Poor with plenty cloy.
16 " Their Priests with my Salvation dress,
　　" And fill their Saints with Joy.
17 " There *Davids* Branches ever strong,
　　" Shall fill the Regal Line,
　The Lamp of my Anointed long
　　" With settled Lustre shine.

18 Shame

18 Shame shall his envious Foes surround,
    But his illustrous Head
With starry Beams of Glory crown'd;
    Fresh Honours round him shed.

PSAL. cxxxiij.

1 HOw sweet, how charming is the Sight,
    Where prudent Christians move
In peaceful Ways, and all delight
    To wear the Chains of Love?
Then Kindness fills their tender Hearts,
    And shoots thro all their Eyes.
Each Tongue a Love unfeign'd imparts,
    And Love's their Exercise.

2 So when those fragrant Oils of old,
    The Head of *Aaron* crown'd,
And down his Head the Bo'som roll'd,
    And drench'd his Garments round.
From him the pleasant Odours thro'
    The Tabernacle flow'd,
And on the sacrificing Crew,
    A thousand Sweets bestow'd.

3 And as soft Rains, and pearly Dews
    On *Sion*'s Mount distill,
And Clouds their Silver Drops diffuse
    On *Hermon*'s fruitful Hill.
So God, where Men his Peace maintain,
    His Blessing largely sends,
And Love to all that heavenly Train,
    From Age to Age extends.

Another

Another Metre, as the 148.

Sweet Peace, bleft Charity,
　　How foft thy heavenly Charms,
When that uniting Tye
　　The Souls of Brethren arms;
　　　And foars above
　　Rough Nature's Jars,
　　And finful Wars,
　　　On Wings of Love!

More fweet than Balfams fhed,
　　By Gods divine Command,
On *Aaron*'s facred Head,
　　Which all his Garments ftain'd:
　　　And thence diftill'd,
　　Gods holy Place,
　　With heavenly Grace,
　　　And Odours fill'd.

More fweet than thofe foft Dews,
　　Which ancient *Hermon* crown'd,
Or Drops which Clouds diffufe
　　Gods holy Mount around.
　　　And all below
　　Kind warmth prevails,
　　And pleafant Dales
　　　With Plenty flow.

Where fuch fweet Concord reigns,
　　The God of Peace defcends;
The Church and State maintains,
　　And every Tribe defends.
　　　His Bleffings fall,
　　And Life and Eafe,
　　And lafting Peace
　　　Extends to all.

PSAL.

PSAL. CXXXIV.

1 YE who before the Lord,
     In nightly turns adore
 With Praise his wondrous Acts record,
     His gracious Smiles implore.
2 Up toward his holy Place
     Your Hands devoutly raise,
 And all those happy Hours embrace,
     To sing his glorious Praise.

3 For he at whose Command
     The World from Nothing rose,
 Great Blessings with a liberal Hand,
     On all his Church bestows.

PSAL. CXXXV.

1 O Praise the Lord, ye Saints, his Name,
     With grateful Anthems raise,
2 Who in his House your Stations claim,
     And fill his Courts with Praise!
3 Praise ye the Lord, the gracious Lord,
     For 'tis a pleasant Thing;
 When Men with Thanks his Name record,
     With Thanks his Praises sing.

4 For God himself his Israel chose,
     His own peculiar Care;
5 Vain Gods, in vain his Strength oppose,
     With him in vain compare.
6 Thro' the vast Deeps, Seas, Earth, and Skies
     God acts his pleasure all.
7 He bids the cloudy Vapours rise,
     And he commands their Fall.

Fierce

 Fierce Lightnings on his pouring Rains,
  At his Commands attend:
 Rough Winds he from his Treasures dreins,
  Which thence in Storms afcend.
8 God, the First-born, from Man to Beast,
  Thro trembling *Egypt* flew,
9 Him, by his dreadful Plagues oppreft,
  Diftracted *Egypt* knew.

 Pharaoh and all his Armies dy'd
  Beneath his weighty Hand
10 He many mighty Kings deftroy'd,
  And many a fruitful Land;
11 *Sihon* and *Og*, and all who reign'd
  Of *Canaan*'s Rea'ms poffeft,
12 Till *Ifrael*'s Race their Kingdoms gain'd,
  And there fecur'd their Reft.

Part 2.

13 Thy Name, and thy Memorial, Lord,
  From Age to Age endures.
14 Thy Juftice all thy Saints record,
  While that their Peace procures;
 For God for all their Sufferings griev'd,
  And their afflicted Cafe,
 Will them, from cruel Foes reliev'd,
  With tend'reft Loves embrace.

15 Idols for Gods, the Gentiles blind,
  Of Gold and Silver ufe,
 Whofe Mouths were ne're for Speech defign'd,
  Whofe Eyes the Light refufe.
16 No found could over-reach their Ears,
  No Breath their Lives declare;
17 Dull as their Gods, their Slaves appear,
  And fuch their Makers are.

19 The Lord, ô ye of *Israel*'s Race,
    O *Aaron*'s House proclaim!
20 Ye Levites, ye who seek his Grace,
    O Praise his sacred Name!
21 With Blessings from his holy Hill
    His Name and Acts record;
    Whose Glories all his Churches fill,
    Praise ye, ô praise the Lord!

PSAL. CXXXVj.

1 O Praise th' Eternal Lord,
2   The God of Gods adore!
    His Mercies sure unchang'd endure
    A never-failing Store.
3   O praise the Lord of Lords,
4   Who Wonders works alone!
    His Mercies sure unchang'd endure
    To endless Ages known.

5   Praise Him whose curious Hand
    Stretch'd out the lofty Skies:
    His Mercies sure unchang'd endure,
    When all expiring lies.
6   He made firm Land above
    The mighty Waters rise:
    His Mercies sure unchang'd endure,
    When Time and Nature dies.

7   Praise Him whose Wisdom first
    Set up the glorious Light:
    His Mercies sure unchang'd endure,
    As that immensely bright.
8   The Sun to rule the Day,
9   The Moon and Stars the Night:
    His Mercies sure unchang'd endure
    In all the Nations sight.

10   He all their eldest Hopes
      Thro' *Egypt*'s Land destroy'd :
  His Mercies sure unchang'd endure,
      O're all his Works employ'd.
11   Thence with an out-stretch'd Arm
12   He lead his *Israel's* Race :
  His Mercies sure unchang'd endure,
      When Time resigns his Place.

Part 2.

13   Praise Him whose powerful Hand
      Made mighty Seas divide :
  His Mercies sure unchang'd endure,
      Thro' endless Ages try'd.
14   Who thro' the sandy Deeps
      All *Israel*'s Armies lead :
  His Mercies sure unchang'd endure,
      In all his Actions read.

15   But o're proud *Pharaoh*'s Host
      Returning Waves prevail'd :
  His Mercies sure unchang'd endure
      On all his own Entail'd.
16   Who thro' the Desert wilde,
      His People march'd secure :
  His Mercies sure unchang'd endure,
      And as his Nature pure.

17   He many powerful Kings,
18   And mighty Princes slew :
  His Mercies sure unchang'd endure,
      To all his Servants true.
19   The surly *Amorite*,
20   And *Bashan*'s Gyant Lord :
  His Mercies sure unchang'd endure,
      As his Eternal Word.

21 Praise Him, who all their Land
22   On *Israel*'s Race bestow'd:
  His Mercies sure unchang'd endure,
    To all his Creatures show'd.
23 He help'd our mean Estate,
24   And us from Foes redeem'd:
  His Mercies sure unchang'd endure,
    By all his Saints esteem'd.

25 He feeds his Creatures all;
    O praise this heavenly King:
  His Mercies sure unchang'd endure,
    Let all his Creatures sing!

Another Metre, as the 148*th.*

1 O Praise th' Eternal Lord!
2   The God of Gods adore,
3 The Lord of Lords record,
4   And all his Wonders store.
    For certainly
    His Mercies sure
    Unchang'd endure
    Eternally.

5 Praise Him whose curious Hand
    Stretch'd out the lofty Skies,
6 And made the solid Land
    Above the Waters rise.
    For certainly, &c.

7 He through Confusions sway,
    Drew out the glorious Light,
8 The Sun to rule the Day,
9   The Moon and Stars the Night.
    For certainly, &c.

10 He all the First-born flew
    Thro' *Egypt*'s mournful Land,
11 And out his *Israel* drew
12   With his victorious Hand.
    For certainly, &c.

13 Praise Him, before whose Rod,
    The Seas divided fled,
14 And thro' strange ways untrod,
    His *Jacob*'s Army led.
    For certainly, &c.

15 Who drowning *Pharaoh*'s Host,
16   His own thro' Deserts train'd,
17 And *Canaan*'s ancient Coast
18   With Blood of Princes stain'd.
    For certainly, &c.

19 The furious *Amorite*,
20   And *Bashan*'s Monster King
21 He slew, that to their Right
22   He might his Servants bring.
    For certainly, &c.

23 Praise Him who helps our Needs,
24   And gives us Victories,
25 Who all his Creatures feeds,
    And reigns above the Skies.
    For certainly, &c.

PSAL. 137. *Proper Tune.*

ON *Babel*'s Rivers Banks we sate,
  O're-whelm'd with Miseries,
And Tears for *Sion*'s ruin'd State,
  O're-flow'd our mournful Eyes.

2 Useless our Harps untun'd, unstrung,
    As our disorder'd Minds,
On Willows unregarded hung,
    Expos'd to wanton Winds.

3 But our too cruel Conquerors there
    Disturb'd our silent Woes,
And bad us change our mournful Cheer,
    Our Thoughts to Songs compose.
" Let's hear, *they cry'd*, that wondrous Song,
  " Which once your God could charm,
" Our Ears for *Sion*'s Musick long,
  " Our heavy Hearts to warm.

4 What shall we sing our holy Songs,
    To please our haughty Foes?
Shall we, what to our God belongs,
    In Heathen Lands expose?
5 No, should we *Salem*'s Woes pass o're,
    Her Desolations slight,
O may our skilful Hands no more
    The curious Ear delight!

6 O may our Tongues be silent quite,
    If we her Walls forget;
Or don't, above our chief Delight,
    Poor *Salem*'s Sorrows set!
7 Think, Lord, on *Esau*'s barbarous Race,
    How at our Fall they cry'd,
Down, down, their mighty Walls deface!
    O're-turn their ancient Pride!

8 Nor sha't thou *Babel* e're avoid
    Our God's revenging Hand,
Since He by whom thy Pride's destroy'd,
    Shall, blest, in safety stand.
9 Gods Blessings on his Arms shall rest,
    Who breaks the tender Bones

Of Babes torn from the Mother's Breast,
    On unrelenting stones.

Another Metre: As the 51th. Proper Tune.

1 WHen on *Euphrates* Banks we lay,
    Poor flaves oppress'd with Cares and Fears,
And thought on *Salem*'s fatal Day,
    Our Sighs burst out at last in Tears,
We saw proud *Babel* firmly wall'd,
    Her Buildings fair, serene her state,
The fight poor *Salem*'s Doom recall'd,
    Augmenting Sorrows dismal weight.

2 Thither in vain our Harps wee'd brought,
    To calm our Thoughts, and ease our Woes,
Such Ease, alass! in vain we sought,
    Our Wounds no Musick's Balm could close.
Careless, at last, we hung them by,
    On mournful Willows planted round,
Where the sad Strings by sympathy,
    Sigh'd, broke, and gave a doleful sound.

3 But they whose cruel Hands had laid
    Our Country waste, our selves in Chains,
A sport of all our Sorrows made,
    And call'd for Musick's pleasing streins.
" Come take your lazy Harps, *they cry*,
" Tune well, tune every sounding string,
" Let's have some godly melody,
" Some chearful Hallelujah sing!

4 Inhumane! should we prostitute
    Our holiest Things to Dogs, or Swine?
Should we God's sacred Name pollute,
    Or treat his Foes with songs Divine?
5 Ah Lord! Ah *Sion*'s ancient Fame!
    Ah *Salem*'s ruin'd Walls! shall we

 Forget Dear *Sion*'s darling Name,
  Or Widdowed *Salem*'s Misery?

 No; rather may our Fingers loose
  Their Relish on the tuneful Lyre;
 Our Hands their sweetest Strokes refuse
  Their softest Touch, and noblest Fire,
6 Oh! may Eternal Hoarseness seize
  Our Throats! our Tongues be always dry!
 No more our charming Anthems please,
  If *Salem*'s sad remembrance dye.

 Nay, should Joys sudden Extasies
  To Heav'n our drooping Tempers raise;
 O may we ne'er approach the Skies,
  If *Sion* crowns not all our Praise!
7 Think, Lord, on *Esau*'s Sons whose Spite
  Unnaturally urged our Fate:
 Down, Down with *Salem*; Rase it quite;
  Down with that Birthright-stealing State!

 Our deathful Cries not one kind Look
  Could from obdurate Brethren gain;
 Our Griefs they for Diversion took;
  Laugh'd at our Cries, and mock'd our Pain.
8 Nor shall thy Doom, proud *Babel*, stay;
  Thy Sword was cruel too.; thy Rage
 Could brutish *Edom*'s Curse obey,
  And against Tears and Cries engage.

 See where God's dreadful Judgments wait,
  To strike the dead revenging Bow!
 And bless'd be He whose mortal hate
  Shall make thee taste of *Salem*'s woe!
9 Thrice happy he whose hands shall tear
  From Mother's Breasts thy Infant Race;
 Nor for their tender Out-cries spare,
  But dash their Brains in every place.

PSAL. CXXXVIij.

1. WIth all my heart, thy Praises I
    Before the Gods will sing,
2. And to thy Temple chearfully
    My grateful Offerings bring:
Before thy Holy Place I'll bow,
    Thy Truth, thy Mercies praise;
For o'er thy Name entirely now
    Thy Word it self displays.

3. I pray'd; thou heard'st my Prayer: restor'd
    To strength my Soul appear'd.
4. All Earthly Kings shall praise the Lord,
    When they his Words have heard.
5. Joy shall enlarge their Hearts, when they
    Shall tread thy sacred Ways:
When they thy Just Commands obey,
    They'll all thy Glories praise.

6. For though the Lord, enthron'd on High,
    The World's vast Empire sways,
On humble Souls He casts his Eye,
    And scorns the Prides haughty ways.
7. Though I, involv'd in mighty Woes,
    As sunk and lost appear,
Thy Hand shall break my angry Foes,
    And save my Soul from fear.

8. Since, Lord, thy Mercies boundless are,
    O don't my Hopes defeat;
But all thy Works, for me, with care,
    Thy Handy-works compleat!

PSAL. CXXXIX.

1 Lord, Thou haſt fully ſearch'd me out,
    And throughly canvaſs'd me!
2 My Reſt, my Riſe, each ſhapeleſs Thought
    Is known long ſince to Thee.
3 Thy wond'rous Art, thy curious Hand,
    My private Path diſplays;
  By Thee my very Sleeps are ſcann'd,
    And all my various Ways.

4 What e'r my ſerious Thought produce,
    Before the Words are fram'd,
  Before my Tongue can find its uſe,
    Is in thy Ears proclaim'd.
5 When I my Shape, ſo clean, ſo fair,
    Behind, Before, ſurvey;
  I know thy Hand, thy skilful Care,
    Thus built my humble Clay.

6 Would I into thy Secrets pry,
    Thy Forming Wiſdom know;
7 For me ſuch Skill is far too high,
    And I, alas! too low.
  Whither, O whither then ſhould I
    Go from thy piercing ſight?
  O whither from thy Spirit's Eye
    Direct my ſecret flight?

8 If I climb high above the Sky,
    Thy Throne of Glory's there:
  If in Hell's gloomy Deeps I lie,
    In Hell thy Powers appear.
9 If I, on Morning's purple Wings,
    Out-ſtrip the fleeting Day,
  And toward the Ocean's Weſtern Springs
    Find out an unknown way,

10 Yet

10 Yet there thy far extended Hand
    Would lead me out at laſt;
And thy Right Hand my Steps command,
    And ever hold me faſt.
11 Nay, ſhould I ſay, the gloomy Night
    Shall ſure my Steps conceal,
Around me ſoon a glorious Light
    Wou'd all my Walks reveal.

12 Should Night condenſe its darkeſt Steams
    One diſmal Gloom to frame,
That Gloom, with more than Mid-days Beams,
    Would Night it ſelf enflame.

Part 2.

13 For in my Mother's Womb, of old,
    Thy Hand my Reins poſſeſt;
And, in a wondrous Covering, roll'd,
    Did all my Limbs inveſt.
14 Since in my Shape, and round me, all
    Thy dreadful Wonders ſhine;
My Thoughts ſhall all my Works recall,
    And in thy Praiſe combine.

15 When in the lower Womb, embrac'd,
    My curious Texture grew;
Thy Wiſdom all that Darkneſs trac'd,
    And all my Subſtance knew.
16 The Lord my formleſs Subſtance view'd,
    And in His Book enroll'd;
And as each Day with Shape endu'd,
    My growing Members told.

17 How dear thy Counſels, Lord, to me!
    How vaſt their Numbers are!
The Sands we round the Ocean ſee,
    Can't with their Summs compare;

18 On then all Day I closely muse;
   And in my Nightly Dreams,
They through my Soul themselves diffuse,
   And are my waking Themes.

19 The Lord shall wicked Men destroy:
   Begone, Blood-thirsty Crew,
20 Who against God your Tongues employ,
   His Name with Lyes pursue!
21 I with a perfect rage at those
   Who hate my Maker, fly;
22 And such, as if my deadly Foes,
   With deadly hate defie.

23 O search me! Try my Heart! and see
   Which way my Thoughts encline!
24 And all ill Thoughts remove, and me
   Conduct in Paths divine!

PSAL. cxl.

1 FRom vile, from godless Men, Dear Lord,
   O save! O rescue me!
2 Whose Hearts in wicked Plots accord,
   And quarrel constantly.
3 Their Tongues more pointed much than those
   Of angry Serpents are;
Their Lips more Venome far disclose,
   Than fretted Asps prepare.

4 From Sinners, and the Violent,
   Me, Lord, in peace bestow!
Whose spite against my ways is bent,
   And would my Steps o'erthrow.
5 Their Nets, their Snares, their Ginns they lay,
   With unsuspected Arts;
And when they quite surround my Way,
   They please their scornful Hearts.

6 Thou

PSAL. cxli.

6 Thou art my God, my Lord, alone:
    Then to the Lord I said,
The Prayers, the Supplications own,
    By me thy Servant made!
7 Thou art my strength alone; from Thee
    My safety, Lord, descends:
When furious Battels compass me,
    Thy Hand my Head defends.

8 Lord, let not wicked Workers thrive,
    Nor gain their base Design!
Lest they their Hearts, if thou connive,
    To haughty Pride resign.
9 But as for all that impious Crew
    Who now my Path surround,
Let the malicious Lyes they brew,
    Themselves at last confound!

10 On them let burning Sulphur rain,
    Hot Flames about them fly,
And they, O never rais'd again,
    In dismal Darkness lie!
11 Ne'er let the dismal Wordy Tool
    On Earth continue long;
Let mischief hurt the Griping Fool,
    Who still delights in Wrong.

12 I know th' afflicted Poor Man's Claim
    The Lord will still maintain:
13 The Righteous then shall praise thy Name,
    And in thy Sight remain.

PSAL. cxli.

1 I Call'd on Thee; Lord, haste and hear,
    And let my Voice, my Cries
2 As Incense prove! my Hands appear
    As Ev'ning Sacrifice!

3 Lord, by thy Grace, my Mouth secure,
    My Lips with Wisdom close!
4 And let my Heart from Sin be pure,
    And wicked Works oppose.

Lest I associate with those
    Who only Sin pursue,
And feast where luscious Plenty flows
    Amongst the scornful Crew.
5 Whene'er I sin, with pity, may
    The Good my Sins reprove;
Their Wounds are kinder far than they
    Who feign deceitful Love.

Let those, Lord, heal my Head, as Oil
    Which heals and mollifies:
And though my Foes attempt my spoil,
    For them my Pray'rs shall rise.
6 May their Great Men in rocky Ways
    Be trampled under so,
That they my prudent Words may praise,
    And Wisdom's sweetness know!

7 As Chips from falling Timber fly,
    Or Ploughs tear up the Ground;
So, Lord, our Bones unbury'd lie
    Our emptied Graves around.
8 To Thee I lift my faithful Eyes!
    O don't my Soul reject!
But from those Snares my Foes devise,
    My Innocence protect!

9 Let not the Sinner's crafty Snare,
    Dear Lord, entangle me!
10 But, while I 'scape, O let his Care
    His own Confusion be!

PSAL. clxij.

1 Lord, from a dismal Place
   I pray'd, I cry'd to Thee,
2 With earnest Prayers before thy Face,
   I lay'd my Misery.
3 My Spirits fainted quite,
   But, Lord, thou know'st my Way,
   And how my Foes with active spite,
   Their Snares about it lay.

4 Where e're I cast my Eyes,
   I stand, alass! unknown,
   Where e're my Soul for Refuge flies,
   It's left forlorn alone.
5 Yet to the Lord, I cry'd,
   And said, " My Hope's in Thee,
   " Thou, Lord, while I on Earth abide,
   " Shalt all my Portion be.

6 " Lord, hear my Cries! my Woes;
   " My lost Condition view,
   " Save me from those too mighty Foes,
   " Who now my Life pursue!
7 " O let my Soul be free,
   " Thy holy Name to praise!
   " The Just with Songs shall compass me,
   " When Thou my Head shalt raise.

Another Metre.

1 I to the Lord devoutly pray'd,
   To him I cry'd aloud,
2 And in his sight my Sorrows laid,
   And all my Sufferings show'd.
3 When my faint Spirits slowly mov'd,
   Thou knew'st my certain way,

PSAL. clxiij.

How Snares by cruel Arts improv'd,
   About my Footsteps lay.

4 I look'd for some Assistance round,
   But was, alass! unknown,
My wretched Soul no shelter found,
   And was esteem'd by none.
5 Then I, in Prayer, to God confest,
   In Thee my Hope's secure,
Thou art, since I my Life possest,
   My Lot, my Portion sure.

6 O let my Cries thy Ears engage,
   My groaning weakness see!
Save me from Persecutor's rage,
   Too strong alass! for me.
7 Lord, set my Soul from Prison free,
   To praise thy sacred Name,
And when the Righteous compass me,
   Thy Bounties I'le proclaim.

PSAL. clxiij.

1 LOrd, hear my Prayers, accept my Cries,
   In Truth and Righteousness!
2 And let not Judgments sharp surprize
   Thy Servant's Soul oppress!
For when thy searching Eyes begin,
   To try our fading Years,
Lord, in thy sight o'rewhelm'd with Sin,
   The purest Saint appears!

3 My Soul pursu'd by cruel Foes,
   My Life quite overthrown,
I ly in Darkness lost, like those
   Who to their Graves are gone.
4 For this my Spirit faints in me,
   My Heart deserted mourns,

PSAL. clxjv.

5. And to my labouring Memory,
   My happier Age returns.

On all thy Acts I daily muse,
   Thy Works run daily o're,
6. And as the parching Earth soft Dews,
   So Thee my Hands implore.
7 I faint, ô quickly, quickly hear,
   Thy smiles, dear Lord, I crave;
Least I, like dying Men, appear,
   Who just approach the Grave.

8 Let me thy Mercies early gain,
   For, Lord, I trust in Thee,
To Thee I lift my Soul, make plain
   The way of Life to me!
9 Save me from all my Foes, who still
   To Thee for shelter fly.
10 Teach me to do thy sacred Will,
   My Lord, my God, most High!

O let thy Spirit lead me to
   The Land of Righteosness,
11 My Soul with active Life renew,
   And for thy Glory bless!
Just Lord, from Troubles set me free,
   And all my Foes destroy,
Thy Mercy, and thy Help, let me,
   Thy Servant, Lord, enjoy!

PSAL. clxjv.

1 BLest be the Lord, my strength, whose Care
   And whose victorious Might,
Instructs my ready Hands for War,
   My Fingers for the Fight,
2 My Goodness, Fort, my Raiser, He,
   My Saviour, and my Shield,

  In Him I trust, thro' Him to Me,
   My willing People yield.

3 Lord what is Man? what Mans weak Race,
  Own'd by the favouring Ey?
4 Meer Vanity! His Age, his Grace,
  Like Shadows swiftly fly.
5 Lord bow thy Heavens, come down, divide
  The Hills, the Hills, shall smoke!
6 Shoot Lightnings, break, destroy their Pride
  With one confounding stroke!

7 Lord, from above thy Arms extend,
  And save and rescue Me,
From Headstrong Crouds, my Crown defend,
  And Forreign Tyranny;
8 From such whose Lips, and Hands in Lyes,
  In Deed and Word agree.
9 So I'll new Songs, new Tunes devise,
  On Lute and Harp to Thee.

Part 2.

10 The Lord his strong Salvation's Guards,
  On Royal Heads bestows,
And from his Servant *David* wards,
  The plotting Traitors blows.
11 Save Me my God! ô rescue Me
  From Forreign Enemies!
Whose Words and Actions all agree,
  In Treachery and Lies.

12 So shall our Sons like Plants alive,
  In Water'd Gardens show:
And with a kindly vigour thrive,
  And daily stronger grow:
Our Daughters like fair Marble Coines,
  Smooth'd by some Curious hand;

PSAL. cxlv.

On which the building sweetly joyns,
    The Roofs securely stand.

13 All kind of Grain shall largely flow,
    And run our Garners o're;
Till none by Numbers force can know,
    Our never ending store.
Our Flocks their Young by thousands near,
    Our very Gates shall lay,
Ten thousands in the rolling Year
    About our Pastures play.

14 Our Cattel to their Work be strong,
    We no Invasions fear,
No Captives know, no Cries among
    Our peaceful Dwellings hear.
15 Happy the Tribes must needs become,
    On whom such Favour flows!
But, ô more happy those on whom,
    Their God himself bestows!

PSAL. cxlv.

1 THy Name, my God, my King, I'll raise
    Above the lofty Skyes,
2 Each Day thy Holy Name I'll praise,
    And Psalms of thanks devise.
3 Great is our Lord, his Glory's great,
    No Bounds his Greatness knows.
4 And Race to Race, his Acts repeat,
    His wondrous Works disclose.

5 I'll all my serious Thoughts address,
    To search thy wondrous ways:
6 The World thy Terrors shall confess,
    While I thy Greatness praise.
7 Thy Righteous Truth the World adores,
    To mind thy Goodness brings,

    And all thy Loves unfailing Stores,
       In grateful Anthems Sings.

8. Our Lord's Compassionate and kind,
       To vengeance only flow,
9. His Goodness all his Creatures find,
       O're all his Mercies flow.
10. Thee all thy Works, ô God, shall Praise
       And celebrate thy Name;
    Thy Saints as gladly all their Days,
       Thy glorious Might proclaim.

Part 2.

11. Thy Might, thy Kingdom's glorious State,
       Thy Servants Talk shall show,
12. Till all thy valiant Acts relate,
       Thy awful Glories know,
13. Beyond Times bounds, thy Kingdom stands,
       Thy Government endures;
14. Thy Help supports the weak; thy Hand
       Their timely Ease procures.

15. To Thee all raise their longing Eyes,
       From Thee they beg their Food,
16. Thy Bounteous Hand, their Wants supplies,
       And satisfies with Good.
17. How Just, blest God, how gentle all
       Thy Ways and Works appear!
11. Kind to those Souls which on Thee call,
       To those who seek Thee near!

19. Thou grantst the pious Suppliants Prayers,
       Thou seest thy Servants Tears.
    Thy Hand relieves their Various Cares,
       And Ends their Doubts and Fears.
20. But all the wicked World shall find,
       Thy Judgments dreadful weight.

    To thy revenging Wrath, resign'd,
      And unrelenting Hate.

2. Thy Name bleft God, my Songs shall raise
      Above the lofty Skyes;
    And all to Thee shall pay their Praise,
      Till Times laſt Moment dyes.

PSAL. cxlvj.

1. PRaiſe ye the Lord! with praiſe my Soul,
      Thy Maker's Glories raiſe!
2. While Breath and Life are in me whole,
      I'll ſing thy lofty Praiſe.
3. On Kings, on Men of mortal Birth,
      For ſafety ne'r rely,
4. Whoſe Breath goes out, who turn to Earth,
      And all whoſe Counſels dy.

5. But happy's He whoſe Hopes, whoſe Aid,
      On God his Lord depends;
6. Who Seas, Earth, Heaven, and all things made,
      Whoſe Promiſe never ends.
7. He for the Poor his Judgment ſhows,
      When preſt by Violence.
    Does Priſoners free, and Food to thoſe
      Of Hungry Souls diſpence.

8. God to the Blind gives Senſe and Eyes,
      And with his healing Art
    Sets up the ſinking Soul; ſupplies
      With Love the faithful Heart.
9. The Widows, Orphans, Stranger's cauſe,
      The Lord himſelf maintains,
    But o're the Stubborn Sinner draws,
      Deſtructions fatal Chains.

PSAL. CXVJ.

10 Thy King, thy Lord, O *Sion* reigns;
　　His Actions all record,
His Throne from Age to Age remains,
　　Praise ye, ô Praise the Lord!

PSAL. CXLVIJ.

1 PRaise ye the Lord! its good to Sing
　　Our Mighty Maker's praise,
Its pleasant, and a comely thing,
　　His Glorious Acts to blaze.
2 The Lord poor *Salem*'s Walls repairs,
　　Her wretched Dust removes,
And home her wandring Outcasts bears
　　Fenced with his tenderest Loves.

3 The Lord finds out with pittying Art,
　　What Man from Man conceals.
And gently binds the bleeding Heart,
　　Its wounds as gently Heals.
4 He names the Stars which fill the Skies,
　　And all their Number Counts,
5 But his great Might and Actions wise,
　　All numbring Art surmounts.

6 The Lord exalts the lowly Heart,
　　But casts the Sinner down,
7 Then Sing to God a grateful part,
　　Your Harps with Praises Crown!
8 With Clouds He covers all the Skies,
　　Which Rains as duely bring,
And makes the buried Plants to rise.
　　The Sun burnt Hills to spring.

9 He feeds the Beasts, and at their Cries
　　For Birds of Prey provides.
10. But strength of Horse, and brawny thighs
　　Of mighty Men derides.

11 But

PSAL. cxlvij.

11 But Loves the Men who fear his Name,
 And for his Mercies wait.
12 O Sion, Sion, ô proclaim,
 Thy God's Majestic State!

Part 2.

13 He strengthens all thy Gates and Bars,
 And blesses all thy Seeds,
14 Thro' Him thy Borders, freed from Wars,
 On Wheats pure fatness feed.
15 He sends his Word, his Word on Earth,
 With wondrous swiftness flies,
16 And gives the Snow its Flaky Birth,
 Which all in Fleeces lies.

His heavy Frosts, like Ashes you
 Spread o're the Fields behold.
17 His Ice like Morsels lies, and who
 Can stand his piercing Cold?
18 He sends his Word again, and streight
 His Ice, his Frosts and Snow!
 Before his Warmer gusts abate,
 And all in Waters flow.

19 The Lord to *Jacob's* chosen Race
 His Sacred Writings gave;
 His Laws, his Judgments, by his Grace,
 His *Israel* only have.
20 So well no other Nation far'd,
 Nor of his sacred Word,
 Nor of his Righteous Judgments heard,
 Praise ye, ô praise the Lord!

PSAL. cxlviij.

1 PRaise ye the Lord! ô Praise the Lord!
 On High his Glories raise!

2 Ye Angel Armys all record,
  His Name with Joyful Praise!
3 Sun, Moon, and lightsome Stars consent,
  To praise his glorious Name;
4 And Heavens high Throne, the Firmament,
  Of Waters praise the same!

5 Let these advance his Name, which He
  Made by his great Command,
6 And fix'd 'um by a sure Decree,
  Unmov'd, unchang'd to stand.
7 Him all ye Earth born Dragons praise,
  And each unfathom'd Deep:
8 Fire, Hail, Snow, Winds, which Tempests raise,
  Yet still his Orders keep!

9 Vast Hills, small Hillocks, Cedars high
  And every Fruitful Tree!
10 Wild Beasts and Tame, and Birds which fly,
  And Insects each Degree.
11 Kings, Princes, Nations, Judges, those
  Who rule the World below,
12 Youths, Virgins, such as strength disclose,
  And Heads adorn'd with Snow.

13 Let all advance their Maker's Name,
  Whose Name excells alone,
  Whose Name is o're the Worlds vast frame,
  On Winds of Glory blown,
14 He only makes his People great;
  His Saints his Praise record,
  His *Israel*, his near Friends repeat,
  Praise ye, ô praise the Lord!

Another Metre. Proper Tune.

1 PRaise ye the Lord! Above
  The Skies his Praises sing!

Let

PSAL. cxlviij.

Let Heaven the Seat of Love,
  With Heavenly Praises ring
    Of his great Name,
    Ye Angel Host
    With Reverence boast;
      His Praise proclaim;

Bright Sun, whose Golden Rays,
  Fill all the World with Light;
Pale Moon, bright Stars which blaze,
  Thro' the dark Fields of Night,
    Heavens outmost Frame;
    Vast Deeps which lie
    Above the Sky,
      His Praise proclaim!

Let these their Maker Praise,
  By whose Command Divine,
The Sky its Wealth displays,
  And all those Beautys shine.
    Fix'd by his Will,
    They all stand fast,
    And Orders past,
      With Joy fulfil.

Ye Dragons, Earth-born Race,
  And all ye Deeps profound.
With every Natural Grace,
  Your Masters Praises sound.
    In Praise agree,
    Fire, Clouds, Hail, Snow,
    And Storms which blow,
      At His Decree.

Let Soaring Mountains now,
  And smaller Hills descend,
Fruit Trees before Him bow,
  And stately Cedars bend.

PSAL. cxlix.

10   Beasts Wi'd and Tame,
Birds airy wings,
And creeping Things,
His Praise proclaim!

11 His Praise all Kings on Earth,
And Subject Nations show.
Great Men of Princely Birth,
And such as Judgment know,
12   Each Youthful Tribe,
Each Virgin Throng,
With Old and Young,
His Praise describe!

13 Let them with one consent,
Exalt their Maker's Name,
And various Ways invent,
To spread his glorious Fame.
His Name shall rise,
With Beams divine,
Thro Earth to Shine,
And reach the Skyes.

14 He makes his *Israel* great,
And Praise is comely, where
Before his Mercy Seat,
His grateful Tribes appear.
O all accord,
Who Worship near,
His Presence there,
To praise the Lord!

PSAL. cxlix.

1 PRaise ye the Lord! with Anthems new,
The great *Jehovah* praise!
His Praise in his Assembly's shew,
On all his Holy Days!

2 With

PSAL. cl.

With Joy let *Israel*'s Faithful Race,
   Their Maker's Power adore,
And *Sion*'s Heirs with humble Grace,
   Their Monarchs Smiles implore!

Where Harp and Timbrel tun'd invites,
   Let all his Praises sing!
To th' Meek, in whom the Lord Delights,
   Beauty and Safety spring.
4 Let then each Pious Soul rejoice,
   With lightsom Glories blest;
And Praise their God, whose happy choice
   Secur'd their Downy Rest

5 To them let God's high Praises yield,
   A Ground for all their Joys;
Then They a two edg'd Sword shall wield,
   Whose very weight destroys:
6 A Sword whose Point just Vengeance bears,
   To all the Nations round,
Whose glittering brandish'd Edge, with Fears
   Will all their Hearts confound.

7 Till They their daunted Kings shall bind,
   With Ease in Slavish Chains!
And till their Noblest Youth confin'd,
   Strong Fetters weight restrains.
8 To execute that Ancient Doom,
   Which Holy Books record,
Such Honour all his Saints assume,
   Praise ye, ô praise the Lord!

PSAL. cl.

1 O Praise the mighty Lord!
   His Holyness proclaim!
His wondrous Acts record.
   And praise his awful Name,

        His dreadful might;
    O celebrate!
  His Power and State,
    In Songs recite!

3 Praise Him with Trumpets sound,
    With sweet Tun'd Harp and Lute!
  Sing all the Chorus round,
    To cheerful Pipe and Flute!
4   Your Voices raise!
  The King of Kings
  With sounding Strings,
    And Organs praise!

5 Wind up the Cymbals high,
    Till with a Shriller sound,
  Wide as the vaulted Sky,
    Your cheerful Notes rebound.
6   With Spritely Flame
  Each living thing,
  His Glories sing,
    And Praise his Name!

Another Metre.

1 PRaise ye the Lord! ô praise the Lord!
    His strength, his Holiness adore,
2 His Name, his Might, with praise record,
    His Majesty with praise implore!

3 Praise him with Trumpets Martial sound,
    With Lute and Harp his praise advance!
4 With Organs, and with Timbrels round,
    And Viols, and a cheerful Dance!

5 With high tun'd Cymbals praise his Name,
    His Name to loudest Cymbals Sing.

                              6 And

6 And all whom Vital Spirits enflame,
O praise the World's Eternal King!

To Father, Holy Ghost and Son,
One bless, one glorious Trinity,
As is, as was e're Time begun,
So endless praise, and Glory be!

The End of the PSALMS.

DOXOLOGIES.

For the 1st. Metre of the 1st. Psalm, &c.

TO Father, Son and Holy Ghost,
  Immense, Eternal, Three in One,
By Us, and all the Heavenly Host,
  Be Glory pay'd, and Homage done!

For the 2d. Metre, and all of 8 and 6 Syllables.

To Father, Spirit, Son, Blest Three,
  In whom we move and Live,
One undivided Trinity.
  Unceasing Glories give!

For the 2d. Metre, of the 8th. Psal. and all of Ten Syllables.

To God the Father, and to God the Son,
  And God the Holy Ghost, blest Trinity,
As is, as was, before the World begun,
  Eternal praise, Eternal Glory be!

For the 2d. Metre of the 11th. Psalm.

To Father Ho'y Ghost and Son,
One God, as was e're Time begun,
    As now We see,
    So ever be
  All Humblest Homage done!

DOXOLOGIES. 317

For the 2d. Metre of the 15th, Pfalm.

To Father, Holy Ghoſt and Son,
   Bleſt Three in One!
Eternal Praiſe and Glory pay,
   His Word obey,
As was of Old, as ſtill we ſee,
And ſhall, when Times extinguiſh'd, be.

For the 17th Pſal, and all Two Sixes, and Eight and Six.

To Father, Spirit, Son,
   One God in Perſons three,
Be Glory paid and Homage done,
   Thro' all Eternity

For the 20th. and 122d. Pſalm, 1ſt. Metre and proper Tune.

To that great Lord above,
   The God of Peace and Love,
In Eſſence One, in Perſons Three,
   To Father, Spirit, Son,
   Each God immenſe alone,
One Undivided Trinity.
   To him your Anthems raiſe,
   And Holy Songs of Praiſe,
And Glories pay, and Reverence ſhew;
   So God of old was bleſs'd
   Of theſe he's ſtill poſſeſt,
And theſe will when Time's done be due.

For the 22d. and 124th. Pſal. 2d. Metre.

To God the Father, and to God the Son,
   And God the Holy Ghoſt, Almighty Three,
   One only God, one Glorious Trinity,

P 3

As shall be, is, and was e're Time begun,
Be lasting Glories paid and Homage done.

For the 23d. Psalm, 2d. Metre.

To Father, Holy Ghost, and Son,
Eternal glorious Three and One,
    Be Glory paid,
    His Word obey'd.
As was before Times Birth begun,
    As is, and still shall be,
    Thro' all Eternity.

For the 24th. Psalm, 2d. Metre.

To one great God, one mighty Lord,
  One Eternal Trinity,
The Father, the Eternal Word,
  And the Spirits Majesty,
    Wee'l gladly raise,
    Unceasing praise,
And his endless Glories sound.
    So Saints of old,
    His Name extold!
So we'll keep th' Eternal round.

For the 29th. Psalm, or 127th. 2d. Metre, or 48th. 2d. Metre.

To Father, Holy Ghost, and Son,
  One blest, one glorious Trinity,
Who fram'd this Universe alone,
  All Honour, Praise, and Glories be,
    So 'twas of Old, at Present too,
    And shall when Time's run out be due.

DOXOLOGIES.

For the 33d. Pfal. 2 Metre.

To Father, Son, and Holy Ghoſt,
By us, and all the Heavenly Hoſt,
   Be equal Glories paid!
Great Three in One! thus bleſt of old,
They ſtill their ancient Honours hold,
   And muſt be ſtill obey'd.

For the 43d. Pfal. 2d. Metre.

To the Father, Spirit, Son,
   One glorious Trinity,
Perſons Three, in Eſſence One,
   Eternal Glory be.
Thus e're Time begun its race,
   The Godhead was obey'd,
This when Time reſigns its place,
   Muſt to our Lord be paid.

For the 3d. Metre of the ſame Pſalm.

To Father, Son, and Holy Ghoſt,
   One bleſt Eternal Trinity,
By us and all the Heavenly Hoſt,
   Be Praiſe aſcrib'd and Majeſty,
   So 'twas at firſt, and ſtill ſhall be,
When Time expires, and Nature's loſt.

For Pfal. 45th. Metre 3d. &c.

To that great Lord who rules above,
The God of Might, of Peace, and Love,
   In Eſſence One, in Perſons Three,
To Father, Holy Ghoſt and Son,
Each God Himſelf, immenſe alone,
   One undivided Trinity.

To

To Him with Hearts exalted raise,
Your Holy Hyms and Songs of Praise,
    And Glories pay, and Reverence shew.
So He before Time's Birth was bless'd,
Of these He's now by Right possest,
    And they'l, when Time's no more, be due.

For the 50th. Psal. 2d. Metre.

To God the Father, and to God the Son,
  And God the Holy Ghost, coæqual Three;
Three Holy Persons, but ador'd in One!
  All equal Honours, equal Glories be,
    His Glory shone e're Time's first Springs could move it,
    And vast Eternity shall more improve it.

For the 51st. Psal. and 137th. Psal. 2d. Metre.

All Glory to that Mighty Lord,
  Who made the World, and all its Host!
The Father, the *Begotten* Word,
  And the *proceeding* Holy Ghost.
As was e're Time's first Race begun,
  As was when Time commenc'd his Score,
As is, and ever shall be done,
  When Nature sinks, and Time's no more.

For the 53d. Psal. 2d. Metre.

To one Almighty Lord,
  One glorious Trinity,
The Father, Spirit, Word,
  Eternal Glories be,
So happy Angels Sung,
  Before the World begun,
So ever Lord among,
  Thy Servants shall be done.

DOXOLOGIES.

For the 58th. Psal. 3d. Metre.

To God alone,
The Mighty Father, Mighty Son,
   And Holy Ghost,
Blest Trinity, great Three in One,
   Be Homage done.
As was before the World begun,
   When th' Angel Host!
O're Rebel Mates the Conquest wonne,
So we at present Sing his glorious Praise,
So All shall Sing when Time it self decays.

For Psalm 60, and 121st. Metre 2d.

To Father, Holy Ghost and Son,
   One God, in Persons Three,
   All Praise and Glory be!
As was before Time's race begun;
   As is now, and sha'l be paid,
   When swift Time its self is laid.

For Psal. 69, 2d. Metre.

To Father and Son,
   And Pure Holy Ghost,
One blest Trinity,
   All Glory be paid,
As e're Time begun,
   By the Heavenly Host,
And by All must be,
   When Time's motions are laid.

DOXOLOGIES.

For Psal. 72, 2d. Metre.

To Father, Holy Ghost and Son,
Blest Trinity, Great Three in One,
Be Glory paid and Homage done,

So 'twas before this All was made,
Nor shall God's Honours ever fade,
But shall when All's consum'd be paid.

For Psalm 76, or 148th Proper Tune.

To Father, Spirit, Son,
  The glorious Trinity,
In Sacred Essence One!
  All Praise and Glory be,
    As now We see,
    As was Time past,
    And shall outlast
      Eternity.

For Psalm 85, 2d. Metre. Proper Tune.

To Father, Son, and Holy Ghost,
  One blest one glorious Trinity,
From all the World's Created Host!
  Eternal Praise and Glories be,
    So 'twas e're Time begun,
    And ever shall be done.

For Psalm 93, 2d. Metre.

To Father, Spirit, Son,
  Eternal Three in One!
    All praise and Glory be,
    As 'twas in Times of old,
    And we shall still behold,
      And thro' Eternity.

DOXOLOGIES. 323

For the 95th. Pfal. 2d. Metre.

To the Father, Spirit, Son,
God Eternal Three in One,
Be all Praife and Glory paid,
When the World in Duft is lay'd.

For Pfal. 97. 2d. Metre.

To God the Father, God the Son,
And God the Spirit, Three,
A glorious Trinity,
In Eternal Effence One.
By all the bright Angelic Hoft above,
By us the Sons of Grace, and Heirs of Love,
Be Praife and Glory paid,
As was in days of old,
As is where God's Command's obey'd,
And fhall as long as Nature Hold,
And when the World's confum'd and all its ruins [cold

For the 98. 2d. Metre.

To Father, Spirit, Son,
Eternal Three in One,
One glorious Trinity,
Unceafing Glory be,
As was e're time begun,
And ever fhall be done.

For the 119th. Pfal. Proper Tune.

God the Father, God the Son,
And God the Holy Ghoft,
Glory paid, and Homage done,
By all the Heavenly Hoft:

By

By us, and all Mankind, as was,
    Before Time's Courſe begun,
As is, and undecay'd ſhall paſs,
    When Time's laſt Moment's run.

For Pſal: 127, Metre 2d.

To Father, Holy Ghoſt, and Son,
    One glorious God, in perſons Three,
    One Undivided Trinity,
Be glory paid, and Homage done,
    'Twas ſo e're Time's firſt race begun,
    And ſhall be when his laſt is run.

Si male quid Cecini me Culpa redarguet Ipſum,
    Si bene quid, redeat Gloria Sola Deo.

www.ingramcontent.com/pod-product-compliance
Lightning Source LLC
Chambersburg PA
CBHW020307240426
43673CB00039B/732